DIVING DEEP *into* NONFICTION

Grades 6–12

To Peter Rabinowitz:

Thanks, Peter, for setting us on a road that has proven to be so generative for our thinking, reading, and teaching.

28 Lessons on *Reader's Rules of Notice*

DIVING DEEP *into* NONFICTION

TRANSFERABLE TOOLS FOR READING **ANY** NONFICTION TEXT

Grades 6–12

JEFFREY D. WILHELM  MICHAEL W. SMITH

http://resources.corwin.com/divingdeep-nonfiction

FOR INFORMATION:

Corwin
A SAGE Company
2455 Teller Road
Thousand Oaks, California 91320
(800) 233-9936
www.corwin.com

SAGE Publications Ltd.
1 Oliver's Yard
55 City Road
London EC1Y 1SP
United Kingdom

SAGE Publications India Pvt. Ltd.
B 1/I 1 Mohan Cooperative Industrial Area
Mathura Road, New Delhi 110 044
India

SAGE Publications Asia-Pacific Pte. Ltd.
3 Church Street
#10-04 Samsung Hub
Singapore 049483

Publisher: Lisa Luedeke
Editorial Development Manager: Julie Nemer
Editorial Assistant: Nicole Shade
Production Editor: Melanie Birdsall
Copy Editor: Melinda Masson
Typesetter: C&M Digitals (P) Ltd.
Proofreader: Christine Dahlin
Indexer: Amy Murphy
Cover and Interior Designer: Rose Storey
Marketing Manager: Rebecca Eaton

Printed in the United States of America

Library of Congress Cataloging-in-Publication Data

Names: Wilhelm, Jeffrey D. | Smith, Michael W. (Michael William)

Title: Diving deep into nonfiction, grades 6-12 : transferable tools for reading any nonfiction text / Jeffrey D. Wilhelm, Michael W. Smith.

Description: Thousand Oaks, California : Corwin, 2017. | Includes bibliographical references and index.

Identifiers: LCCN 2016027863 | ISBN 9781483386058 (pbk. : alk. paper)

Subjects: LCSH: Reading (Secondary) | Reading comprehension—Study and teaching (Secondary) | Content area reading—Study and teaching (Secondary)

Classification: LCC LB1632 .W497 2017 | DDC 428.4071/2—dc23
LC record available at https://lccn.loc.gov/2016027863

This book is printed on acid-free paper.

SFI label applies to text stock

16 17 18 19 20 10 9 8 7 6 5 4 3 2 1

CONTENTS

Visit the companion website at
http://resources.corwin.com/divingdeep-nonfiction
for videos, handouts, and other downloadable resources.

LIST OF VIDEOS

Note From the Publisher: The authors have provided video and web content throughout the book that is available to you through QR codes. To read a QR code, you must have a smartphone or tablet with a camera. We recommend that you download a QR code reader app that is made specifically for your phone or tablet brand.

Videos may also be accessed at the companion website, **http://resources.corwin.com/divingdeep-nonfiction**

(Continued)

(Continued)

Chapter 4. Noticing Varied Nonfiction Genres

Video 4.1. Rules of Notice in the Content Areas

Video 4.2. Noticing Different Genres

Chapter 5. Noticing the Text Structures in Nonfiction Texts

Video 5.1. Teaching Compare and Contrast With Think-Aloud in Science

Video 5.2. Teaching Three Rules of Structure: Martin Luther King Jr.'s "I Have a Dream" Speech

Video 5.3. Noticing Patterns: Martin Luther King Jr.'s "I Have a Dream" Speech

Chapter 6. Why This Method Words

Video 6.1. Reader's Rules of Notice: Frequently Asked Questions

ACKNOWLEDGMENTS

We'd like to especially thank Lisa Luedeke, our acquisitions and development editor, for her careful and responsive guidance at all stages of the process of composing this book. We'd also like to thank editor Julie Nemer and editorial assistant Nicole Shade at Corwin. We explored new terrain in this book, theoretically but especially in terms of instructional practice, and they helped us navigate this terra nova by pushing us to clarify both our thinking and our prose. Thanks, too, to the entire design team at Corwin for making our work look so good. Finally, a team of teacher reviewers whom Corwin enlisted provided very valuable feedback as we were working on our final revisions.

A forty-one-gun salute to the Boise State Writing Project Teacher Inquiry Community in thanks for implementing and testing these ideas through their teacher research projects into text complexity: Ramey Uriarte, Micah Lauer, Jerry Hendershot, Nancy Chaffin, Cathy Adams, Mandy Hardan, Janna Davis, Cathy Keys, Erin Gatfield, Anne Stevenson, Jody Billiard, Raylene Dodson, Amanda Michelletty, Shauna Steglich, and Serena Hicks.

A special thanks and Air Force fly-by for Paula Uriarte for carefully reviewing the manuscript, for helping to shape the lessons, and for organizing our video shoot. Thanks too to Erika Boas for providing insights about the Australian approach to teaching genre and for evaluating and validating our approach here.

Many heartfelt thanks as well to everyone who worked on the video production: Paula Uriarte, Jonelle Warnock, Rhonda Urquidi, and Micah Lauer—not to mention all the kids who gave up three days of their summer vacation to learn about rules of notice!

Thanks, as always, to our families for their kindness, forbearance, and inspiration. Jeff wishes to thank his wife, Peggy Jo, and his daughters, Jazzy and Fiona Wilhelm, for always being willing to listen and to test out ideas in their own reading. Michael wants to thank his wife, Karen Flynn, and his granddaughter, Gabrielle White, for their love and support.

Publisher's Acknowledgments

Corwin gratefully acknowledges the contributions of the following reviewers:

Sara K. Ahmed
Educational Consultant
New York, NY

Lydia Bowden
Assistant Principal; Former Instructional Coach and Language Arts Teacher
Gwinnett County Public Schools
Atlanta, GA

Cindy Gagliardi
Teacher Chatham High School
Westfield, NJ

Michael Rafferty
Director of Teaching and Learning
Region 14 Schools
Woodbury, CT

Melanie Spence
Assistant Principal/Curriculum Coordinator; Educational Consultant
Sloan-Hendrix School District
Imboden, AR

Sayuri Stabrowski
Director of Instruction
KIPP Infinity Middle School
New York, NY

Jennifer Wheat Townsend
Director of Learning
Noblesville Schools
Indianapolis, IN

Chapter 1

Reader's Rules of Notice

Reading is both our passion and our work.

We've dedicated our professional lives largely to the teaching of reading. But some time ago, we became aware that we're considerably better at teaching students how to read *literature* than how to read *complex nonfiction*.

And when we recognized how many complex nonfiction texts we read each and every day and how much this reading contributes to the various kinds of formal and informal work we do—and to the various pleasures and passions we enjoy—it gave us a start. When we monitored our nonfiction reading in the context of our jobs, our lives as citizens, and our lives as parents, spouses, friends, and family members, we realized that if we were going to better prepare students for their lives both in school and out, we needed to focus our attention more closely on nonfiction and the ways that experts make meaning of such texts.

This book is our effort to do just that. In it, we share our understanding of what it takes to become a consciously competent reader of nonfiction, along with useful lessons that help students develop that competence and continue to develop expertise consciously over time. Our focus is on helping students learn and apply what we, following Peter Rabinowitz (1987), call reader's rules of notice—that is, the cues in a text that help us recognize what authors expect us to attend to and then use to construct meaning.

What Skilled Readers Do

Our work is based on two central insights. The first is that reading is simultaneously a top-down and bottom-up process. The second is that not everything in a text is of equal importance. We address these one at a time in the following pages.

Expert Reading Is Simultaneously Top Down and Bottom Up

The first insight is that comprehending what we read is simultaneously a top-down and bottom-up process (see Figure 1.1). This may sound complicated, but it's really quite simple: Expert readers start constructing an overarching understanding about the text as soon as they begin reading. This overarching understanding

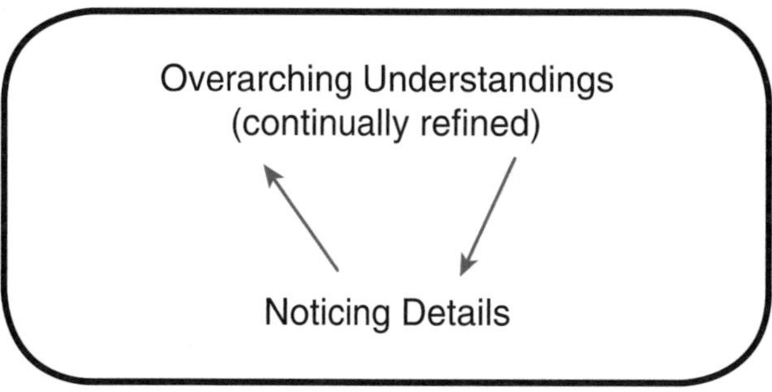

Figure 1.1

The Top-Down Bottom-Up Process of Reading Comprehension

points them to the details they notice (top down), and these details, in turn, refine the overarching understanding (bottom up), which helps them recognize other details that lead to a further refined understanding (more top down), in a continuing process.

As Kintsch (2005) explains, top-down processes "guide" comprehension, and bottom-up processes "constrain" it (p. 128). The influential reader-response theorist Louise Rosenblatt (1978) makes much the same point: As we read, we develop a "tentative framework" that influences the "selection and synthesis of further responses" (p. 54) that then reinforce or revise the framework.

We can illustrate this idea using the reading with which we begin our day: the newspaper. Michael subscribes to the *New York Times*, Jeff to the *Idaho Statesman* (or, as he'd prefer it to be called, the *Idaho StatesPERSON*). On the day we drafted this paragraph, the Supreme Court affirmed the right of same-sex couples to marry. We were both eager to read the reporting and commentary on this important issue. Michael began reading a *Times* editorial knowing it would endorse the decision and critique the dissenting justices' opinions. Jeff was unsure what position the *Statesman* would take and looked for details revealing that position. Both of us read in ways that were mindful of the ongoing cultural and historical conversations about civil rights and the rights of same-sex couples, conversations of which the decision and newspapers' reporting of it are a part. To guide us, we used our overarching understandings of the topic, the cultural conversation, and the kinds of texts (newspaper editorials, in this case) we chose to read to explore the issue.

Noticing the Conversation

This illustration reveals the importance of the *schemas*—which can be thought of as bookshelves in our brain—we use to store and organize information. Readers use background schemas to make sense of text. Reading research has long made clear the power of this schematic understanding.

Consider this short passage from a classic study by Bransford and Johnson (1972):

> A newspaper is better than a magazine. A seashore is a better place than the street. At first it is better to run than to walk. You may have to try several times. It takes some skill but it's easy to learn. Even young children can enjoy it. Once successful, complications are minimal. Birds seldom get too close. Rain, however, soaks in very fast. Too many people doing the same thing can also cause problems. One needs lots of room. If there are no complications, it can be very peaceful. A rock will serve as an anchor. If things break loose from it, however, you will not get a second chance. (p. 722)

Despite being composed of uncomplicated words, without schema markers to activate background knowledge, this paragraph was difficult for readers in the Bransford and Johnson study to understand. In contrast, readers who were told before they read that the topic of the passage was making and flying a kite had a much easier go of it—in fact, they experienced no comprehension problems whatsoever. That overarching conceptual understanding allowed them to activate their prior schematic knowledge about kites so they could use that knowledge to comprehend the text. Without activating that knowledge, even expert readers struggled mightily with the text. They couldn't figure out the local-level meaning of words without some sense of the whole. The above passage is what textbooks and much complex nonfiction texts look like to students who lack or fail to apply the background knowledge that would help them make sense of their reading.

Experienced readers necessarily employ *a priori* conceptual understanding to aid in their reading of new texts. One reason we're able to do so is because we tend to read to deepen existing areas of expertise rather than to develop entirely new ones. We know a lot about the cultural and historical conversations to which most of the texts we read are contributing. Our students don't have that advantage in the reading they do in and for school. They don't have schemas that are as well developed as those of adults; they have to read what's assigned; and they are often learning about something totally new to them. Noticing the conversation a text is part of and activating or building the background knowledge necessary to comprehend that turn in the conversation are prerequisite steps to effective reading. This book therefore begins with lessons that help students notice the conversation a text is part of. If readers don't notice this, they can't activate whatever necessary background knowledge they have, and they can't build new schematic knowledge about the topic that might be necessary to understand what is being said.

Noticing Key Details

Now, for the second central insight: Not everything in a text is of equal importance. Skilled readers know how to separate the wheat from the chaff; less accomplished readers have difficulty doing so. Reynolds (1992) provides a comprehensive review of research establishing that more successful readers self-consciously identify and pay more attention to important information than less successful readers do and that more successful readers continuously adapt their understanding of what's most important as they read.

Noticing Genre and Text Structure

In addition to the *a priori* conceptual understanding we bring to our reading, we bring *a priori* understanding of how texts work. Let's return to our newspaper example. We know that news stories have headlines but that these headlines are likely not written by the author of the story. We know that news stories, features, editorials, reviews, and so on all work a bit differently. We know that stories that appear above the fold are regarded as more important than stories on the same page that appear below the fold. We know that news stories are a genre and that this genre often employs text structures like comparison, definition, or process analysis. In short, we know how to notice both genres and the text structures embedded in those genres to guide our reading.

Peter Rabinowitz (Rabinowitz & Smith, 1998) applies a useful metaphor in thinking about genre and structure. He writes that reading a text is like putting together an item that arrives from the manufacturer unassembled—you have to have at least some sense of what it is you're making (top down). You don't just follow step-by-step directions without a clear sense of what you're going to end up with. The steps only make sense *if you know what the end product will look like*. In that light, each individual piece needs to be understood in terms of how it connects to neighboring pieces and how everything contributes to the purpose and shape of the whole (bottom up).

What This Noticing Means for Us as Teachers

First, because understanding a text requires readers to approach that text with some general understanding both of the cultural and historical conversation of which it is a part and of its structural features and genre, we have to teach students to *notice* the way in which a particular turn in the conversation is framed and shaped. Fortunately, authors do specific things to help readers orient themselves to the conversation, the genre, and the text structures they employ. We have found that we need to teach students how to notice and attend to these *orienting moves*. If we do, students are much more able to enter into texts and make meaning of them. In fact, we have found that they do so with the enthusiasm and joy of a knowing insider, someone who is in the process of developing new forms of expertise.

Second, because skilled reading requires readers to notice key details—to sort out what's important from what is less so—we have to teach students (1) to notice and use the *signaling moves* authors use to indicate what is most important and (2) to sort the important stuff they notice into categories that help them get a sense of the whole.

The lessons in this book are designed to teach students the rules of notice that expert readers employ, often unconsciously, as they read.

Principles of Effective Instruction

The lessons in this book are informed by four key principles.

1. The Importance of Teaching *How*

The first recommendation of the *Reading Next* report on adolescent literacy (Biancarosa & Snow, 2006) is that teachers ought to provide "direct, explicit comprehension instruction" (p. 4). Students need to understand *how* to do what we want them to do. This seems obvious, but many common instructional practices don't provide explicit instruction about how to do what we want students to do. Asking questions, for example, teaches students neither how to answer our questions nor how to ask their own. (Key principle 2 shows why this is true.)

2. The Importance and Difficulty of Transfer

Understanding any individual text is not that important. It would be nice if students remembered all the nuances of what we taught them about, say, *Narrative of the Life of Frederick Douglass*—but they won't. What is important is that they are able to apply what they learned from reading the *Narrative* to their subsequent reading and to their thinking about civil rights issues in their lives. What matters is that students *transfer* what they learn—both conceptually and strategically—to new reading and real-life situations.

Unfortunately, the data on transfer aren't that inspiring. Transfer typically doesn't occur. For example, students don't automatically apply strategies required by one reading to subsequent readings. The good news is that they can be taught to transfer new strategies if certain conditions are met. Haskell (2000) presents eleven of those conditions, which we have reduced to four:

1. Students must have command of the knowledge that is to be transferred.
2. Students must understand the principles to be transferred.
3. The classroom culture must cultivate a spirit of transfer.
4. Students must deliberately and repeatedly practice applying the meaning-making and problem-solving principles to new situations.

Byrnes's (2008) discussion of transfer is remarkably similar. He too argues that if students can develop deep, principled knowledge of what they do, they can then apply it to new situations. As Jeff has argued previously (Wilhelm, Douglas, & Fry, 2014):

> All instruction must involve service to self. After all, how can we call something "learning" if it does not lead to self-regulation and independence, to understanding new ways of doing things that can be applied right now and developed and further used in the future, both in school and out? (p. 30)

3. The Importance of Practice

How do students develop conscious competence that can be transferred? First of all, they need plenty of a particular kind of practice.

The research on the importance of practice was made famous by Malcolm Gladwell (2008) when he argued that ten thousand hours of practice are necessary to become an expert in a field. In an article that's adapted from a recent book, Anders Ericsson, the author of the study on which Gladwell bases his claim, and a colleague (Ericsson & Pool, 2016a) explain that Gladwell got the study wrong. Ten thousand isn't a magic number; although lots and lots of practice is needed to become an expert, the actual amount needed varies by field. But more importantly, they explain, Gladwell fails to consider the nature of the practice that moves people toward expertise. They call that practice *deliberate practice*. Such practice

> involves constantly pushing oneself beyond one's comfort zone, following training activities designed by an expert to develop specific abilities, and using feedback to identify weaknesses and work on them. (Ericsson & Pool, 2016a)

That's the kind of practice we hope to provide in our lessons. How often do schools provide students the kind of deliberate practice they need in mindfully applying what they have learned to new reading situations? How often do students develop conscious and transferable strategic competence? In our experience: very seldom.

Rules of Notice

Video 1.1

http://resources.corwin.com/divingdeep-nonfiction

To read a QR code, you must have a smartphone or tablet with a camera. We recommend that you download a QR code reader app that is made specifically for your phone or tablet brand.

4. The Importance of Promoting a Dynamic Mindset

The lessons in this book teach students transferable strategies they can apply to the reading and writing of ever more complex texts over time.

Working consciously toward this kind of development helps cultivate an attitude that Carol Dweck (2006) calls the *growth* or *dynamic* mindset—a validating attitude that one *can* and *will* learn, through targeted effort and strategic practice, to become ever more competent and proficient. This process begins with the learners engaging in what Lave and Wenger (1991) call *legitimate peripheral participation* in which the learner becomes competent enough to participate as a novice expert and eventually an actual expert in the ongoing disciplinary conversations and the knowledge making and problem solving that are generated by these conversations.

The most important service we can provide our students is to help them develop and cultivate a dynamic mindset. The dynamic mindset—on the part of teachers *and* students—is a prerequisite to achieving the kind of expertise required by complex texts—and modern life.

The bottom line: Our abilities are not inborn and fixed; they are cultural and dynamic. The dynamic mindset is based on the understanding that intelligence and abilities are developed and cultivated with practice over time. In contrast, the fixed mindset, expressed through information-driven teaching, assumes that abilities and intelligence are static. We need to convey to students that they—that anyone—can master the next available challenge if they embrace their capacity to learn and if a few minimal conditions are met. And we need to believe this ourselves.

Figure 1.2 summarizes the fixed versus growth/dynamic mindset. The descriptions are based on Carol Dweck's *Mindset* (2006) and Peter H. Johnston's *Opening Minds* (2012).

The Current Educational Climate

We haven't yet mentioned the Common Core State Standards, because we wanted to argue the importance of teaching students how to read complex nonfiction texts independent of this mandate. However, the CCSS and all next-generation standards worldwide provide even more forceful justification for the lessons that follow.

Next-generation standards worldwide, including the anchor standards of the Common Core, are entirely strategic; they focus on *what*—the outcome—but implicitly require that students learn *how* by foregrounding words that ask them to *do* things like argue, analyze, and explain. Next-generation standards therefore insist on the transfer of expert reading processes, as well as those of composing, speaking, and listening.

While we endorse the importance of teaching students to read complex nonfiction (something stressed by the CCSS), we have significant concerns with some of the instructional ideas that have sprung up surrounding these standards. We discuss those concerns in great detail in *Uncommon Core* (Smith, Appleman, & Wilhelm, 2014), but we'll mention a couple of them here.

One concern is the emphasis on text-dependent questions and the way these questions are used in instruction. There are two problems here. The first

Fixed Mindset	Growth (or Dynamic) Mindset
Intelligence and abilities are static.	Intelligence and abilities can be developed and cultivated.
Tends to lead to avoiding challenges.	Tends to lead to embracing challenges.
Tends to be defensive or give up easily when faced with challenges.	Tends to be persistent in the face of setbacks.
Tends to see effort as fruitless or worse.	Tends to see effort as the path to mastery.
Tends to ignore useful feedback, particularly when it is negative—sees it as judgment.	Tends to learn from criticism, framing it in causal or procedural terms informing principles of how to do things in the future.
Tends to feel threatened by the success of others.	Tends to find lessons and inspiration in the success of others.
Learning goal tends to be to look as smart as one can.	Learning goal tends to be to learn as much as one can.
The most important information is whether one is successful. It shows who is smart and more valuable. *How* is irrelevant.	The most important information is *how* someone did (or could do) something, because that's what one can learn from.
When encountering difficulty, views the difficulty as failure, questions one's ability, assigns blame for failure, and ceases acting strategically.	When encountering difficulty, engages in self-monitoring and self-instruction, increases strategic efforts, and doesn't see oneself as failing. Says, "I don't have it quite yet." Consciously builds a toolbox for problem-solving success. Sees learning as a process.
When asked, "When do you feel smart?" says things like: "When I don't make any mistakes." "When I finish something fast and it's perfect." "When something is easy for me, but other people can't do it."	When asked, "When do you feel smart?" says things like: "When it's really hard, and I try really hard, and I can do something I couldn't do before." "When I work on something a long time and I start to figure it out."
Everything is about the outcome.	Everything one is doing has value regardless of the outcome.
When teaching, asks questions like: "Can I teach them?" "Are they able to learn?"	When teaching, asks questions like: "How can I teach them?" "How will they learn best?"

Source: Based on Dweck (2006) and Johnston (2012).

Figure 1.2

The Fixed Mindset Versus the Growth (or Dynamic) Mindset

is that text-dependent questions are typically relevant to only one text and so cannot be transferred to new reading situations. The second is that teachers are too often the only ones asking the questions, which means that teachers are the only ones noticing what's worth asking about. If we want students to become highly expert readers (as the standards and the world demand), we must help them become independent and attentive noticers, questioners, and interpreters on their own. Text-dependent questions can help achieve this goal only if they teach students something that students can apply on their own to their future reading.

Rules of Notice and Transfer of Learning

Video 1.2

http://resources.corwin.com/divingdeep-nonfiction

Our second concern is a related one: the emphasis on close reading and how that is being interpreted in connection with instruction. Most discussions of close reading suggest that reading is an entirely bottom-up process. As we explained earlier, it isn't. You can't notice the details that are worth attending to unless you are guided by a conceptual framework and a familiarity with genre.

How This Book Works

The lessons in this book are built on the four kinds of noticing we have outlined in this chapter:

1. Noticing the conversation
2. Noticing key details
3. Noticing genre
4. Noticing text structure

Chapter 2 provides seven lessons that help students *notice the conceptual conversation* of which the text is a part. Chapter 3 provides seven lessons on *noticing key details*. Chapter 4 provides seven lessons on *noticing and making meaning based on genre*. The seven lessons in Chapter 5 focus on *noticing and making meaning based on text structure*, with an emphasis on comparison and contrast.

Each chapter comprises a series of seven lessons that proceed similarly:

Lesson 1: Reading Visual Texts

Students examine some kind of visual text. Visual texts get learners into the game, allowing them to focus on what they must do to understand the author's message without attending to the demands of vocabulary and complex syntax. Visual texts are accessible to struggling readers and English learners, helping all students to name the rules of notice—direct statements, ruptures, calls to attention, and reader's response—and to see and develop their strategic facility using these rules.

Lesson 2: Thinking Aloud

We explicitly model the kind of expert procedures we want our students to apply and mentor students into practicing these strategies, naming specific rules of notice that will assist them.

Lesson 3: Practice in Miniature

Students have the opportunity to practice what we've modeled by deliberately and consciously applying the strategy to short texts we have written or selected.

Lesson 4: Questioning

Students apply a procedure for questioning to the text that focuses their attention on noticing and interpreting in ways that can be transferred and applied to all texts.

Lesson 5: Writing and Responding

Students are cast as writers or respondents to the writing of others to practice and monitor the use of focal strategies using the rules of notice.

Lesson 6: Search and Find

Students pay attention as they read and watch *outside school*, looking for ways to apply the rules of notice that they've learned in class. They see the relevance of their learning as they transfer it to other texts and situations.

Lesson 7: Putting It All Together

Students pull together everything they've learned in the instructional sequence as they consider a complete nonfiction text, consolidating their learning of the strategies associated with the rules of notice.

Each lesson is ready to teach but is also a model for other lessons you'll create for your own students based on the same principles. For additional lessons and extensions, visit this book's companion website at **http://resources.corwin.com/divingdeep-nonfiction.**

How to Use This Book

Although the lessons we present in this book are classroom tested and we think you could teach them as written, we suspect that you might want to adapt them to meet the needs of your own students. We designed the lessons to be usable from late elementary through high school, but depending on your students, you might want to move faster or slower than we suggest. You might want to substitute one of the texts we suggest for one that's easier or more difficult. You might want to use different grouping procedures than the ones we suggest. You might want to break the lessons up and offer them on consecutive days instead of in a single period.

That said, we think it's crucially important to maintain the principles of practice at play here. That is, it's crucial that the lessons provide explicit instruction in the ways authors cue their readers to notice and make meaning with what's most important, that students get plenty of deliberate practice in applying those rules of notice, and that the lessons require students to deliberately transfer their strategic learning and in so doing cultivate a growth mindset.

Although you may choose to modify the lessons in some way, we do advise that you teach them in the order that we suggest. Doing so will guarantee that you enact the principles we discuss above. However, following the sequence doesn't mean that you need to teach the lessons one after another, uninterrupted by any other instruction. In fact, if you've read one or more of our other books (e.g., Smith, Appleman, & Wilhelm, 2014; Smith & Wilhelm, 2002, 2006, 2010; Wilhelm, 2007; Wilhelm, Douglas, & Fry, 2014; Wilhelm, Wilhelm, & Boas, 2009), you know we advocate embedding instruction within inquiry contexts that require and reward the use of new strategies. In inquiry, the curriculum is reframed, usually with an essential or existential question (Wilhelm & Novak, 2011) that poses a personally and socially/culturally compelling problem to be solved. We believe that strategies for reading, composing, speaking, listening, and problem solving are best learned in the context of addressing and solving such problems. Courtney Cazden (1992) offered a metaphor that we have long found compelling: the instructional detour. That is, the lessons we provide can be used to focus students' attention on particular strategies that they can then employ on the main road of the inquiry. If we practice the strategies with texts and content relevant to the inquiry, we get a twofer. But we can also take a meaningful detour *if* the students see how they are practicing a strategy that they will immediately apply in the context of a meaningful inquiry. Indeed, the value of the lessons will be most obvious to students when they are rewarded for applying them to pursue an inquiry that matters to them.

Let's get started.

Getting Started Using Rules of Notice

Video 1.3

http://resources.corwin.com/divingdeep-nonfiction

Chapter 2

Noticing the Conversation

In Chapter 1, we explained how expert readers place the text they are reading into an ongoing conceptual conversation. We wish we could take credit for this important concept, but we can't. It comes from Kenneth Burke (1941), who used it to talk about entering ongoing cultural conversations about important issues. Here's how he spins out his metaphor:

> Imagine that you enter a parlor. You come late. When you arrive, others have long preceded you, and they are engaged in a heated discussion, a discussion too heated for them to pause and tell you exactly what it is about. In fact, the discussion had already begun long before any of them got there, so that no one present is qualified to retrace for you all the steps that had gone before. You listen for a while, until you decide that you have caught the tenor of the argument; then you put in your oar. (pp. 110–111)

The idea that texts are part of an ongoing conversation changes, in fundamental ways, how we view, approach, and understand them. In this way, noticing the conversation is a threshold concept. Meyer and Land (2003) use the term *threshold knowledge* to describe "core concepts and processes that once understood, transform perception of a given subject" (p. iii). In other words, a *threshold concept* gives learners an entirely new way of looking at what they are studying, and a *threshold process* gives learners a new and powerful way of doing a discipline or solving a problem. Threshold concepts are powerful, but they can be troublesome, too, because they are likely to challenge learners' preconceived ideas. In our experience, when students read, most think only about the particular text they are reading. For such students, the concept that texts are part of an ongoing conversation will change the way they think about reading—and the strategies with which they pursue it.

If we want our students to enter these ongoing conversations, we need to help them learn how to "listen for a while," using strategies to identify the conversational topic and construct the nature of the conversation on their own. That is, we want students to understand that the texts they read are written in response to other texts already out in the world. We want them to realize that putting a written work in its textual context will help them understand it. That's what the lessons in this chapter are designed to help them do.

Noticing the Conversation
READING VISUAL TEXTS

PURPOSE

- To recognize textual topics and infer how texts speak to issues and to each other

LENGTH

- Approximately 90 minutes (can be split into two 45-minute classes)

MATERIALS NEEDED

- A means of projecting images from the Internet onto a larger screen
- A class set of handouts:
  - Handout 2.1, "*Beer Street* and *Gin Lane*"
  - Handout 2.2, "Two Views of Children's Play"
- Chart paper or other means of displaying a list

Introduction

As we noted in Chapter 1, each set of lessons begins with a lesson using visual art. As you'll see, we use artwork that's old enough to be in the public domain, for two reasons: First, we can publish the images without having to purchase rights. But second, we want to give students practice in identifying and entering conversations about topics that are distant from them in time, place, and experience. They'll have to do this whenever they read about a new topic—throughout their lives in school and often outside of school as well.

Lesson Steps

Step 1

Introduce the lesson and its purpose:

- Ask students to imagine overhearing a conversation on a bus or in a doctor's office.
- Note that when you do that kind of overhearing, you have to imagine how what you overhear fits or makes sense in the lives of the people whose conversations you are overhearing. What is happening or has gone on in the people's lives that you *aren't* hearing? What can you infer?
- Explain that reading is often like overhearing a conversation in that it's useful to imagine how the text you're reading fits in with other texts about the same topic. Readers must infer what's happened before and where things might be going.
- Explain that identifying or imagining the conversation a text is part of is an important way to come to understand it.

Step 2

Introduce the practice of studying a visual. Model and guide students to identify and justify topics of conversation:

- Project so that all students can see it the prints *Beer Street* and *Gin Lane* by William Hogarth. Explain that the prints are placed next to each other so that students can see both at the same time. If you can, zoom in on one of the prints first and ask students what they notice about it. Then zoom in on the other print and ask them to do the same.
- Allow students to get up to look at the image more closely if they would like to.
- Ask students what details they notice. Record these details on chart paper or in any place visible to all students.
- When your discussion of both halves of the painting is complete, divide students into small groups and have them work together on Handout 2.1, "*Beer Street* and *Gin Lane*." Tell them that the scale has seven points and that they should mark the scale with an X or by circling one of the points to indicate where they stand.
- Ask groups to discuss reasons for their ratings on the scales. What details led them to their conclusion(s)? If students disagree on a rating, ask each of them to explain how they came to their conclusions and try to come to agreement.
- Circulate to check their understanding. If students are not elaborating their responses, point to how they marked a scale and ask:
    - *What makes you say so?*

Step 3

Lead a whole-class discussion of how details make conversational points:

- Bring the class back together and tally responses from the groups' scales.
- Ask the groups for details that support their choices and to explain how these details support their position on the scale.
- As students provide these details, list them (if new) or check them off (if already on the list that the class constructed together in Step 2). Ensure students provide the details as well as their interpretations of how the details work for meaning and effect.

- After students provide each detail, ask what Hogarth would have done differently if he had wanted to make a different point:
    - *What details might he have used instead?*
    - *How would these details change the meaning of the painting?*
- List students' answers to these questions as well. For example, if students notice the young child falling over the railing in the lower right-hand corner of the engraving, say:
    - *If he wanted to show the gin wasn't so destructive, the mother would be holding her child or at least would seem upset that the child fell.*
- Explain that Hogarth's print *Gin Lane* was one factor that led the Parliament of Great Britain to pass the Gin Act of 1751, which was designed to reduce the illegal production and drinking of gin. Ask students how they think this print might have made an argument and done some work toward changing social attitudes and policy.

Topic–Comment Strategy: Bruegel's *Children's Games*

Video 2.1

http://resources.corwin.com/divingdeep-nonfiction

Step 4

Provide additional practice to give students increased independence in noticing conversational topics:

- Project so that all students can see it the 1560 painting *Children's Games* by Flemish painter Pieter Bruegel the Elder.
- Have students work in groups to make notes on what they notice in this painting.
- Allow students to look at the image more closely if they would like to and make notes.
- If they are struggling, zoom in on various quadrants of the painting, and ask students to make notes on each one before returning to view the whole.
- When they have adequate notes, ask the groups to work on the first two pages of Handout 2.2, "Two Views of Children's Play."
- Circulate to listen to their conversations and check their understanding.
- If students are not elaborating their responses, point to how they marked a scale and ask:
    - *What makes you say so?*
- If students disagree on how to mark the scale, ask them to explain to each other how they came to their conclusions and try to reach agreement. Make sure they use details from the painting to support their conclusions.

Step 5

Provide additional practice with a second painting, giving students an opportunity to compare two different messages on the same topic:

- Project so that all students can see it the engraving by Pieter van der Borcht produced in 1559: *The Cobbler's Unruly Family*, also called *The Cobbler and His Wife as a Teacher.*
- Have students work in groups to make notes on what they notice in this painting.
- Allow students to look at the image more closely if they would like to and make notes.
- If they are struggling, zoom in on various quadrants of the painting, and ask students to make notes on each one before returning to view the whole.
- When they have adequate notes, ask the groups to work on the remainder of Handout 2.2, "Two Views of Children's Play."
- Circulate to listen to their conversations and check their understanding.
- If students are not elaborating their responses, point to how they marked a scale and ask:
  - *What makes you say so?*
- If students disagree on how to mark the scale, ask them to explain to each other how they came to their conclusions and try to reach agreement. Make sure they use details from the painting to support their conclusions.

Step 6

Lead a whole-class discussion to review the process of noticing conversational topics:

- Ask: *How does Bruegel's attitude toward children compare to van der Borcht's? How do you know?* See the sample exchange in the "Voices From the Classroom" box that follows.
- When students respond, make sure they provide details from the painting and engraving to back up what they say. Ask: *How do you know? What makes you say so?* Record students' main points on the board or chart paper.
- Ask the class to consider this: *What discussions about children must have been going on at the time to motivate Bruegel and van der Borcht to create their works?* If students are not responding, ask them to turn and talk to a partner about this first, then bring the class back together and pose the question again.

Teaching Parody: Bruegel's *Children's Games*

Video 2.2

http://resources.corwin.com/divingdeep-nonfiction

- Ask students to consider to what extent we are having similar discussions and debates about children's games today.

Step 7

Conclude the lesson by reviewing and considering how to move forward:

- Explain to students that when they read a visual text, they should apply what they learned in this lesson to understand the work—think about the conversation that the visual text is part of, the turns in that conversation, and how the text is responding to other texts and perspectives.
- Explain that they'll be practicing this strategy in the next several lessons.

Extension

Have students research the Gin Act of 1751 or European attitudes toward children in the 16th and 17th centuries and report their findings. As an alternative, have students identify and report on modern conversations that resemble the ones the have just considered (e.g., the legalization of marijuana or whether schools should require physical education).

Voices From the Classroom

WHAT STUDENTS SAID ABOUT
Two Views of Children and Play

TEACHER: So how does Bruegel's attitude toward children compare to van der Borcht's?

STUDENT: That van der Borcht guy likes children a lot less.

TEACHER: What makes you say so?

STUDENT: Well, just look at the guy and his wife.

TEACHER: What do you mean?

STUDENT: Their expressions.

TEACHER: Tell me more.

STUDENT: Well, the wife especially looks like she's going to cry or something.

TEACHER: And in Bruegel's painting?

STUDENT: You can't really see the faces of the adults too well.

TEACHER: So what?

STUDENT: So you can't see the disapproval or something. If Bruegel had wanted to show that he had a bad attitude toward kids, they'd all be frowning or something.

Beer Street and Gin Lane

The prints *Beer Street* and *Gin Lane* were created by William Hogarth in 1751. They were meant to be viewed side by side.

Source: Wikimedia Commons/Yomangani

Look carefully at the images and respond to the questions that follow:

1. How does Hogarth feel about Gin Lane? What makes you say so? Look at specific details and explain how they work to establish Hogarth's meaning and what effect they were designed to have on his audience.

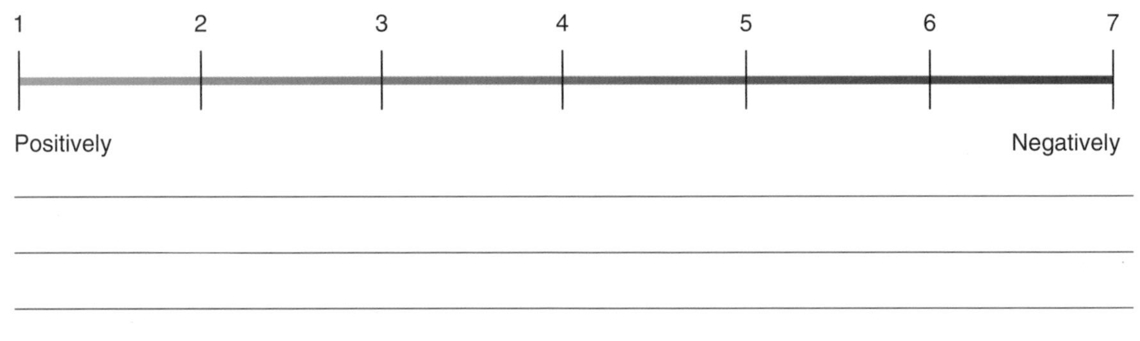

(Continued)

2. How does Hogarth feel about Beer Street? What makes you say so? Once again look at specific details and explain how they work to establish Hogarth's meaning and what effect they were designed to have on his audience.

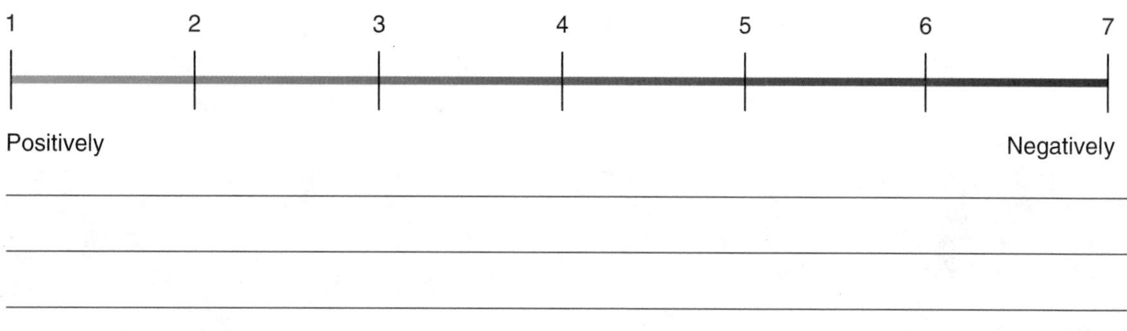

____

____

____

____

3. Think about and write down two or three details in the image you would change if you wanted to communicate a more positive or negative attitude toward Beer Street or toward Gin Lane.

____

____

____

____

4. What must have been going on at the time to motivate Hogarth to make his engraving? What conversation is his engraving entering into? And what comment is it making or turn is it taking in this conversation?

____

____

____

____

Handout 2.2

Two Views of Children's Play

Please look carefully at the painting *Children's Games*, which was painted by the Flemish painter Pieter Bruegel the Elder in 1560, and respond to the questions that follow it. You should mark the scales the same way you did on Handout 2.1.

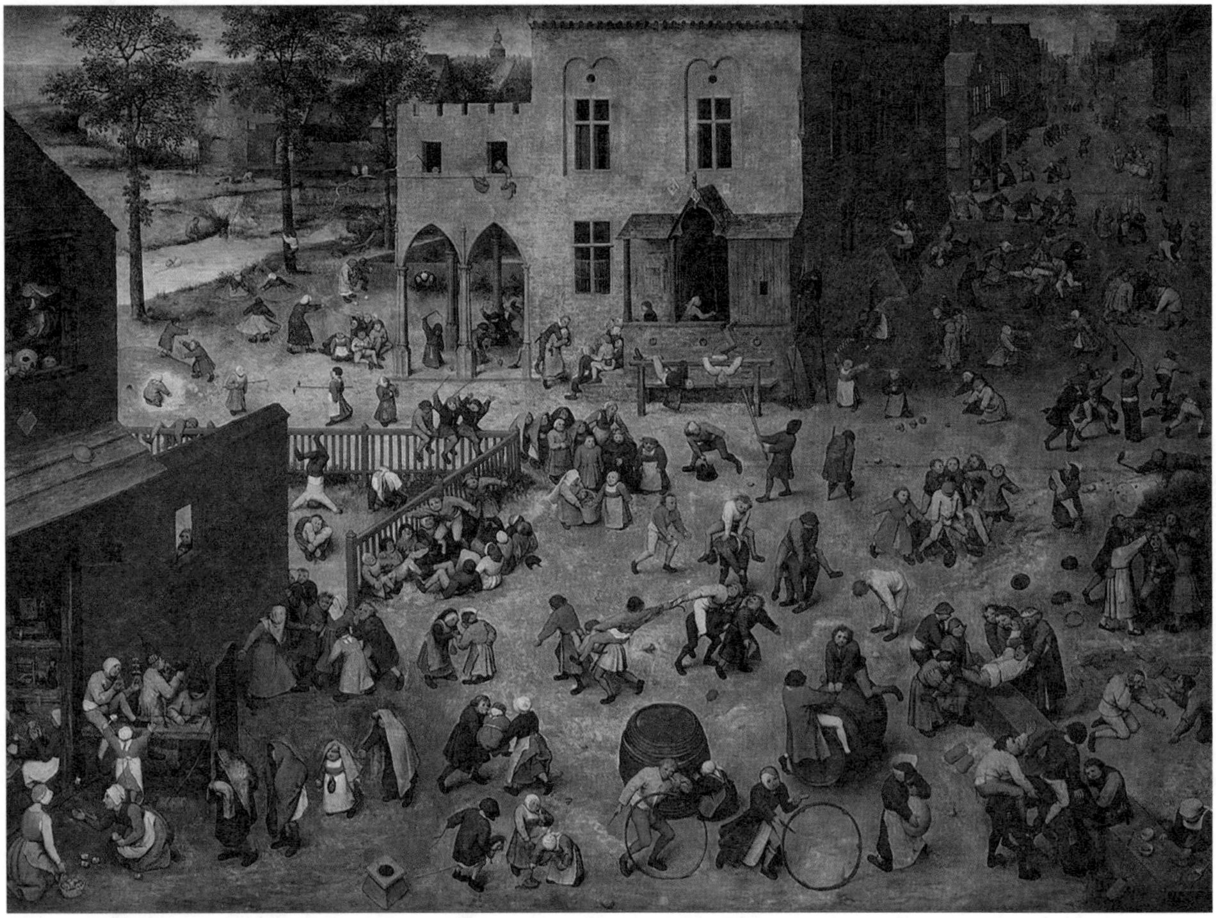

Source: Wikimedia Commons

Look carefully at the image and respond to the questions that follow:

1. How does Bruegel feel about children? What makes you say so? Look at specific details and explain how they work to establish Bruegel's meaning and what effect they were designed to have on his audience.

1	2	3	4	5	6	7
Positively						Negatively

___

___

___

___

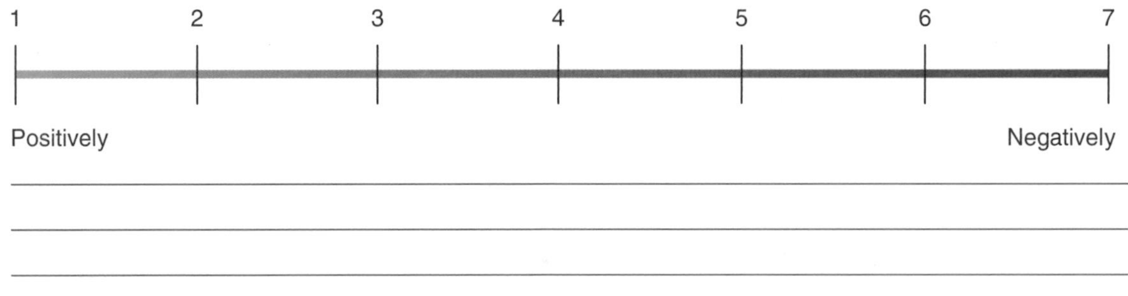

(Continued)

2. How does Bruegel feel about play? What makes you say so? Once again, look at specific details and explain how they work to establish Bruegel's meaning and what effect they were designed to have on his audience.

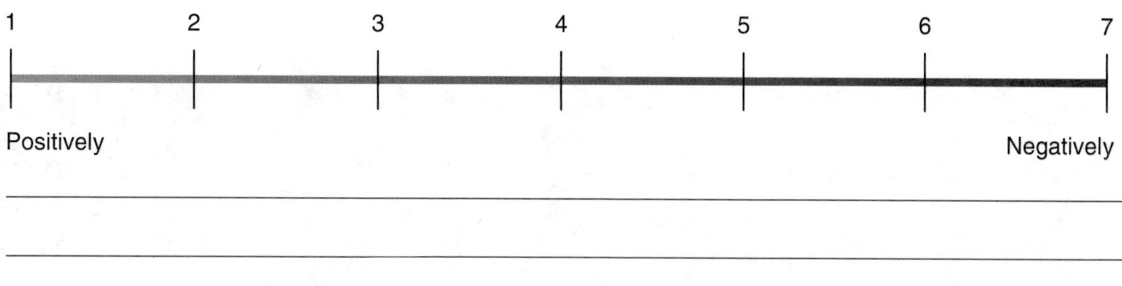

3. Think about and write down two or three details in the image you would change if you wanted to communicate a different attitude toward children or play.

4. What conversations is this painting entering into? And what comment is it making or turn is it taking in this conversation?

(Continued)

The next piece of art for you to examine, composed around the same time as Bruegel's, also depicts children at play. Pieter van der Borcht produced this engraving in 1559. It's called *The Cobbler's Unruly Family* or *The Cobbler and His Wife as a Teacher.*

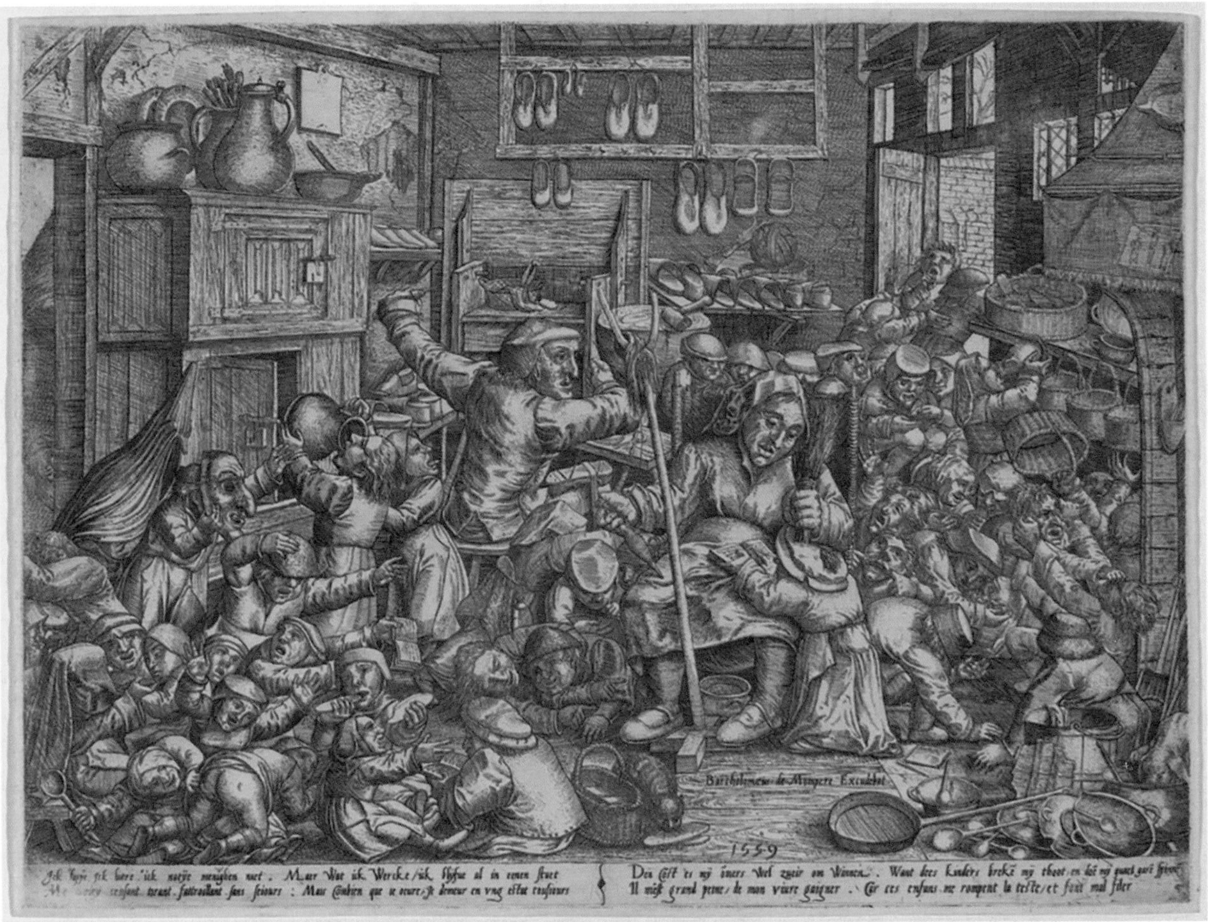

Source: Courtesy of the National Gallery of Art, Washington, DC

Look carefully at the image and respond to the questions that follow:

5. How does van der Borcht feel about children? What makes you say so? Look at specific details and explain how they work to establish van der Borcht's meaning and what effect they were designed to have on his audience.

1 — 2 — 3 — 4 — 5 — 6 — 7

Positively — Negatively

____

____

____

____

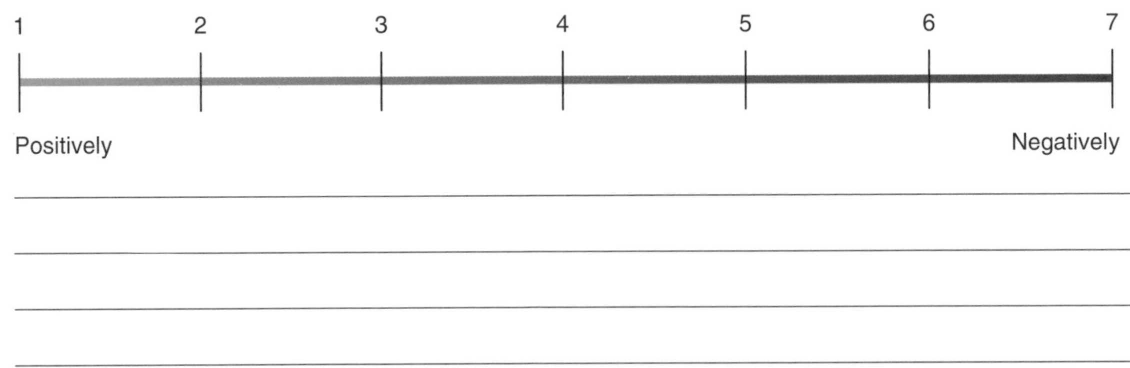

(Continued)

6. How does van der Borcht feel about play? What makes you say so? Look at specific details and explain how they work to establish van der Borcht's meaning and what effect they were designed to have on his audience.

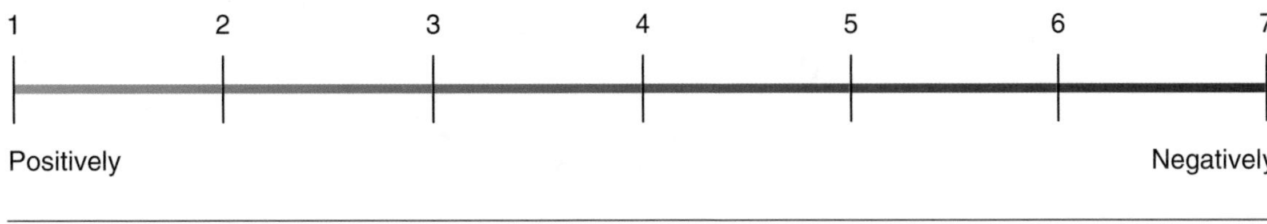

7. What details in the engraving support your judgments?

8. Think about and write down two or three details in the image you would change if you wanted to communicate a different attitude toward children or play.

9. What conversations is this engraving entering into? And what comment is it making or turn is it taking in this conversation? How does this compare to the perspective, comment, and turn that Bruegel's work offers?

Lesson
2

Noticing the Conversation
THINKING ALOUD

PURPOSE

- To notice conversational topics and get oriented to the conversation

LENGTH

- Approximately 45 minutes

MATERIALS NEEDED

- Class sets of two texts (at the level of complexity appropriate for your students) that you will use to do your think-alouds *or*
- A class set of Handout 2.3, "*Intelligence: A Brief History* (Excerpt)"
- Chart paper for an anchor chart that you will create with students after you have done the think-aloud—ideally, in a maintainable format that you can revise and add to throughout your work on noticing conversations
- Different colored pens, pencils, or highlighters for each student

Introduction

Whenever we read any text, we understand that it's *about something*. Our desire to understand that something is probably what caused us to pick up the text in the first place. Typically, people read about things that they already know about—and that they have an interest in or questions about—so they understand how what a particular text is saying relates to what others have said on the same topic. But our students don't have the luxury of reading only to deepen existing areas of expertise. They also have to read to develop new areas of expertise. That means orienting themselves to the text by constructing the topic and textual conversation that it's part of. The lesson that follows is designed to help students do just that.

Think of it this way: Being assigned to read a text is like being dropped from a helicopter into unfamiliar terrain. Before you know what to do or where to go, you have to get the lay of the land. The technique we use to help students do so in this lesson is the think-aloud.

We hope that the thinking aloud that we share is useful to you as a model for your think-aloud, but it's important for *your* students to see *your* modeling. That is, you should use our suggestions as a guide rather than a script.

In this lesson, we suggest ways to model how experienced readers orient themselves to unfamiliar textual terrain. We use two very different and complex texts from different disciplines with the hope that it will help students apply what they learn in their own diverse reading experiences.

An important note: In this lesson, we also introduce the four primary rules of notice we'll be working with throughout the text. See Figure 2.1 for a couple of examples of each; however, we don't recommend reproducing this as a handout for students. Discussing rules of notice as they occur and creating a class anchor chart is a much more effective means for students to learn to notice and use these rules and to feel ownership over this technique, as the examples will come from texts you are reading together. The Appendix provides a much more exhaustive collection of examples compiled by Jeff and fellows of the Boise State Writing Project.

1. Direct statements of a principle or generalization

Examples:

- *Sentences with beginnings such as "In summary" or "Putting it all together"*
- *Sentences with colons, especially when what follows begins with a capital letter as that typically introduces an answer or direct statement*

2. Ruptures

Examples:

- *Surprising attention to a detail that doesn't seem so important at first—something you don't expect*
- *A change in style—for example, a short sentence used among long ones*

3. Calls to attention

Examples:

- *Direct questions—and their answers*
- *Typesetting conventions such as italics, bold text, and bullets*

4. Reader's response

Examples:

- *Strong or extreme words (like* must*)*
- *Any writing that seems designed to evoke an emotional response from the reader*

Figure 2.1

The Four General Reader's Rules of Notice

In the course of the lessons in the book, we will dig deeper into what these rules mean and provide plenty of additional examples of each one.

Lesson Steps

Step 1

Introduce the lesson and its purpose:

- Explain to students that much of the reading they do relates to what they know. They might read about a favorite musician or athlete, to which they bring their knowledge of what others have said about that musician or athlete. Or they might read the next book in a series they love and already be familiar with many of the characters, their challenges, and the setting.

- Provide an example from your own reading, such as the following from Michael (written before Cleveland's comeback NBA Finals victory):
    - *As a sports fan, when I read a headline like this one from* USA Today*—"LeBron James' Legacy Fades With Each NBA Finals Loss"—I know that the article is part of an ongoing conversation about LeBron's place among the game's greatest players and that Michael Jordan and his six titles (compared to LeBron's two) are lurking in the background. Or if I read the headline "Why Did Taylor Swift Go Pop?" I know that it will be part of a conversation about the relationship between pop music and country.*
- Explain that in school, and sometimes in life, you might have to read something that you don't know much about, which means you have to figure out the conversation as you read and orient yourself toward that conversational topic.
- Illustrate how to go about figuring out the conversation and orienting yourself to it by thinking aloud as you read a text.

Step 2

Model the think-aloud illustrating how to notice and get oriented to the conversation of which the text is a part:

- Distribute copies of Handout 2.3, "*Intelligence: A Brief History* (Excerpt)."
- Do a think-aloud to model the process of orienting oneself to the conversation. See the sample think-aloud that follows, and remember to use our suggestions as a guide rather than a script. Note also that we interrupt the think-aloud from time to time to ask students to do something. We don't want them to be passive observers of their teacher!
- Tell students that you will ask for their help in recording what you call "rules of notice" on an anchor chart after you have done the think-aloud.
- Tell students that you will also be asking them to annotate the texts using different colored pens, pencils, or highlighters.

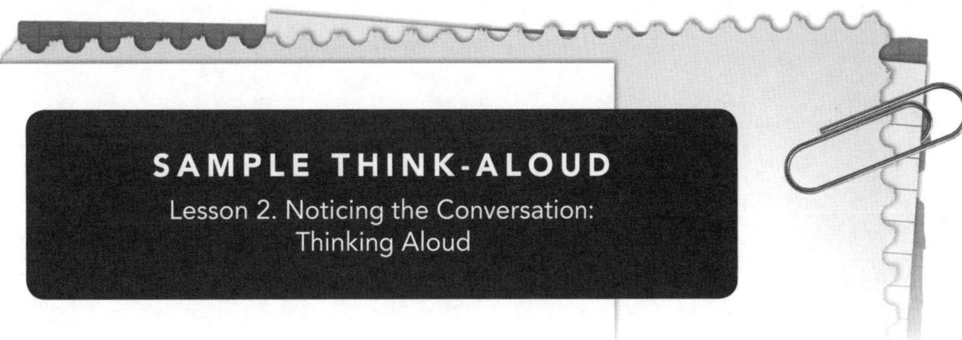

SAMPLE THINK-ALOUD

Lesson 2. Noticing the Conversation: Thinking Aloud

Intelligence: A Brief History (Excerpt)

By Anna T. Cianciolo and Robert J. Sternberg

In the now classic tale, three blind men approached an elephant

OK, this is the first chapter of a history book. But it starts out with a legend or something. I didn't expect that. When something unexpected happens like this, I know I have to notice it. I call such things ruptures. Ruptures are one rule of notice. So I know that this little story is going to be something important.

Tell students to mark this rupture with one of their colored pens.

and were curious about its nature. Having never encountered an elephant before, the men each had a different impression.

So I'm thinking that maybe this book's going to be about different ideas about intelligence. I wonder if some people think that there's only one kind.

For the man holding the elephant's thick legs, the elephant was like a tree. The elephant was snakelike to the man who had the elephant's lively trunk in his hands. The third blind man, feeling the elephant's sturdy side, exclaimed it was like a wall.

Another thing I know is that you have to notice metaphors. And the description of the classic tale is going on for a bit. I know I need to notice whenever an author seems to provide undue attention. I'm going to call such things calls to attention.

Have students mark this rule with a different-colored pen.

Who was right? And what does this story have to do with intelligence?

Questions are another call to attention.

Just like the blind men in our story, people exploring the nature of intelligence cannot see the object of their study and so

"So" is a little word. But it often announces some kind of conclusion. I know that I should be on the lookout for anytime an author directly states a conclusion. I'll call those things direct statements. I wonder whether some people have more confidence in their ability to understand intelligence than these authors seem to.

Tell students to mark this rule of notice with one of their colored pens.

(Continued)

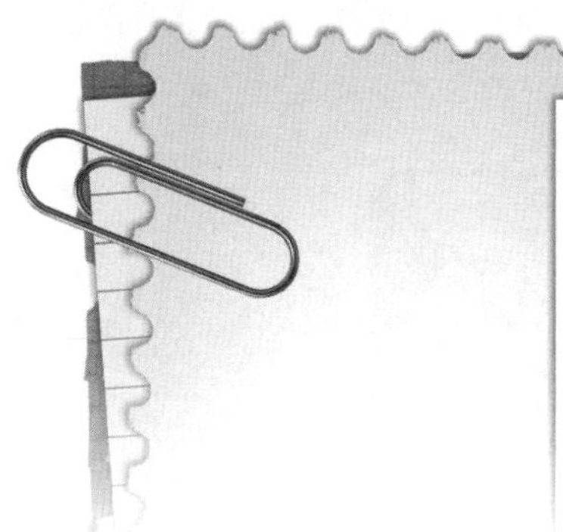

SAMPLE THINK-ALOUD
(CONT.)

have used metaphors to help them conceptualize intelligent behavior (Sternberg, 1990). In this chapter we describe some of the earliest notions of intelligence, which predate scientific study by hundreds, even thousands, of years.

Tell students to mark this rule with one of their colored pens.

Wow, that's really interesting to me. I know whenever my interest is really piqued, I have to notice why. I'll call this rule of notice the reader's response. In this case, I find it interesting that these ideas existed before scientists studied intelligence. I wonder whether modern science is consistent or inconsistent with these early understandings. I'm going to read to find out.

Next we present seven metaphors that underlie modern intelligence research: geographic, computational, biological, epistemological, sociological, anthropological, and systems. We briefly describe each metaphor, highlighting the major theories of intelligence associated with each one.

Ask students what rule or rules might be in operation in the preceding two sentences.

Source: Cianciolo, A., & Sternberg, R. (2004). *Intelligence: A brief history.* Hoboken, NJ: Wiley-Blackwell.

Step 3

Lead a whole-class discussion about the think-aloud:

- Ask students to name and define the four rules of notice you mentioned in the think-aloud. Record their responses on the anchor chart, which you might call "How We Notice the Conversation." See Figure 2.2 for an example. (Students compiled the chart, complete with a few misspellings.)
- Set up the anchor chart in a maintainable format and add to and revise it as you continue the class discussion on the rules of notice.
- Ask students to select what they think is the single most important sentence in the first two paragraphs. Lead a discussion on their answers. Probe for why they say what they say. Their responses will vary, but it should be clear that some details are less important than others. For example, their responses should reveal that the idea that intelligence has been conceived of in different ways is way more important than the parts of the elephant the different blind men hung onto.
- Ask students to name the conversation(s) of which this text is a part. Students might say "intelligence." If they do, probe for more detail—for example, "different ideas about intelligence" or "the problem of describing or measuring intelligence."
- Explain that students will have an opportunity to apply this strategy in a follow-up lesson.

Extension

Have students record a think-aloud on a text of their own selection to share in pairs, naming the rules they use to notice the conversation and explaining how that works for them. Newspaper articles are often good choices since such articles enter into a conversation that is ongoing and typically issue-oriented. The reader is expected to know what has happened previously in regard to the news item, and what various perspectives might exist.

Look for models of think-alouds using more difficult texts on this book's companion website at **http://resources.corwin.com/divingdeep-nonfiction**.

RRN: Noticing the Conversation/Topic

1) Direct Statements of Principls/Generalizations
Notice colors = what follows
In summary, in conclusion, most importantly
does the text say what or who it's for? Against?
Statements of certainty: we know...

2) Ruptures/Surprises/shifts
Repeating the obvious - or going against the obvious
Shifts in tone, time, emotion...
Shat sentance among long one. Shovt 1
Sentance TP among long one.

3) Calls to Attention!!!
Direct questions + Answers to them. What do I have to offer?
Allusions/Refrences to things outside the text:
former, past, literature, sango, e.t.c. Titles: Intros! Repetition!
Parallelism. Connections- intra tettra texual - Throughlines
(connect the dots!)

4) Reader Response
Extreme words. Emotional words when YOU feel
emotional, shoked. Seek a personal connection. Ask a big
question applied to your life or the world. Ask what you alrady know.

Figure 2.2

Anchor Chart: Noticing the Conversation

Intelligence: A Brief History (Excerpt)

By Anna T. Cianciolo and Robert J. Sternberg

Handout 2.3

In the now classic tale, three blind men approached an elephant and were curious about its nature. Having never encountered an elephant before, the men each had a different impression. For the man holding the elephant's thick legs, the elephant was like a tree. The elephant was snakelike to the man who had the elephant's lively trunk in his hands. The third blind man, feeling the elephant's sturdy side, exclaimed it was like a wall.

Who was right? And what does this story have to do with intelligence? Just like the blind men in our story, people exploring the nature of intelligence cannot see the object of their study and so have used metaphors to help them conceptualize intelligent behavior (Sternberg, 1990). In this chapter we describe some of the earliest notions of intelligence, which predate scientific study by hundreds, even thousands, of years. Next we present seven metaphors that underlie modern intelligence research: geographic, computational, biological, epistemological, sociological, anthropological, and systems. We briefly describe each metaphor, highlighting the major theories of intelligence associated with each one.

Source: Cianciolo, A., & Sternberg, R. (2004). *Intelligence: A brief history*. Hoboken, NJ: Wiley-Blackwell.

Noticing the Conversation
PRACTICE IN MINIATURE

PURPOSE

- To learn how to practice reading to notice conversational topics—specifically, how to apply the rules students learned in Lesson 2

LENGTH

- Approximately 45 minutes

MATERIALS NEEDED

- A class set of Handout 2.4, "Noticing the Conversation"
- A class set of Handout 2.5, "More Practice Noticing the Conversation"

Introduction

As we noted in Chapter 1, one of the foundational instructional principles of our work is the importance of deliberate practice—practice that is geared toward what real experts do. Reading, we think, is similar to most other human activities. If you're going to become an expert, you need to practice, approximating ever more closely what experts do. The *New York Times Magazine* (Dubner & Levitt, 2006) reported that studies of expertise including investigations of such different activities as

> soccer, golf, surgery, piano playing, Scrabble, writing, chess, software design, stock picking and darts . . . make a rather startling assertion: the trait we commonly call talent is highly overrated. Or, put another way, expert performers—whether in memory or surgery, ballet or computer programming—are nearly always made, not born. And yes, practice does make perfect.

One problem that teachers often face in providing this practice is that it takes students so long to read texts. That's why we think it makes sense to provide a series of shorter texts for students to apply what they are learning in different reading contexts as we illustrate in this lesson. Another problem is that reading is somewhat mysterious and hidden, and that what experts actually do is very underarticulated and not well understood by students. That's why we name the rules of notice, another principle of our practice: *Knowing is always helped by naming*. We've found in our work with teachers and students beginning in the upper elementary grades that naming and practicing the rules of notice fuels their engagement and development because it gives them such a clear, specific pathway. This specificity helps students express a growth mindset and provide procedural feedback to themselves and others.

Lesson Steps

Step 1

Introduce the lesson and highlight the importance of practicing how to notice and use orienting details and moves:

- Remind students that they have previously experienced and heard you thinking aloud about how you notice the conversation that a text is part of. Point out that every text is part of a larger conversation on a topic.
- Explain that this means identifying the subject of the text and then thinking about how it fits in with what others have written or said about it.
- Note that sometimes they'll already know how a text fits in with the larger conversation (and just need to remind themselves) but other times they'll have to figure it out from the text itself.
- Explain that today they're going to practice identifying textual topics and orienting themselves to conversations about these topics.

Step 2

Prepare students for their group work:

- Write the following clause on the board: "I know it's a school night . . ."
- Ask students to pretend that these are the first six words of a text that a middle schooler is sending to his or her parent or guardian.
- Challenge students to predict which of the following is most likely to be the next word of that text—*and, but,* or *so*—and ask them to explain how they know. Students may have a variety of answers, though it's likely most will say "but."
- Probe for why they are making their prediction. Whatever they choose, it will come down to how they see this text in relation to an ongoing conversation and differences of opinion between the parent and the child.
- Reinforce that to understand the opening of the text we have to infer an ongoing conversation between the child and the parent that helps us think about where that conversation has been and where it will go next.

Step 3

Provide independent practice in identifying and orienting oneself to topics:

- Divide students into groups of three.
- Distribute Handout 2.4, "Noticing the Conversation."
- Circulate as the class is working, monitoring student work and providing help as needed.

Step 4

Lead a whole-class discussion to reflect on the process:

- Have groups share their responses to the sentence frames by either writing them on the board or displaying them electronically.
- Ask the students to identify similarities and differences among their sentences.
- Ask them to identify areas of success and of *productive struggle*—that is, how they made sense of something that wasn't immediately apparent.

Step 5

Provide additional practice to consolidate the strategies:

- Distribute Handout 2.5, "More Practice Noticing the Conversation."
- Explain that this task may be a bit harder because students have longer segments of text to deal with, but note that the process is the same: Together with their group they must identify the subject of the text and then think about how it might fit into an ongoing conversation.
- When all of the groups have finished, ask them once again to share their responses to the sentence frames by either writing them on the board or displaying them electronically. Ask the students to identify similarities and differences among their sentence frames and discuss the potential impact of the differences on readers. For example, consider these two frames:
    - *Rather than songs that made people feel they were "born to lose," Woody Guthrie composed songs that made people feel they weren't losers at all.*
    - *Rather than songs that focused on the lives of the wealthy, Woody Guthrie composed songs that all people could see themselves in.*

  Focus on how the first frame employs Guthrie's own words but the second suggests a meaning for those words. Some students might say that the informal tone of the first one is in line with Woody Guthrie's language. Others might say that it's inappropriate for an academic paper. It doesn't matter where students come out on these issues. What's important is for them to see that the choices writers make impact their readers.
- Have students discuss how they felt working with the rules of notice. Listen for students to say the rules helped them pay attention to what's really important, but also note their struggles. For example, a student might say, "I have trouble knowing for sure the difference between a call to attention and a rupture." That would allow you to explain that categorizing what rule a detail might exemplify isn't nearly as important as noticing and remembering the detail and then using it to help make sense of the whole. Note also that the rules may overlap or that an author's move may exemplify more than one rule.

Step 6

Conclude the lesson and set the task ahead:

- Remind students that they should remember that texts are always part of an ongoing conversation and that they have to be understood in the context of that conversation.
- Explain that students should work to identify the textual conversation whenever they read, especially when they start reading about a topic that they aren't very familiar with.
- Explain that sometimes texts may be participating in more than one conversation, so if students notice more than one conversation going on, that's okay.

Extension

Ask students to choose a topic in which they are interested, but about which they haven't read much. Have them find a short text on the topic and identify the conversation that the text is contributing to, sharing in partners or in small groups to get feedback from peers.

Handout 2.4

Noticing the Conversation

A. "With sincere apologies to the old song, the children are not the future. They are the present. They are not going to lead the way one day. They are leading it right now" (Feil, 2007).

Questions for Group Discussion

1. On the basis of these sentences, what do you think is the subject of the text on which they were based? What rules of notice helped you?

   ____

   ____

2. How do you expect this text to fit in with the ongoing conversation about this subject? What makes you think so?

   ____

   ____

3. Please complete the following sentence frame based on the prediction you made above.

   Although conventional wisdom has it that ____________________,

   the author of this statement points out instead that ____________________.

B. It is already understood that technology has a huge effect on shaping the human brain and changing how it functions, but the effects of cell phone use while driving is an especially scary case (based on Richtel, 2014).

Questions for Group Discussion

1. On the basis of this sentence, what do you think is the central topic of the book on which it is based? What rules of notice helped you?

   ____

   ____

2. How do you expect this text to fit in with the ongoing conversation about the topic?

   ____

   ____

3. Please complete the following sentence frame based on the prediction you made above.

   Although we already know that ____________________,

   the author of this statement argues that the problem is extended and exacerbated when

   ____

(Continued)

C. "Whenever there is a mass shooting in the United States, it doesn't take long before pundits suggest violent video games might be to blame" (Casey, 2015).

Questions for Group Discussion

1. On the basis of this sentence, what do you think is the subject of the text from which it was taken? What rules of notice helped you?

   ____

   ____

2. How do you expect this text to fit in with the ongoing conversation about this subject? What makes you think so?

   ____

   ____

3. Please complete the following sentence frame based on the prediction you made above.

   Although some people believe ______________________________,

   the author of this statement believes ______________________________.

D. "We often talk about soldiers, firefighters and fictional characters with supernatural powers as heroes. Recently, the news media have used the term to describe three Americans who helped foil an attack on a speeding train in Europe. But what really is a hero? Does heroism always involve physical strength, or are there other qualities that define being a hero?" (Gonchar, 2015).

Questions for Group Discussion

1. On the basis of these sentences, what do you think is the subject of the text from which they were taken? What rules of notice helped you?

   ____

   ____

2. How do you expect this text to fit in with the ongoing conversation about this subject? What makes you think so?

   ____

   ____

3. Please complete the following sentence frame based on the prediction you made above.

   Although conventional wisdom has it that ______________________________,

   the author of this statement argues that ______________________________.

E. "I really didn't think my two fourth graders could complete their homework assignment on their own: 'Prepare a five-minute-long speech from a biography, to be delivered, not read, from notes on index cards, in costume and in character and with at least one prop.' An impossible task for a 10-year-old,

(Continued)

I thought, as I braced for the battle that would surely be involved in dragging them both through the project" (Dell'Antonia, 2016).

Questions for Group Discussion

1. On the basis of these sentences, what do you think is the subject of the text from which they were taken? What rules of notice helped you?

 ____

 ____

2. How do you expect this text to fit in with the ongoing conversation about this subject? What makes you think so?

 ____

 ____

3. Please complete the following sentence frame based on the prediction you made above.

 Although this author initially believed ______________________________,

 she eventually came to understand that ______________________________.

F. "There are many men who have argued over the ages that women don't have enough mental strength to become morally good on their own: they need the guidance of men" (Wollstonecraft, 1792).

Questions for Group Discussion

1. On the basis of this sentence, what do you think is the subject of the text from which it was taken? What rules of notice helped you?

 ____

 ____

2. How do you expect this text to fit in with the ongoing conversation about this subject? What makes you think so?

 ____

 ____

3. Please complete the following sentence frame based on the prediction you made above.

 Although throughout the ages men have contended ______________________________,

 the author of this statement argues ______________________________.

Sources: Casey, M. (2015, August 17). Do violent video games lead to criminal behavior? *CBS News.* Retrieved from http://www.cbsnews.com/news/do-violent-video-games-lead-to-criminal-behavior; Dell'Antonia, K. J. (2016, March 22). "Impossible" homework assignment? Let your child do it. *The New York Times.* Retrieved from http://well.blogs.nytimes.com/2016/03/22/fourth-grade-book-report-let-your-fourth-grader-do-it; Feil, E. (2007). The world is in their hands. In D. W. Moore, D. J. Short, M. W. Smith, & A. W. Tatum (Eds.), *Hampton-Brown EDGE Level B.* Carmel, CA: National Geographic School Publishing/Hampton Brown; Gonchar, M. (2015, August 25). What is a hero? *The New York Times.* Retrieved from http://learning.blogs.nytimes.com/2015/08/25/what-is-a-hero; Richtel, M. (2014). *A deadly wandering.* New York, NY: HarperCollins; Wollstonecraft, M. (1792). *A vindication of the rights of women.* Boston, MA: Peter Edes.

More Practice Noticing the Conversation

> "I hate a song that makes you think that you're not any good. I hate a song that makes you think you are just born to lose. I am out to fight those kind of songs to my very last breath of air and my last drop of blood."

Woody Guthrie could never cure himself of wandering off. One minute he'd be there, the next he'd be gone, vanishing without a word to anyone, abandoning those he loved best. He'd throw on a few extra shirts, one on top of the other, sling his guitar over his shoulder, and hit the road. He'd stick out his thumb and hitchhike, swing onto moving freight trains, and hunker down with other traveling men in flophouses, hobo jungles, and Hoovervilles across Depression America.

He moved restlessly from state to state, soaking up some songs: work songs, mountain and cowboy songs, sea chanteys, songs from the southern chain gangs. He added them to the dozens he already knew from his childhood until he was bursting with American folk songs. Playing the guitar and singing, he started making up new ones: hard-bitten, rough-edged songs that told it like it was, full of anger and hardship and hope and love. Woody said the best songs came to him when he was walking down a road. He always had fifteen or twenty songs running around in his mind, just waiting to be put together. Sometimes he knew the words, but not the melody. Usually he'd borrow a tune that was already well known—the simpler the better. As he walked along, he tried to catch a good, easy song that people could sing the first time they heard it, remember, and sing again later.

Source: Partridge, E. (2002). *This land was made for you and me: The life and songs of Woody Guthrie.* New York, NY: Penguin Group.

(Continued)

Questions for Group Discussion

1. On the basis of these three paragraphs, what do you think is the subject of the text from which they were taken? What rules of notice helped you?

____

____

____

____

2. How do you expect this text to fit in with the ongoing conversation about this subject? What makes you think so?

____

____

____

____

3. Please complete the following sentence frames based on the prediction you made above.

Rather than songs that ______________________________,

Woody Guthrie composed songs that ______________________________.

Rather than musicians who ______________________________,

Woody Guthrie ______________________________.

Available for download at **http://resources.corwin.com/divingdeep-nonfiction**

Lesson 4

Noticing the Conversation
QUESTIONING

Introduction

In the mid-1990s, Isabel Beck and her colleagues (Beck, McKeown, Sandora, Kucan, & Worthy, 1996) introduced an instructional strategy they call Question the Author (QtA). In brief, this strategy asks students to employ a series of teacher-created queries as they are reading. In so doing, they engage actively in constructing meaning with their reading. What Beck and her colleagues found is that the use of QtA resulted both in much more collaborative classroom conversations and in much more engaged and capable reading by students. The approach highlights that texts are written by authors who expect their readers to notice and do certain things. However, the queries that Beck and her colleagues cite seem to us to treat texts as separate things instead of part of an ongoing conversation, so in this lesson we modify and simplify them.

In this lesson, we also introduce students to the topic–comment strategy, which we'll work with much more in the next section of the book. As any teacher can tell you, students often have difficulty articulating the main idea of a text. We think part of that difficulty resides in the fact that they don't know exactly what we want them to do. As Johnston and Afflerbach (1985) point out—and as illustrated in Figure 2.3—main ideas always have two components: a statement of the topic of a text and a statement of the comment on that topic.

For example, one inquiry we pursue with students is centered on the essential question "What does it really mean to be smart?" So the topic is intelligence. The texts that we read make many different comments on that topic. Here are some examples of main ideas that students came up with for various articles using the topic–comment strategy:

- Intelligence is shown by the ability to be successful in a variety of school subjects.
- Intelligence is shown by superior achievement in one domain.

PURPOSE

- To identify both the topic and the comment of a text

LENGTH

- Approximately 45 minutes

MATERIALS NEEDED

- A class set of Handout 2.6, "*Narrative of the Life of Frederick Douglass, an American Slave, Written by Himself* (Excerpt)"
- A computer and projection device to project the three paintings from Lesson 1
- Chart paper and magic markers for small groups

- Intelligence means street smarts as much as book smarts.
- Intelligence cannot be effectively measured by tests.
- Intelligence is a function of heredity.
- Intelligence is a function of the environment.
- Intelligence is a function of the complex interplay of heredity and environment.

We could go on and on, but we think you get the idea.

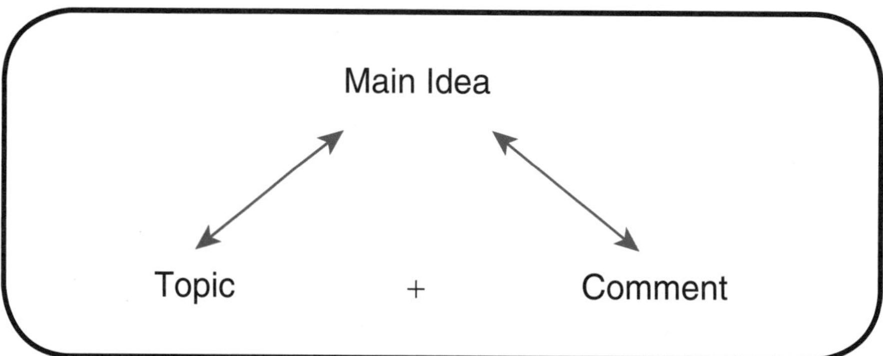

Figure 2.3

Components of a Main Idea

The QtA queries we want the students to apply are listed in Figure 2.4; however, we don't recommend reproducing this as a handout to students. We build this discussion protocol into the following lesson, and recommend creating a class anchor chart at the same time. This process allows the students to feel ownership over the protocol and helps them commit it to memory as well.

Question the Author (QtA)

- What topic is the author addressing?
- What is the author's comment on that topic?
- What other comments on that topic are possible?
- What does the author do to convince you that his or her comment is the best one or at least a justifiable one worthy of consideration?
- How did the rules of notice help you in this process?

Figure 2.4

Question the Author Queries

Lesson Steps

Step 1

Introduce the lesson and highlight the topic–comment strategy for finding and expressing main ideas:

- Recall how each work of art (from Lesson 1) made a particular comment on a particular issue. Display *Beer Street* and *Gin Lane* again.
- Have students fill in this sentence on paper: "According to Hogarth, gin has the effect of/results in/is ______________________."
- Ask them:
  - *What is the topic?* (Gin or gin consumption)
  - *What is the comment about that topic?* (It is bad, has the effect of drunkenness, results in laziness and debauchery, etc.)
- Point out how the verb phrase leads to the comment on the topic—it's important to highlight this for students and to provide various ways of expressing the comment.
- Have students share and justify their responses in pairs or triads, then in the large group.
- When they share, probe by noting that more specific statements are much more useful in understanding what a text is about. See a sample exchange in the "Voices From the Classroom" section that follows.
- Lead a similar discussion on the other pieces of art from Lesson 1 to help students consolidate this process.
- In pairs or groups, encourage the students to ask probing questions of each other and request more specificity and detail in their comments.

Step 2

Provide independent practice using the topic–comment strategy:

- Explain that figuring out the main point of a written text works similarly, but because readers can't experience all written texts at the same time, they have to think about what is happening in smaller sections of text.
- Explain that you want to give students practice in asking a set of questions that will help them do just that.
- Introduce the five key questions and have a student record them on chart paper that can be seen by everyone in the class.
  - *What topic is the author addressing?*
  - *What is the author's comment on that topic?*
  - *What other comments on that topic are possible?*
  - *What does the author do to convince you that his or her comment is the best one?*
  - *How did the rules of notice help you in this process?*

Voices From the Classroom

WHAT STUDENTS SAID ABOUT *Beer Street* and *Gin Lane* by William Hogarth

TEACHER: So what does Hogarth think about gin?

STUDENT: He doesn't like it.

TEACHER: You mean he doesn't like the taste. Is that the topic?

STUDENT: I don't know if he likes the taste or not. But I do know he thinks it's bad for you.

TEACHER: What makes you say so? Let's see if we can make the comment more specific.

STUDENT: Just look at the picture.

TEACHER: Give me an example.

STUDENT: Well, there's a baby falling over a railing. And a guy in a wheelbarrow who can't even walk.

TEACHER: So the comment is . . . ?

STUDENT: Gin is so bad for you that the people who drink it can't even perform the basic things they need to do in life.

- Distribute copies of Handout 2.6, "*Narrative of the Life of Frederick Douglass, an American Slave, Written by Himself* (Excerpt)."
- Divide students into groups of four or five and give them time to read silently before they work together to apply the set of questions to the excerpt. Tell them to be thinking about the topic and comment this text makes and the rules of notice that helped them identify the topic and comment as they read.
- Circulate as groups are working.
- Encourage specificity in both their topics and their comments. Ask students to go back to the text to show how their topic–comment statement is based on what they learned by employing the rules of notice as they read.
- Have groups write answers in some kind of maintainable format (e.g., using chart paper).

Step 3

Lead a whole-class discussion to review how to notice topics, details, and comments in order to identify and articulate main ideas:

- Ask:
  - *What is Douglass's comment on the topic of slavery?*
  - *What other comments on that topic are possible?*
  - *What does the author do to convince you that his comment is justifiable?*
- Probe for details that support student conclusions.
- Encourage students to explain what Douglass would have done differently had he wanted to suggest a different comment.

  See the sample exchange in the "Voices From the Classroom" section that follows.

Step 4

Apply understandings to writing:

- Note that Douglass comments on more than one topic. Write or project this frame: "Although some people believe reading is only _________, Douglass points out that reading can be _________."
- Explain to students that they can modify the frame as long as they indicate both Douglass's comment and an alternative comment.
- Circulate to note variation in responses and to encourage students to make a comment that mirrors the topic and details of the text.

Step 5

Lead a whole-class discussion to consolidate understanding about the topic–comment strategy:

- Ask students to share by writing their topic–comment sentences on the board or through some electronic means. Discuss the pros and cons of the sentences. Some possible examples follow:
  - *Although some people believe reading is only beneficial, Douglass points out that reading can be a negative experience.*
  - *Although some people believe reading is only a positive, Douglass points out that reading can be negative because it teaches you things you might not want to learn.*
  - *Although some people believe reading is only a benefit because it teaches you so much, Douglass points out that reading can be hurtful because you might not want to learn what it teaches.*
- Remind students of the set of five questions from Step 2 and encourage them to use it whenever they read.

Extension

Challenge students to apply the set of five questions and write topic–comment sentences with other photos, cartoons, or short texts relevant to the inquiry unit in which the class is engaged.

Voices From the Classroom

WHAT STUDENTS SAID ABOUT *Narrative of the Life of Frederick Douglass, an American Slave, Written by Himself* (Excerpt)

TEACHER: So how does Douglass feel about reading? Where'd you mark your scale?

STUDENT: I gave it a 5.

TEACHER: What makes you say so?

STUDENT: He says it made him miserable.

TEACHER: Wait, I don't remember that. What exactly did he say?

STUDENT: He said reading stung his soul.

TEACHER: So what rule of notice made you pay attention to that?

STUDENT: Well, I think it's a rupture. You expect reading to bring you benefits or something.

STUDENT: I think it's the rule of reader's response because the language is so emotional.

TEACHER: I think it's both actually. But if it stung his soul, why'd you give it a 5 and not a 6?

STUDENT: 'Cause it also gave him knowledge.

STUDENT: That's why I gave it a 2. I think he's more positive. What about that stuff he read about the slave? The arguments the slave made. Why would he explain so much about that if all he wanted to do is say reading is negative? I think the comment is that reading may hurt but it's worth it.

Narrative of the Life of Frederick Douglass, an American Slave, Written by Himself (Excerpt)

The plan which I adopted, and the one by which I was most successful, was that of making friends of all the little white boys whom I met in the street. As many of these as I could, I converted into teachers. With their kindly aid, obtained at different times and in different places, I finally succeeded in learning to read. When I was sent on errands, I always took my book with me, and by going one part of my errand quickly, I found time to get a lesson before my return. I used also to carry bread with me, enough of which was always in the house, and to which I was always welcome; for I was much better off in this regard than many of the poor white children in our neighborhood. This bread I used to bestow upon the hungry little urchins, who, in return, would give me that more valuable bread of knowledge. I am strongly tempted to give the names of two or three of those little boys, as a testimonial of the gratitude and affection I bear them; but prudence forbids;—not that it would injure me, but it might embarrass them; for it is almost an unpardonable offence to teach slaves to read in this Christian country. It is enough to say of the dear little fellows, that they lived on Philpot Street, very near Durgin and Bailey's ship-yard. I used to talk this matter of slavery over with them. I would sometimes say to them, I wished I could be as free as they would be when they got to be men. "You will be free as soon as you are twenty-one, but I am a slave for life! Have not I as good a right to be free as you have?" These words used to trouble them; they would express for me the liveliest sympathy, and console me with the hope that something would occur by which I might be free.

I was now about twelve years old, and the thought of being a slave for life began to bear heavily upon my heart. Just about this time, I got hold of a book entitled "The Columbian Orator." Every

(Continued)

opportunity I got, I used to read this book. Among much of other interesting matter, I found in it a dialogue between a master and his slave. The slave was represented as having run away from his master three times. The dialogue represented the conversation which took place between them, when the slave was retaken the third time. In this dialogue, the whole argument in behalf of slavery was brought forward by the master, all of which was disposed of by the slave. The slave was made to say some very smart as well as impressive things in reply to his master—things which had the desired though unexpected effect; for the conversation resulted in the voluntary emancipation of the slave on the part of the master.

In the same book, I met with one of Sheridan's mighty speeches on and in behalf of Catholic emancipation. These were choice documents to me. I read them over and over again with unabated interest. They gave tongue to interesting thoughts of my own soul, which had frequently flashed through my mind, and died away for want of utterance. The moral which I gained from the dialogue was the power of truth over the conscience of even a slaveholder. What I got from Sheridan was a bold denunciation of slavery, and a powerful vindication of human rights. The reading of these documents enabled me to utter my thoughts, and to meet the arguments brought forward to sustain slavery; but while they relieved me of one difficulty, they brought on another even more painful than the one of which I was relieved. The more I read, the more I was led to abhor and detest my enslavers. I could regard them in no other light than a band of successful robbers, who had left their homes, and gone to Africa, and stolen us from our homes, and in a strange land reduced us to slavery. I loathed them as being the meanest as well as the most wicked of men. As I read and contemplated the subject, behold! that very discontentment which Master Hugh had predicted would follow my learning to read had already come, to torment and sting my soul to unutterable anguish. As I writhed under it, I would at times feel that learning to read had been a curse rather than a blessing. It had given me a view of my wretched condition, without the

(Continued)

remedy. It opened my eyes to the horrible pit, but to no ladder upon which to get out. In moments of agony, I envied my fellow-slaves for their stupidity. I have often wished myself a beast. I preferred the condition of the meanest reptile to my own. Anything, no matter what, to get rid of thinking! It was this everlasting thinking of my condition that tormented me. There was no getting rid of it. It was pressed upon me by every object within sight or hearing, animate or inanimate. The silver trump of freedom had roused my soul to eternal wakefulness. Freedom now appeared, to disappear no more forever. It was heard in every sound, and seen in everything. It was ever present to torment me with a sense of my wretched condition. I saw nothing without seeing it, I heard nothing without hearing it, and felt nothing without feeling it. It looked from every star, it smiled in every calm, breathed in every wind, and moved in every storm.

Source: Narrative of the life of Frederick Douglass, an American slave, written by himself. Boston, MA: Anti-Slavery Office, 1845. (1845)

Questions for Group Discussion

1. How does Douglass view reading at the end of this piece?

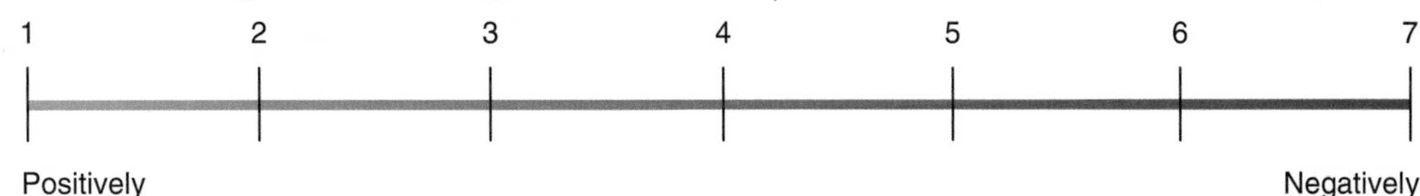

2. How do you know? What makes you say so?

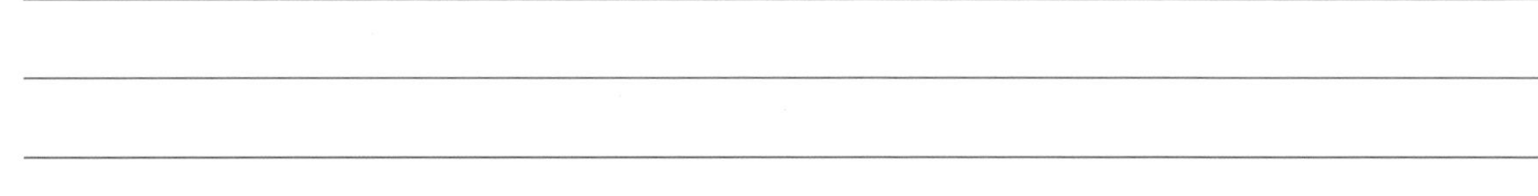

Noticing the Conversation

WRITING AND RESPONDING

PURPOSE

- To think about what students do as writers to help their readers, and to reflect on how thinking about their writing helps them become better readers

LENGTH

- Approximately 90 minutes (can be split into two 45-minute classes)

MATERIALS NEEDED

- A computer for at least every three students
- Seating arrangements that accommodate students working individually or in groups of three
- Chart paper or electronic means to record student observations

Introduction

One characteristic of writing in the digital age is that it is so obviously interactive. And so digital writing (think of fanfics, social media posts followed by comments, and so on) provides a great vehicle to help students see that texts are part of an ongoing conversation. This lesson will engage students in textual conversations to further their understanding of that threshold concept and the threshold process of using rules of notice for conversation; help them be writers who think about what readers need from a text; and help them employ rules of notice to navigate and make meaning of a text.

In teaching this lesson, we motivate students by showing them why what we're doing matters. In *"Reading Don't Fix No Chevys"* (Smith & Wilhelm, 2002), we cite a very disturbing comment from one of our study participants, who, when asked how he feels about English, said the following:

> English is about NOTHING! It doesn't help you DO anything. English is about reading poems and telling about rhythm. It's about commas and crap like that for God's sake. What does that have to DO with DOING anything? It's about NOTHING!

This lesson is also designed to help students see that English is most definitely about something—something incredibly significant and substantive—and that the work we're doing will help them succeed not only in school, but out of school as well.

Lesson Steps

Step 1

Introduce the lesson and highlight how writing and reading are two sides of the same coin—writers have to signal what they want readers to notice, and readers must notice these details to make meaning:

- Remind students that texts are part of an ongoing conversation, and determining the conversation will help them understand what they are reading.

- Recall that in the last lesson, they wrote some sentences that illustrated this point by explicitly placing a text into a conversation.
- Explain that the conversational aspect of texts is never more apparent than online, where comments follow many postings. The comments are in conversation both with the initial posting and with each other.
- Explain that in today's lesson, the students will work on writing a post about something that they care about that others might have a different opinion about.

Step 2

Model how you respond to texts in your writing:

- Explain that you want students to respond to a posting about something they deeply care about.
- Illustrate with an example of your own. Note that the following is one Michael might have provided, but you should substitute your own favorite book or movie, with details.
    - Share that one of your favorite recent books is Anthony Marra's *A Constellation of Vital Phenomena* (2013). Note that although most reviewers really liked it, some didn't.
    - Explain that one Amazon reviewer gave it one star and called it "brutal, depressing. Our book club slogged through this, but it was not a pleasure."
    - Note that you want to respond to that review, but while you agree that the book describes some terribly brutal situations, you think it is mostly about how people can act with grace and courage even in the most desperate of circumstances.
    - Ask students to help you think about how to begin your post to make that point. Discuss their suggestions as they make them. See the sample exchange in the "Voices From the Classroom" section that follows.
- Use the board or computer projection as you and the students coauthor the beginning of the response.

Step 3

Provide independent practice in responding appropriately to a post:

- Thank students for helping you get off to a good start in your writing. (Complete and post your contribution to provide a model—either immediately if you are comfortable, or before the next class.)
- Explain that now you want the students to do the same thing.

Voices From the Classroom

WHAT STUDENTS SAID ABOUT *A Constellation of Vital Phenomena* by Anthony Marra

TEACHER: So how should I start this?

STUDENT: You have to refer back to the review.

TEACHER: Right. But how? How have you referred to what others think in the writing you've been doing?

STUDENT: How about "Although some people"?

TEACHER: OK. "Some people" what? You have to be specific, right?

STUDENT: "Although some people think the book is brutal and depressing."

STUDENT: Now you have to say what you think.

TEACHER: OK, how about "Although some people think Anthony Marra's *A Constellation of Vital Phenomena* is brutal and depressing, the book really is hopeful in the way it portrays people's acting with grace, love, and courage in the very worst of times"?

- On board or on chart paper, brainstorm with students a list of criteria that would make a good post. These might include the following:
  - A clearly stated position
  - A clear and accurate summary of what you're responding to
  - Uptake of ideas from the original post and perhaps even subsequent comments on it
  - A well-developed response justifying your own position and why you hold that position in contrast to other positions
  - An appropriately respectful tone
- Have students identify a posting they have found and want to respond to, and begin drafting their response.
- Circulate as they are writing, reminding them of the criteria.
- As you read over their shoulders, ask them to explain why they are doing what they are doing. Make sure they focus on the rules of notice they employ.
- If a student articulates an interesting strategy (perhaps a rule of notice to use) or understanding, tell that student that you'll be calling on him or her to share with the class.

Step 4

Have students respond to each other's writing:

- Divide students into groups of three to respond to each other's writing.
- Stress that they should encourage each other to use the criteria that the class has developed and to consider how rules of notice are used in their writing to help the reader understand the conversation.

Step 5

Lead a whole-class discussion to clarify and consolidate understanding of how texts indicate the conversational topic:

- Have students share moves that they made or that they liked in the student writing to which they responded.
- Make a list in a maintainable format (e.g., using chart paper).
- Collect students' writing. In responding to what they have written, highlight when students employed a rule of notice—for example, "This is a clear call to attention."

Extension

Ask students to monitor a website that features ongoing responses to identify what moves they think are most effective.

Lesson 6

Noticing the Conversation
SEARCH AND FIND

PURPOSE

- To apply what students have learned to texts that they choose and name the strategies and rules of notice they use to interpret these texts

LENGTH

- Approximately 45 minutes

MATERIALS NEEDED

- Internet access or access to a variety of print texts: nonfiction books, magazines, newspapers, and so on
- An easel pad or electronic way to record student observation

Introduction

In Chapter 1, we discussed the importance and difficulty of transfer and noted that students must have a deep understanding of the knowledge to be transferred and plenty of practice making the transfer. We hope that the lessons we have presented thus far have demonstrated how we've created those conditions. In an article that has been a significant influence on our thinking, Perkins and Salomon (1988) argue that if we want students to apply what they learn in new contexts that differ from the ones in which they initially learn the material, we have to give them conscious control over what they learn. Perkins and Salomon call this *high-road transfer*. We think of it this way: "If you can name it, then you can tame it"; that is, if you can name a strategy, then you can use it as a tool for subsequent work.

The ability to name what it is you're doing is especially important in instances of *far transfer*. If problem-solving situations are very similar, transferring knowledge from one situation to the next may happen almost automatically, a situation that's called *near transfer*. *Far transfer*, in contrast, means applying knowledge learned in one context to a markedly different context. The purpose of the following lesson is to cultivate far transfer by asking students to identify and respond to texts of their own selection that demonstrate different ways of making a place in the conversation of which they are a part.

As you'll see, the texts for this lesson are ones that the students themselves have selected. We've long argued about the importance of providing meaningful choice for students (cf. Wilhelm & Smith, 2014). Sometimes the teachers with whom we work despair about doing so given all that they have to cover. We'll save our critique of the pressure of coverage for another time, but that pressure is one of the reasons that John Guthrie's notion of *micro choices* is so compelling to us. Guthrie, perhaps the leading scholar in the area of reading motivation, and his colleagues (Guthrie, Klauda, & Morrison, 2012) argue that giving students choice is extremely motivating. They note that because "teachers believe they must cover topics by traveling quickly over broad domains, they tend to believe they have little opportunity to afford choice to learners. Although this obstacle is prohibitive, teachers have many opportunities to provide micro choices" (p. 28). One example would be letting students choose the texts the class will examine as in the lesson that follows.

Lesson Steps

Step 1

Introduce the lesson and its purpose—to apply rules of notice for conversations to a variety of texts outside of school:

- Recall for students that identifying the conversation of which the texts they read are a part is a way of getting oriented to the texts.
- Recall the tools for employing in that effort, especially sentence frames, topic–comment sentences, and QtA. Write the tools on chart paper and display them for easy reference.
- Explain that the purpose of this lesson is for students to apply what they've been learning to texts that they select.

Step 2

Model what students will do to select and interpret a text:

- Explain that students should select a text that they think does an especially good, bad, or interesting job of indicating the conversation of which it's a part. Song lyrics, ads, memes, YouTube videos, and the like are often favorite choices of our students.
- Share your own example from popular culture to illustrate that you want students to look broadly. What follows is an example using lines from MCA on the Beastie Boys song "Sure Shot":

  I want to say a little something that's long overdue
  The disrespect to women has got to be through
  To all the mothers and the sisters and the wives and friends
  I want to offer my love and respect to the end

- Explain that you think MCA is putting this song in conversation with rap lyrics that degrade women.
- Explain how in the first two lines MCA seems to be talking to other hip-hop artists but in the second two lines moves to female members of his audience.

- Note how in the third line he doesn't talk about girlfriends, which seems to be a deliberate omission. That is, the roles he cites are not celebrated in other hip-hop songs. MCA is differentiating his position in the conversation about the roles of women and how women should be regarded.

Step 3

Provide independent practice in selecting texts and identifying the conversations they are part of:

- Have students work in groups of three to find a text that they want to share.
- Circulate as students are working.
- Probe for how they know what the larger conversation is and what rules of notice they might be using.

Step 4

Lead a whole-class discussion:

- Ask students to share what they found and the rules of notice used.
- Record their answers on the anchor chart you've been compiling on chart paper or in some electronic format. If you used the Beastie Boys song, for example, a student might identify "I want to say something that's long overdue" as a direct statement. *You would then make some sort of note on the anchor chart to remind students of this example.*

Extension

Challenge students to write the first page of a book for beginning readers in which they explain and illustrate both why readers need to notice the textual conversation and how readers go about doing that noticing.

Lesson 7

Noticing the Conversation
PUTTING IT ALL TOGETHER

Introduction

According to historian Garry Wills in *Lincoln at Gettysburg: The Words That Remade America* (1992), the Gettysburg Address changed the way the nation felt about itself:

> Up to the Civil War "the United States" was invariably a plural noun: "The United States are a free country." After Gettysburg it became a singular: "The United States is a free country."

The final lesson in this section of the book will ask students to apply what they've learned about noticing the textual conversation in order to understand the rhetorical choices Lincoln made in the Gettysburg Address and the meanings and effects he hoped to achieve about the topic of the United States through these choices.

Lesson Steps

Step 1

Introduce the lesson:

- Recall for students that to understand the texts they are reading they must notice the textual conversation that they are a part of.
- Recall that doing so helps readers anticipate what's to come and to understand the major ideas the author is trying to communicate, as well as the potential significance of these ideas.
- Note that today students will do this by looking closely at one of the most famous texts of all time: the Gettysburg Address.

PURPOSE

- To apply what students have learned about noticing conversations in complex nonfiction by comparing what a writer did with what he *could* have done; to independently use all of the strategies necessary for noticing and orienting oneself to a textual conversation

LENGTH

- Approximately 75 minutes (can be split into two classes if needed)

MATERIALS NEEDED

- A class set of Handout 2.7, "The Gettysburg Address"

Step 2

Develop background knowledge:

- Put these two sentences on the board or display them in some way:
  - "The United States are a free country."
  - "The United States is a free country."
- Discuss with the class the difference between the sentences and why it is significant.
- Explain that one famous historian has argued that the Gettysburg Address moved people from saying the first to saying the second.
- Explain that they'll be looking closely at the address to see just how Lincoln tried to foster such a tremendously significant change of thinking.
- Explain that you'll want them to put on two hats as they do their work: one of an observer from the North who lived close to the battlefield and heard the terrible roar of the guns, and another of someone from the South who only read about the battle and the text of the speech days later.
- To help them put on those hats, show a couple of pictures of the battle.
- Note that there were as many as 51,000 casualties.
- Explain that Lincoln's Gettysburg Address was the second of two speeches that day.
- Explain that a famous speaker, Edward Everett, spoke for two hours before President Lincoln spoke. Note that much of the speech was an explanation of what happened. To give them a sense of the tone of the speech, however, share a short excerpt:
  - And now, friends, fellow-citizens, as we stand among these honored graves, the momentous question presents itself, Which of the two parties to the war is responsible for all this suffering, for this dreadful sacrifice of life,—the lawful and constituted government of the United States, or the ambitious men who have rebelled against it?

Step 3

Provide independent practice:

- Ask students to put on their Northern hats and to pretend that they went home after the oration and wrote in their journals about their feelings about what they saw and heard. Give them five minutes or so for this in-role writing.
- Invite volunteers to read what they wrote. The entries will vary, but the prevailing emotion will likely be anger and/or sadness, and

students are likely to express some agreement with Everett. Ask what rules of notice they applied in responding to Everett's speech.

Step 4

Lead a whole-class discussion:

- Read the entire Gettysburg Address aloud.
- Have students count off by twos and cast the ones as Northerners and the twos as Southerners.
- Ask students to put on their Northerner and Southerner hats and consider the feeling they would have had if the first sentence read as follows: "Four score and seven years ago *the* founding fathers brought forth on this continent, a new nation, conceived in Liberty, and dedicated to the proposition that all men are created equal."
- Explain that you know the change is a small one, but you think it might have had a significantly different effect on Lincoln's listeners than the way Lincoln said it: "*our* fathers."
- Ask them to share their perspectives as Northerners and Southerners. Be sure they recognize that Lincoln's version makes a gesture toward connection and a shared history and vision between North and South. It includes everyone, and evokes a sense that we have worked together from the start to create a great nation.

Noticing the Conversation: Reading the Gettysburg Address From Two Perspectives

Video 2.3

http://resources.corwin.com/divingdeep-nonfiction

Step 5

Provide additional practice:

- Divide students into groups of four or five.
- Ask them to identify two instances where Lincoln's language worked to accomplish the grand goal of a sense of one united country. Ask them to be prepared to explain what rules of notice they employed in making that identification.
- Have them illustrate their point by inventing language he could have used that would have been less effective in achieving that goal.
- Circulate as students work, probing them to focus on alternative ways Lincoln could have expressed himself.

Noticing the Conversation: How Does Lincoln Reveal His Theme?

Video 2.4

http://resources.corwin.com/divingdeep-nonfiction

Step 6

Lead a whole-class discussion:

- Invite groups to share their work.
- Together, compile a list of moves that Lincoln made throughout his speech and record them on chart paper. Refer to the rules of notice anchor chart and note how students employed the rules when they identified the moves.

Step 7

Apply understandings to writing:

- Have students work individually on the following frame:
    - I know that President Lincoln's goal in the Gettysburg Address was ______________________ because he ______________________. Had he wanted to ______________________ [name a different goal], he would have ______________________.
- Pair up students to share their sentences.

Step 8

Conclude the lesson:

- Explain once again that understanding the conversation of which a text is a part helps readers recognize the author's purpose and perspective.
- Note that another valuable tool for understanding an author's purpose is to imagine what he or she could have done differently.

Extension

Invite students to select another historically significant speech, or a modern speech, and rewrite part of it in a way that would change its impact. Challenge them to also write a parody of a popular song or speech and compare the meaning and effect of the parody with that of the original.

The Gettysburg Address

By Abraham Lincoln

Four score and seven years ago our fathers brought forth on this continent, a new nation, conceived in Liberty, and dedicated to the proposition that all men are created equal.

Now we are engaged in a great civil war, testing whether that nation, or any nation so conceived and so dedicated, can long endure. We are met on a great battle-field of that war. We have come to dedicate a portion of that field, as a final resting place for those who here gave their lives that that nation might live. It is altogether fitting and proper that we should do this.

But, in a larger sense, we can not dedicate—we can not consecrate—we can not hallow—this ground. The brave men, living and dead, who struggled here, have consecrated it, far above our poor power to add or detract. The world will little note, nor long remember what we say here, but it can never forget what they did here. It is for us the living, rather, to be dedicated here to the unfinished work which they who fought here have thus far so nobly advanced. It is rather for us to be here dedicated to the great task remaining before us—that from these honored dead we take increased devotion to that cause for which they gave the last full measure of devotion—that we here highly resolve that these dead shall not have died in vain—that this nation, under God, shall have a new birth of freedom—and that government of the people, by the people, for the people, shall not perish from the earth.

Source: Lincoln, A. (1863, November 19). The Gettysburg address. Retrieved from http://avalon.law.yale.edu/19th_century/gettyb.asp

Chapter 3

Noticing Key Details

In Chapter 2, we explored how to get students into the inner game of reading: how to help them as readers orient themselves to the text by noticing the conversational topics that the reading takes up. *Why?* Because before students can play the game of reading, they have to be in the ballpark and know what game they are in.

The way we notice key details is informed by our purpose—by how we think we might use the information. As we argued in the last chapter, being assigned to read an unfamiliar text is like being dropped by a helicopter into unfamiliar terrain. You first have to get the lay of the land. But once you get oriented, you have to pay attention to the specific details of that terrain. Your noticing those details determines the actual journey you'll make.

In this chapter, we explore how students must learn *how to notice* what is most essential in a text. To continue our metaphor, we explore how to help students recognize the signposts and landmarks necessary to their meaning-making journeys.

To help them do this, our lessons focus on *conceptual detail* and *authorial moves—that is, how authors cue readers to attend to critical details.* We then focus on teaching students to use what they notice to make meaning. Expert readers notice and remember key details, connecting what they notice to other details and overall patterns. The ability to notice and connect details is a major characteristic of expert readers. Poor readers may be able to decode and understand text at the local level, but experts build knowledge throughout their reading by connecting what they have read before to what they are reading in the moment—they make meaning globally. Poor readers often do not differentiate between details that are just texture and those that are significant to remember; expert readers know how to do this.

Novice or developing readers like our students need to learn how to say: *Here's what I know is important in this text and* why *I know it's important in this context and for this purpose*. They then need to be able to add what they notice to other details so that they can weave the accumulated details into patterns. Doing so is necessary to identify the overall trajectory of a piece of writing. Readers can then use their understanding of key details to comprehend what they all add up to in terms of total meaning and effect.

Think about a kind of reading often portrayed as being relatively easy: reading an excerpt, a kind of reading often required during information searches or on tests. Reading an excerpt requires even more alert noticing and unpacking than does reading a complete text because the reader has to infer what came before the excerpt (the pretext) and what will come afterward. Reading an excerpt requires students to see, in a short burst of text, the patterning of the larger text, where that pattern came from, and where it will lead.

It's crucial to know what's key.

We want to enable our students to do what expert readers do: attend to the most important details during reading and put them together in order to understand the main ideas of a text so they can carry the ideas forward into their lives. If we can do this, we will have achieved something profound, something that will help our students as readers, writers, and humans both in school and out.

What happens if we can't accurately notice all the crucial details and what they add up to? Our reading will become associational and off point—we won't be in conversation with the authors and their texts about meaningful issues in life and society. This is a problem we often see students experiencing. If they aren't oriented to the conversational topic(s), then they have no idea what to notice and no purpose for noticing. They become overburdened trying to attend equally to every detail in a text. Since they can't remember everything, they forget everything. On their reading journey, they can't see the forest *or* the trees.

Reading Visuals for Topic and Topic–Comment

Video 3.1

http://resources.corwin.com/divingdeep-nonfiction

Before Reading: A Tool for Noticing Key Details

One of the most profound insights of Peter Rabinowitz (1987), whose work has inspired the teaching we describe here, is that writers write with expectations about how readers are going to read. He argues that writers and readers, experienced readers anyway, have shared assumptions about how texts are constructed to be communicative and impactful—to have meaning and effect. We regard this insight as a *threshold concept* and strategies for enacting it as *threshold processes*. Our work here is to articulate those shared assumptions between writer and reader and so gain the following payoffs:

1. Students become more powerful and consciously competent readers.
2. They become better writers in two ways:
    a. By being better readers, they get more grist for their own writing, using reading to develop their own ideas and understandings.
    b. By coming to understand and articulate the expectations writers have of readers, they can put these same codes and structures into their own writing.

In other words, students must learn to notice both *what* writers want them to notice and *how* writers code their texts to cue this noticing.

As we explained in the last chapter, through our own self-studies and teacher research on student reading, we've identified four general rules of notice. Not only do they help readers recognize the conversation of which the text is a part; these four rules of notice also help students identify what's most important as they read. These lessons are designed to help students apply the rules of notice—to help them identify what they need to pay special attention to in order to make sense of what they are reading and to do work with what they are reading.

Lesson 1

Noticing Key Details
READING VISUAL TEXTS

Introduction

In our lessons, we follow a central principle of instructional sequencing from cognitive science: start with the concrete before moving to the abstract, and start with the visual and visually supported before moving to texts without such support. Using visuals also makes the modeling more concrete and accessible, something that is especially important for struggling readers, English learners, and the refugee students with whom we work.

We've had great success modeling how to notice key details using the painting *American Gothic* by Grant Wood. This painting works conceptually in inquiry units about relationships, gender roles, trouble, work, the American character, and many other topics.

Lesson Steps

Step 1

Set the purpose for learning the reader's rules of notice for key details:

- Review with students the purpose of today's lesson. Include a review of the four general rules of notice. Perhaps point the students to an anchor chart of the rules that you made in a previous lesson (for an example, see Figure 2.1 on page 23).
- Tell students that you'll be "reading" a painting together, Grant Wood's *American Gothic*, focusing first on noticing key details and then on using the topic–comment strategy (introduced in Chapter 2, Lesson 4, page 39) to figure out what the painting means and how it was structured to communicate that meaning and effect.

PURPOSE

- To discover, name, and practice the reader's rules of notice for key details, including attention to all four general rules, and to use the rules of notice to identify main ideas and thematic generalizations. The four general rules include
  - Direct statements of a principle or generalization
  - Ruptures
  - Calls to attention
  - Reader's response
- To apply these rules to a painting to discover the key details of the painting and how these key details are structured to work together to communicate meaning and effect

LENGTH

- Approximately 75–90 minutes (can be split into two 45-minute classes)

MATERIALS NEEDED

- A way to project Grant Wood's *American Gothic* on a screen so all students can see and study it
- Chart paper to create an anchor chart in a place that all students can see
- A way to look at zoomed-in sections (quadrants) of the painting for students to see up-close

- Share with students that *Gothic* can mean "prototype" or "typical example."
- Point out that titles are always a rule of notice—they are a call to attention. (We often discuss how the title *American Gothic* might be seen as a kind of direct statement as well—i.e., that the two subjects are quintessential American "types." *Gothic* can also refer to the strange, frightening, or mysterious if you want to go there!)
- Project the painting one quadrant at a time, if possible, to see what students notice, or simply ask them what details jump out at them and why. For a link to an interactive version of *American Gothic*, visit **http://resources.corwin.com/divingdeep-nonfiction**.

Step 2

Get started with naming understandings:

- Ask students to quickly list all the things that jump out at them in the painting.
- Invite them to explain how they know to notice these things, and what rules of notice are being employed.
- Ask them:
  - *What does Wood want you to notice in the painting? How do you know?*
  - *What do you see that is surprising? What do you not see that you may have expected?*
  - *How do you know to "see" these things—what rules of notice has the painter used?*
- Have students draw a line down the middle of a notebook page. On the left, have them list what they noticed; on the right, have them write how they knew to notice this detail. Compare their reasoning to the rules of notice for key details.
- Ask:
  - *What did the painter do to draw your attention to particular details?*
  - *What was the tip-off or cue to notice them?*
- Allow students to work for a few minutes on their own list of details. As they write, encourage them to use the four general rules of notice, but also to be as specific as they can in identifying the cue that enacts each rule (e.g., *title* for call to attention, or *emotional charge* for the nature of their intense reader's response).
- Next, have them share in pairs or triads what they noticed and how they knew to notice it.

Noticing Details in a Painting: Wood's *American Gothic*

Video 3.2

http://resources.corwin.com/divingdeep-nonfiction

Step 3

Consolidate students' understanding and add specific details to the anchor chart:

- Invite student groups to share their ideas with the whole class. Create a chart for rules of notice for key details, adding specific examples of the general rules of notice to the chart as the students share.
- Ask: *How did the artist prompt us to notice these things?*
- Help the students to name the rules of notice both generally and specifically. For example:
  - *That is "repetition," and you always notice things that are repeated. We have to notice repetition as the artist is using that detail to bring our attention to it. Repetition is a kind of "call to attention" rule of notice.*
- Point out an example of repetition such as the vertical lines on the barn, the house, and the man's shirt or how the pitchfork design is repeated on his pocket and in the dormer window.

  For a link to an interactive version of *American Gothic* and an example of what a classroom conversation about it might sound like, visit the companion website at **http://resources.corwin.com/diving deep-nonfiction**.

Step 4

Ask the class to consider connections and patterns among the key details:

- As needed, prompt noticing that students may have missed—for example, by asking them to make comparisons and contrasts. Ask:
  - *How do the woman and man compare?*
  - *How are they portrayed similarly and differently?*
  - *What are their separate worlds? How do you know?*
  - *What are their shared worlds? How do you know?*
  - *What shared worlds do they inhabit?*
- Cue students to look at the corners of the painting from left to right and from bottom to top.
- Ask: *How do things change as you move across the painting in these ways? What other things do you notice?*

Discussing Possible Topics: Wood's *American Gothic*

Video 3.3

http://resources.corwin.com/divingdeep-nonfiction

Step 5

Invite students to identify and share topics, and to justify them with reference to key details:

- Ask students to confer with their small groups and discuss the class list of key details. Have them consider:
  - *How do the details all relate to each other?*
  - *What common topics might all of the details comment on?*
- Remind students that all texts have multiple topics, but that they must confirm any topic by showing how all of a text's major details relate to it in some way.
- Circulate as students try out topics together, and ask them to justify their choices. Students also should justify their topics to each other.

Step 6

Ask students to report and justify topics to the larger group:

- Invite the student groups to report to the class. As they share, probe groups for how major details relate to the topic. If necessary, help them to revise their topics to match the patterns of details.
- On chart paper, compile a list of topics brought up by the students (e.g., marriage, relationships, gender roles, farm life, religious influence). Comment on how topics can be more general (e.g., farm life) or more specific (e.g., farm life in the early 1900s).
- Lead a whole-class discussion. Ask:
  - *How specific do you think the artist is trying to be?*
  - *Why do you think so? [You might remind students that the painting's title is* American Gothic, *which can mean "American types or icons."]*
  - *How does the title give clues to possible topics?*
- Mention that identifying a topic is akin to setting a purpose and creating applications for what we read. If a topic of the painting is gender roles, then what can we learn from the painting, and how might we apply and use this in our life? It's also important for students to understand that even seemingly simple texts, including a painting, will potentially explore multiple topics that all key details comment on in some way.

Step 7

Apply the topic–comment strategy (see Chapter 2, Lesson 4) to show how patterns of details express the comment about the topic:

- Model topic–comment statements with one of the topics (e.g., gender roles). Emphasize that the statement must begin with the topic and then make a comment about the topic:
  - *Gender roles are . . .*
  - *Gender roles require . . .*
  - *Gender roles can often . . .*
  - *Gender roles can result . . .*
- Try out the following model topic–comment statements:
  - *Gender roles regulate genders to different worlds of work and influence.*
  - *Gender roles require the woman to be positioned behind the man and at home instead of out in the world.*
  - *Gender roles can often be stifling for both males and females.*
- Follow up by explaining how the details of the painting work together to justify the comment that's been expressed.

Step 8

In small groups, try out various other topics and topic–comment statements to show that even a simple work like a painting can cover multiple topics:

- Invite students to confer in their small groups. Ask:
  - *What other topic do you want to try out, and what comment is the painting making about that topic?*
  - *What makes you say so? How do the details form a pattern of meaning that makes that comment?*
- Have students list commentary verbs they can add to the topic to make their statement (e.g., *is/are, require/s, can/may, results in/leads to*). Have them add one of these to their topic to complete the thought (e.g., "Marriage is . . .").

Step 9

Review the process with the whole class:

- Ask the student groups to report what the painting expresses about relationships, marriage, gender roles, farm life, or whatever other topic they have justified.
- Remind students that the topic–comment statement is a theme or generalization that the work of art can be said to be making about the world. Remind them to ask themselves what key details, working together, led to the expression of their theme.
- Record their topics and comments on chart paper.

Step 10

Look at parodies to show how changing a detail changes the topic and the theme—all of these elements work together to express meaning and effect:

Practicing Topic–Comment With *American Gothic* Parodies

Video 3.4

http://resources.corwin.com/divingdeep-nonfiction

- Tell students that you are going to look at some parodies of *American Gothic* and remind them that a parody mimics and changes an iconic work in some significant way.
- Explain that parodies rupture the original text and it is precisely that rupture that readers must notice. This change in details or structuring of details introduces a new topic and therefore makes a new comment. Help students to see how specific details and structurings lead to specific topics and comments.
- Note that parodies make use of comparison and contrast because the artist is asking us to compare his or her version to the original and to see how a new topic and comment are being expressed by the changes.
- Project a parody of *American Gothic* (examples are available on the book's companion website at **http://resources.corwin.com/divingdeep-nonfiction**). Ask:
    - *What are the new details?*
    - *How do these new details express a new topic?*
    - *A new comment?*
- Show another parody if you wish and ask the same questions. Students enjoy these parodies, as they are often funny. They also enjoy getting the "inside joke," which they wouldn't if they hadn't studied the original work.
- If you have time and access to computers, have students find additional parodies and quickly come up with new topics and comments, sharing as they do so.

Step 11

Review and consolidate students' learning:

- Work together as a class to review and consolidate the anchor chart on the rules of notice for key details. Ask the students to think about how they worked to unpack what they noticed by using the topic–comment strategy.
- Ask:
    - *How did this help you to see patterns?*
    - *How can we apply this process to reading other situations and texts?*
    - *What besides paintings could you try to "read" in this way between today and tomorrow?*

Extensions

- Have students create memes of their topic–comment statements. Some sites that work well for students include the following:
  - Imgflip: https://imgflip.com/memegenerator
  - Meme Maker: www.mememaker.net
  - Quick Meme: www.quickmeme.com/caption
- Use the same lesson plan sequence with another classic painting. (Jan van Eyck's *The Arnolfini Marriage*, shown in Figure 3.1, is a great one to use after *American Gothic*, as it's also a double portrait of a man and woman.)

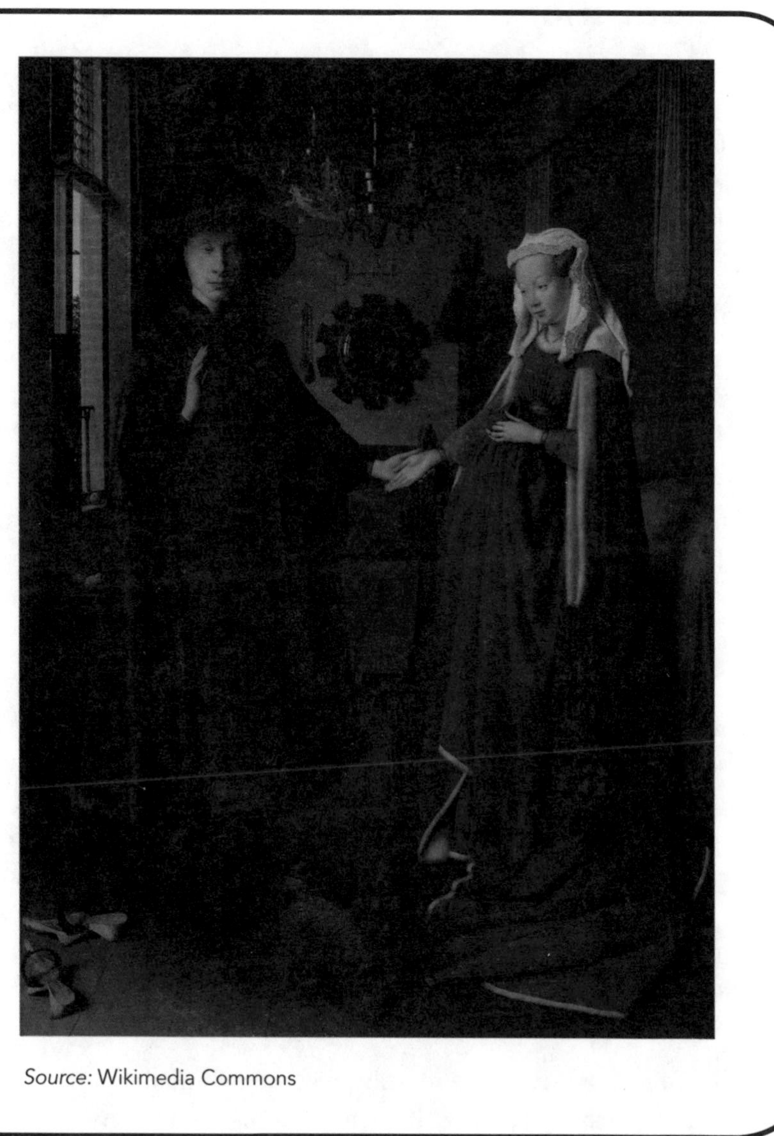

Source: Wikimedia Commons

Figure 3.1

Jan van Eyck's *The Arnolfini Marriage*

Lesson 2

Noticing Key Details
THINKING ALOUD

PURPOSE

- To learn how key details work together inside a text to create meaning and effect, including thematic generalizations, and then to practice noticing key details in a nonfiction text

LENGTH

- Approximately 60 minutes

MATERIALS NEEDED

- A class set of Handout 3.1, "*The Great Fire* (Excerpt)," and an excerpt from Jim Murphy's *The Great Fire* or a complex nonfiction text of your own choosing
- Chart paper or another means of recording examples from the text

Introduction

We previously referenced the idea of *threshold* knowledge. We think that rules of notice are both a threshold concept and a threshold process that give us a transformative view of what writers do to code their texts with meaning. We also believe this knowledge provides a gateway process (Hillocks, 1995) for reading and writing in new and more powerful ways.

As students engage in inquiry over time, we want them to learn transferable, generative, and unconstrained *concepts* and *processes* that will inform how they understand and participate in disciplinary meaning making and apply disciplinary knowledge throughout their lives. We want them to learn concepts that allow them to see and think as experts about the world.

The consideration of threshold knowledge to organize and focus curriculum can be especially useful in areas where curriculum tends to be overloaded (and where isn't it?)—where curriculum becomes a mile wide and an inch deep, as Wiggins and McTighe (2005) express it.

The takeaway is that understanding threshold knowledge can inform teachers' thinking about organizing curriculum and about what texts to choose for or make available to students: those that provide threshold concepts for thinking differently and more generatively about the topic at hand, and those that require and reward using threshold processes, like the reader's rules of notice. Threshold concepts are often expressed in direct statements of generalization. They are always expressed in ruptures as they are troublesome and address misconceptions. And threshold knowledge always gives a radical new way of seeing the topic or doing the discipline.

Thinking aloud is a tremendously powerful technique for modeling and mentoring expert reading, then monitoring strategy use by students, including the use of threshold strategies (Wilhelm, 2012a). Thinking aloud is also great for discovering, with students, what we do and need to do as we read. We use think-alouds to do self-studies, to engage in teacher research with students, and to model and practice how to engage in expert reading with particular strategies.

We like to model the processes of noticing with short texts or excerpts that are concentrated samples of the use of particular rules of notice. In this way, we can make our own reading "visible" and available to students, give students repeated modeling and practice with a short excerpt, and provide a platform to begin including and mentoring students in the process of using a particular strategy like noticing key details. It is important to note that the rules of notice in most nonfiction texts are not as densely packed as they are in the concentrated samples we use in this book to do initial modeling and practicing of strategies with students.

Lesson Steps

Step 1

Model the think-aloud process and name the rules of notice and key details being noticed, and mentor students into participating in the process with you:

- Provide a print copy of the text, with the text on the left so that students can write in the right-hand column what they notice and think.
- Model the think-aloud. Note that this is the modeling phase of the think-aloud and should be done only until students are ready to be mentored into participating in the think-aloud process.
- As you read and think out loud, have students underline the text details that you notice and record *why* you notice each feature, naming what rule of notice is in play.
- Have one student keep an anchor chart of the specific examples of each rule of notice that comes up. See Figure 3.2 for an example.
- Invite students to participate in the think-aloud, stopping often to ask questions or pausing to see how students will participate.

A sample think-aloud of an excerpt from *The Great Fire* follows. We provide it as a generative model to guide you in creating your own think-aloud on this or other texts highlighting rules of notice.

Rules of Notice: Key Details
1) Direct Statements
The great fire
Def
article judgment
You gotta know
What's Key!
Remember the Wheat
Not the Chaff
2) Calls to Attention!
Titles, intensifiers, explanations, metaphors, intros,
repost connections.
Names: Pg-Leg
Intensifiers, unusually warm
Referes to heat, Fire, Wood.
Characteristics of characters and setting
Example: Shingled cottage, little house
3) Ruptures
One-legged-unusual already in lead
different
Surprising - unusually warm
4) Reader Response
Emotional change, questions I have, why start with pg leg
What I want to know, what I already know
about Irish

Figure 3.2

Anchor Chart: Noticing Key Details

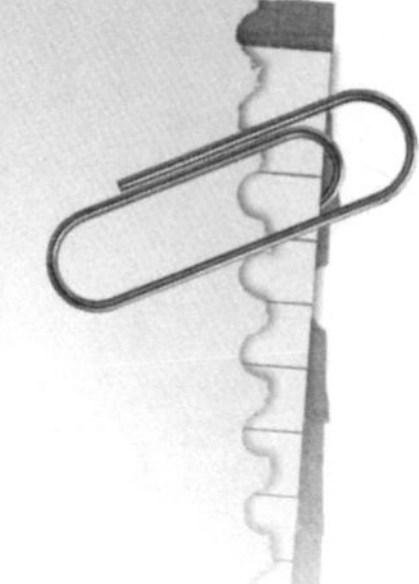

SAMPLE THINK-ALOUD

Lesson 2. Noticing Key Details: Thinking Aloud

The Great Fire

By Jim Murphy

The title is a call to attention.

> Tell students to mark this call to attention with one of their colored pens or pencils and to label it as "Title, always a call to attention."

So this will be about a fire and a great one, the great one. I like the idea of learning more about disasters. It's an important topic. "The Great" is an intensifier, and I should notice it because it's a call to attention.

> Tell students to mark this with the same colored pen or pencil as "Intensifier: call to attention."

The title is also a direct statement because we have a definite article and a judgment. If something is called "The Great" something, then it's being named, and I want to notice names. I happen to know that this fire is the one in Chicago. I also could figure that out from the back cover. But I am wondering what angle Mr. Murphy will take. Lots of rules of notice in play already!

> Tell students to mark this with a different colored pen or pencil for direct statements and label it as "Naming: direct statement of evaluation."

OK, I want to go slow now. We know that beginnings are always important and have a privileged position and give privileged information. This is a call to attention.

> Tell students to mark this with their colored pencil for calls to attention and label it "Beginnings: call to attention through a privileged position."

It was Sunday and an unusually warm ending for October eighth, so Daniel "Peg Leg"

I know names are important, especially nicknames. Why this nickname? One leg? That is another call to attention: Having one leg is a rupture from the norm.

> Tell students to mark this with a new color and to label it "Unusual: rule of rupture." They could label it as "Names and Nicknames: call to attention" and underline it with the colored pencil for call to attention as well.

Sullivan left his stifling

Connects to title, heat. So this is a call to attention using repetition or connection providing a kind of throughline—*that is, an idea that runs through the text, is repeated, and connects and develops other ideas.*

> Tell students to underline this text with the color for calls to attention and to label it as "Repetition, throughline connections: calls to attention."

little house

So he's poor?

> Tell students that it's call to attention when details of setting are mentioned, and readers are being asked to infer what that setting might reveal about character and how the setting might encourage or constrain certain behaviors.

on the West Side of Chicago

Confirms this is about the Great Chicago Fire and where it started.

> Tell students to underline Chicago and note "Repetition, throughline: call to attention."

(Continued)

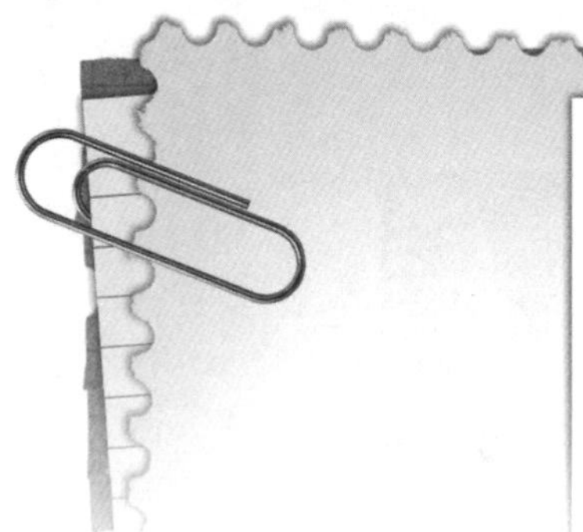

SAMPLE THINK-ALOUD
(CONT.)

and went to visit neighbors. One of his stops was at the shingled cottage

Tell students to underline shingled cottage and note: "Throughline/ invitation to infer: call to attention."

Wood, and we know wood burns. This is another call to attention using repetition and connection.

of Patrick and Catherine O'Leary.

Tell students to underline O'Leary and to note "Names/invitations to infer about character: calls to attention and to underline as well with a new color and label: 'Activation of prior knowledge: rule of reader's response.'" You might also remind students that even the most expert readers don't notice everything—if they notice half of what an author wants them to notice, then they will be very successfully reading.

Sullivan and O'Leary—both Irish. This calls to attention names as well as connections. I bet they are in the Irish part of town. I know that the Irish came to this country after the potato famine, and often lived together in the same parts of cities like New York, Boston, and Chicago. They were hard workers and famous for their fighting in the Civil War. And O'Leary: O'Leary's cow, who kicked over the lantern! I've heard about this! This is my reader's response: a personal connection to prior knowledge.

The one-legged

Tell students to underline one-legged with the colors both for rupture and for call to attention and to label it "Unusual: rupture" and "Repetition, connection to throughline: call to attention."

One-legged—so I'm right about the nickname. That's unusual. Given the time period, could he be a Civil War veteran? So it's a rupture and an invitation to infer. It's also another call to attention using repetition and connection.

Sullivan remembered getting to the O'Learys' house at around eight o'clock,

Tell students to underline remembered and label it as "Reference to pretext: call to attention."

Ah, so someone asked him his memories after the fire—reporters? Investigators? This call to attention is a reference to the pretext*—that is, a reference to something that must have happened before the text begins in order for the text to make sense.*

but left after only a few minutes because the O'Leary family was already in bed.

Tell students to underline eight and already in bed and label the text as "Unusual: rupture."

This is a rupture: Eight is pretty early for bed. They must be hard workers.

Both Patrick and Catherine had to be up very early in the morning: he to set off for his job as a laborer; she to milk their five cows

Tell students to underline with the colors for both reader response and call to attention and label the text as "Activation of prior knowledge: reader response" and "Character activity: call to attention about character."

There's that cow. Another reader's response to prior knowledge, plus a call to attention: a character inference about these two being working class.

and then deliver the milk to neighbors. . . . Fifteen minutes later, Sullivan decided to go home. . . . [He sat down to adjust his leg.] It was while pushing himself up that Sullivan first saw the fire—a single tongue of flame

(Continued)

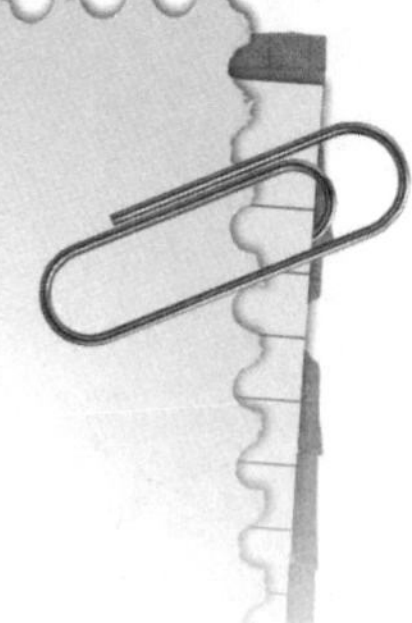

SAMPLE THINK-ALOUD
(CONT.)

I have to notice all figures of speech, comparisons and contrasts, and exaggerations in this case as they are all calls to attention.

> Tell students to underline with the color for call to attention and label the text as "Figures of speech, comparisons, hyperbole: all calls to attention."

shooting out the side of the O'Learys' barn. Sullivan didn't hesitate a second. "FIRE! FIRE! FIRE!"

Here the calls to attention are repetition and emotional charge.

> Tell students to underline with the color for call to attention and note: "Repetition, exclamation marks, emotional charge: all calls to attention."

he shouted as loudly as he could. . . .

Another call to attention: intensity.

> Tell students to underline with the color for call to attention and note: "Intensity: call to attention."

The building was already burning fiercely . . .

And another call to attention: repetition, emotional language.

> Tell students to underline with the color for call to attention and note: "Repetition and intense emotional language: calls to attention."

The barn's loft held over three tons of timothy hay, delivered earlier that day.

Hay would burn like . . . well, wildfire! That connection is a call to attention. I should notice causality.

> Tell students to underline with the color for call to attention and note: "Connection, throughlines, articulated or implied causality: all calls to attention."

Flames from the burning hay pushed against the roof and beams . . .

Here's a call to attention that is intensely visual and personal—we know the people involved. Now, I notice this is a story. It involves real people. I'm wondering at the pace. It meanders. Why did Murphy start this way? To get us into the personal aspects and effects?

> Tell students to underline this phrase with the color for call to attention and note: "Visual; personal connection: calls to attention." Encourage students to mark this as well as a reader's response if they have an intense visualization or personal reaction to the scene.

Source: Murphy, J. (1995). *The great fire.* New York, NY: Scholastic.

Step 2

Mentor students to take part in the think-aloud in pairs or triads and in the larger group:

- Continue reading and thinking aloud until students begin to show readiness for the next step. They will start to join in, name what they notice, cite rules of notice, unpack interpretations, write on their own, or finish sentences. This is all good as this moves the group to a collaborative think-aloud.
- If they need more encouragement and assistance, point out a key detail and then ask students in pairs or triads to consider what rule was used, what meaning they make of it, or how they connect that detail to other details. After a minute or so, have them report their small-group thinking to the class.
- Or, read a paragraph, cite a rule, and see if students can notice another specific word or phrase tipped off for special notice as a key detail by that rule.
- Stop before the think-aloud is complete, once the students have gained some confidence in this mentoring phase of the process.

Step 3

Invite students to work in pairs or triads, or individually, without the teacher's help, then report to the whole class:

- Have students work in pairs or triads for a page or so of the text.
- Lead a whole-class discussion in which students can compare and add to each other's work. Record their noticings and rules on the anchor chart.

Extensions

- Have students do their own written group think-alouds with other texts using Google Docs (see Wilhelm [2012a] for specific examples of models for how to do this).
- Ask students to think aloud about different short excerpts for homework and then get together to share their close readings. You can use a short chapter or section of text that they've read.
- Challenge students to change a sentence or several details in an excerpt. Ask:
    - *How does this deleting, adding, moving, or changing of details affect the reading and what is noticed?*
    - *How does this change affect meaning and effect?*
    - *What would you expect to follow this revision, and how would it be different from the original?*
    - *How would things change, for example, if the excerpt from* The Great Fire *was told through the perspective of Catherine O'Leary?*

The Great Fire (Excerpt)

By Jim Murphy

It was Sunday and an unusually warm ending for October eighth, so Daniel "Peg Leg" Sullivan left his stifling little house on the West Side of Chicago and went to visit neighbors. One of his stops was at the shingled cottage of Patrick and Catherine O'Leary. The one-legged Sullivan remembered getting to the O'Learys' house at around eight o'clock, but left after only a few minutes because the O'Leary family was already in bed. Both Patrick and Catherine had to be up very early in the morning: he to set off for his job as a laborer; she to milk their five cows and then deliver the milk to neighbors. . . .

Fifteen minutes later, Sullivan decided to go home. . . . [He sat down to adjust his leg.] It was while pushing himself up that Sullivan first saw the fire—a single tongue of flame out the side of the O'Learys' barn.

Sullivan didn't hesitate a second. "FIRE! FIRE! FIRE!" he shouted as loudly as he could. . . .

The building was already burning fiercely . . .

The barn's loft held over three tons of timothy hay, delivered earlier that day. Flames from the burning hay pushed against the roof and beams . . .

Source: Murphy, J. (1995). *The great fire.* New York, NY: Scholastic.

Noticing Key Details
PRACTICE IN MINIATURE

PURPOSE

- To practice the rule of notice regarding direct statements of a principle or generalization

LENGTH

- Approximately 60–90 minutes (can be split into two 45-minute classes)

MATERIALS NEEDED

- Class sets of short movie reviews—if the movies are related to the class inquiry, you get a twofer! If you like, you can begin with the review we provide in Handout 3.2, "Movie Review: *Avengers: Age of Ultron* (Excerpt)."
- Class sets of two short texts of your selection, or copies of Handout 3.3, "*Harriet Tubman: Conductor on the Underground Railroad* and *Narrative of the Life of Frederick Douglass, an American Slave, Written by Himself* (Excerpts)"

Introduction

It's pretty clear from survey research that on average students don't read or write nearly enough, and they certainly don't get the kind of focused assistance and practice they need with the strategies necessary to read, write, and problem-solve in the ways that experts do. The research compels us that teachers need to provide lots of assisted practice in meaningful contexts of use, and then help students to develop independence and expertise that they can continue to develop throughout a lifetime. Students can do this if they have processes for comprehending text that are both flexible and transferable. Our aim is to transfer what cognitive scientists call "knowledge"—in contrast to "one size fits few" algorithms that are informational, limited, nongenerative, and not transferable to new situations. If we want students to gain mastery with the flexible processes we provide, we have to give them lots of chances to use them. This lesson provides those chances through practice in miniature.

To provide that practice, we often use materials and texts from popular culture that are familiar to kids. It's best if the texts you choose (or write) relate in some way to a larger inquiry the class is pursuing. In that way, you get a twofer and build both conceptual and procedural knowledge through the activity.

Lesson Steps

Step 1

Introduce the lesson and its purpose in providing practice using one kind of rule of notice: that of direct statements of generalization, principle, or value.

- Tell students you will focus on one rule of notice: attending to direct statements of generalization.
- Explain that one way an author tells you something is important is to phrase it as a direct statement of generalization, principle, or value. For example, if an author is writing in favor

of schools' starting later, he or she might tell a story about a middle or high school student who just couldn't make it to first-period class. If the author then said something like, "If schools really cared about the learning of their adolescent students, they'd start later," you'd need to pay special attention because the author would be directly stating what he or she wants you to learn from the details provided.

Step 2

Provide a short movie review to students to prepare for a think-aloud:

- Distribute Handout 3.2, "Movie Review: *Avengers: Age of Ultron* (Excerpt)," or another short review of a current movie—or, even better, a review of a movie that speaks to the topical conversation being pursued in your current inquiry unit.
- Do a think-aloud focusing on the featured rule of notice. Once again, we provide an example as a guide for you to use in the pages that follow.

Step 3

Ask students to point out any other rules of notice they saw operating in the review.

Step 4

Move from modeling to mentoring the identification of direct statements with a new movie review:

- Distribute another movie review excerpt and mentor students to work individually to identify, articulate, share, and defend their selected direct statements of generalization, principle, or value.
- Divide students into pairs or triads to compare what they chose and how they knew it was a direct statement or generalization.
- If students have difficulty, highlight the first generalization to get them started, but then ask them to find additional generalizations on their own.
- Ask students to return to the review and identify any other rules of notice they found. If students have difficulty, model by identifying the first example of each.
- Repeat this process with other movie reviews until students have demonstrated that they are able to apply the rules of notice regarding direct statements of generalization, principle, or value.

Step 5

Teach to transfer by working with students to apply the process to more complex texts:

- Integrate the noticing and interpretation of direct statements with calls for attention, ruptures, and reader's response.

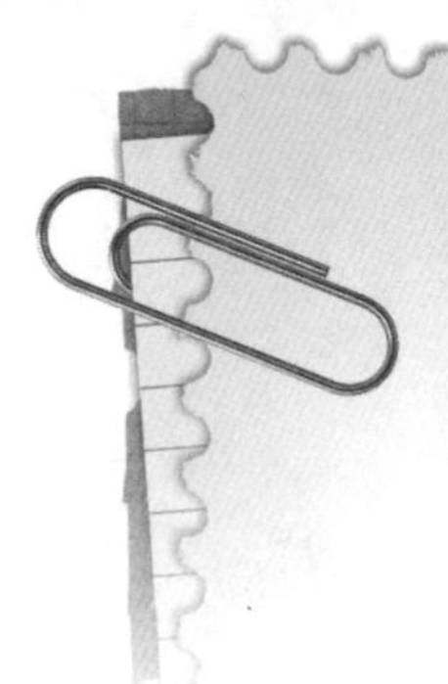

SAMPLE THINK-ALOUD

Lesson 3. Noticing Key Details: Practice in Miniature

Movie Review: *Avengers: Age of Ultron* (Excerpt)

By Cary Darling

It's perhaps appropriate that the summer movie season kicks off with *Avengers: Age of Ultron*. It checks all the right boxes: It's long, loud, larded with effects and sporadically witty, and it sets up events for yet another sequel.

What it doesn't have is any sense of going above and beyond.

This is a direct statement: Good movies go above and beyond, and this review directly states that this movie just doesn't do that.

Unlike some other entries in the Marvel universe—the first *Iron Man, Captain America: The Winter Soldier, Guardians of the Galaxy*, or even the original *Avengers*—it doesn't transcend its boundaries.

Here the author is making another direct statement: Good movies transcend their boundaries and go beyond the expected.

Fans of the franchise will be pleased, but those looking in from the outside of comic-book culture may find themselves also looking at their watches.

Source: Darling, C. (2015, April 29). Movie review: "Avengers: Age of Ultron." *Star-Telegram*. Retrieved from http://www.star-telegram.com/entertainment/arts-culture/article19881744.html

- Distribute two short text excerpts of your next text selection to the class, or use the excerpts in Handout 3.3, "*Harriet Tubman: Conductor on the Underground Railroad* and *Narrative of the Life of Frederick Douglass, an American Slave, Written by Himself* (Excerpts)." Clean copies of these for your students can also be found on this book's companion website at **http://resources.corwin.com/divingdeep-nonfiction**.
- Tell students that they may work to identify rules of notice in the texts individually or in pairs if they are comfortable with using them. Invite students who need more help to gather around you for more guided assistance and mentoring, thus achieving differentiation based on need, grouping, and level of support provided.

In the pages that follow are sample think-alouds that can be used to model or prompt students' thinking aloud. We've highlighted what we identified as rules of notice used in this concentrated sample. Your own model may vary.

Step 6

Consolidate students' understanding of the process for noticing key details:

- Bring students back together as a class to share what they found in the two text excerpts.
- As they share, record their thinking on the anchor chart.
- Encourage them to add specific examples of each rule of notice to the anchor chart.
- Ask: *How might you use the rules of notice in the future?*
- Explain that these are concentrated samples and introductions to books, and that in most texts, and in longer texts, the rules of notice will be less dense and farther apart.

Extensions

- Have students find their own concentrated samples of text that use the reader's rules of notice.
    - Invite them to bring the excerpts into class to share and for others to practice on.
    - Keep them in a classroom file of practice excerpts.
- Match the excerpts to the inquiry and essential question being studied to achieve a twofer. Your students are contributing to archives of both conceptual and strategic material for use in the unit, now and in the future!

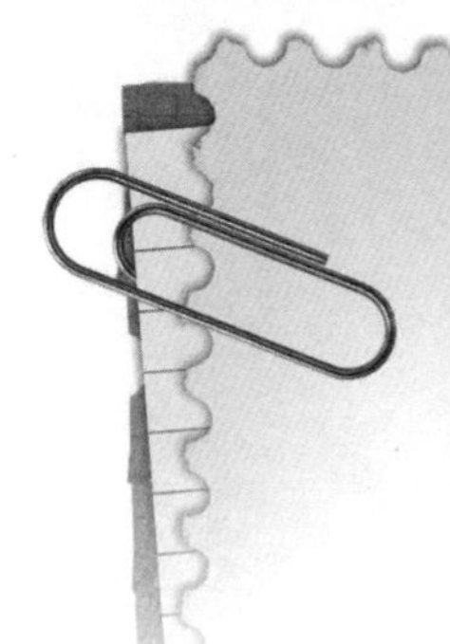

SAMPLE THINK-ALOUD

Lesson 3. Noticing Key Details: Practice in Miniature

Harriet Tubman: Conductor on the Underground Railroad and *Narrative of the Life of Frederick Douglass, an American Slave, Written by Himself* (Excerpts)

Excerpt 1

From *Harriet Tubman: Conductor on the Underground Railroad*, Chapter 3: "Six Years Old"

By the time Harriet Ross was six years old, she had unconsciously absorbed many kinds of knowledge, almost with the air she breathed.

That's a direct statement of generalization that she had unconsciously done lots of learning.

She could not, for example,

The word example *is a call to attention.*

have said how or at what moment she learned that she was a slave.

She knew that her brothers and sisters, her father and mother, and all the other people who lived in the quarter, men, women and children, were slaves.

This is another direct statement of generalization that everyone she was related to was a slave.

She had been taught to say, "Yes, Missus," "No, Missus," to white women, "Yes, Mas'r," "No, Mas'r," to white men. Or, "Yes, sah," "No, sah."

Calls to attention here include the emotional charge of positionality and relationship in regard to others—in this case, an inferior position to oppressors or slaveholders.

(Continued)

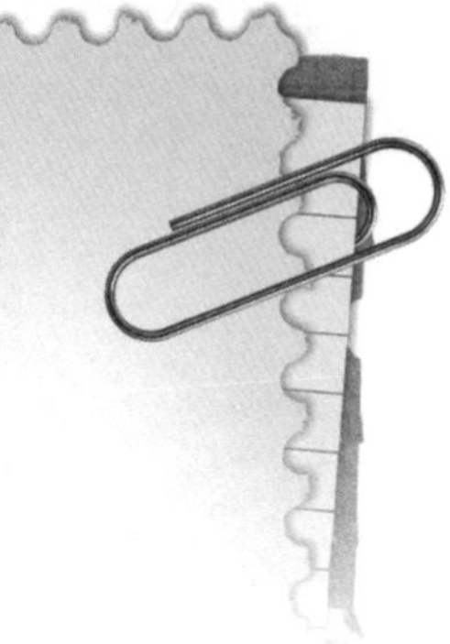

SAMPLE THINK-ALOUD
(CONT.)

At the same time, someone had taught her where to look for the North Star, the star that stayed constant, not rising in the east and setting in the west as the other stars appeared to do; and told her that anyone walking toward the North could use that star as a guide.

That was a rupture: Contrast, surprise, and resistance are introduced with "at the same time" to show the shift. And as for a reader's response, I must activate my background knowledge about the Underground Railroad and how slaves would navigate northward.

She knew about fear, too.

That's a direct statement. And its emotional charge is a call to attention.

Sometimes at night, or during the day, she heard the ***furious***

An emotional word!

galloping of horses, not just one horse, several horses, thud of the hoofbeats along the road, jingle of harness.

More calls to attention: visual and sensory.

She saw the grown folks freeze into stillness, not moving, scarcely breathing, while they listened.

The emotion and intensity here are both a rupture and a call to attention.

She could not remember who first told her that those furious hoofbeats

Another call to attention: repetition.

meant the patrollers were going past, in pursuit of a runaway. Only the slaves said patterollers,

That's a rupture in dialect; slaves use different terms than others.

whispering the word.

And a final rupture here: whispering instead of talking to show how fearsome the patrollers were.

Source: Petry, Ann. *Harriet Tubman: Conductor on the Underground Railroad.* New York: HarperCollins, 1983. (1955)

(Continued)

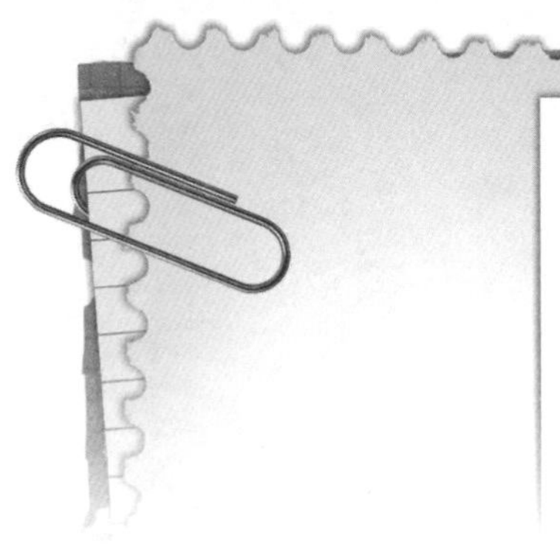

SAMPLE THINK-ALOUD (CONT.)

Excerpt 2

From *Narrative of the Life of Frederick Douglass, an American Slave, Written by Himself*

I preferred the condition of the meanest reptile to my own.

This is a direct statement of the author's condition and feelings.

Any thing, no matter what, to get rid of thinking!

Calls to attention here are emotional charge and exclamation.

It was this everlasting thinking of my condition that tormented me.

Here's a direct statement of generalization—knowing he was a slave tormented him.

There was no getting rid of it.

This direct statement has finality: He absolutely could not get away from it; the repetition and emotional charge are calls to attention.

It was pressed upon me by every object within sight or hearing, animate or inanimate.

The repetition, relentlessness, and parallelism are calls to attention.

The silver trumpet of freedom had roused my soul to eternal wakefulness.

This sentence is visual and sensory, and the metaphor serves as a call to attention.

Freedom now appeared, to disappear no more forever.

Calls to attention also include the varied repetition and contrast of appear *and* disappear. *Finality of "no more forever" is intense and another call to attention.*

It was heard in every sound, and seen in every thing.

More calls to attention: repetition and parallelism.

It was ever present to torment me with a sense of my wretched condition.

(Continued)

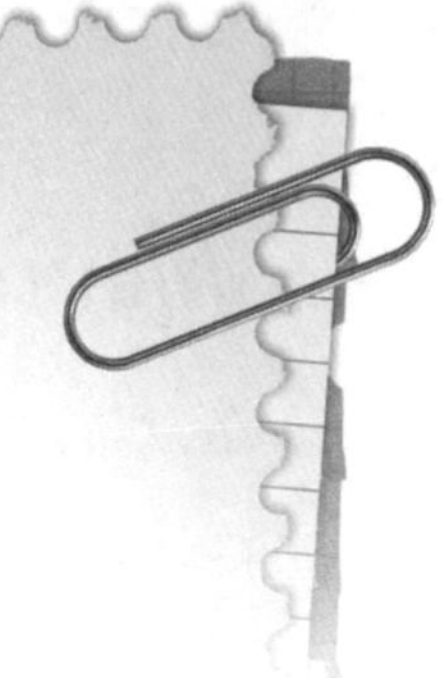

SAMPLE THINK-ALOUD
(CONT.)

The continued repetitions—for example, "torment"—and these emotionally charged words are also calls to attention.

I saw nothing without seeing it, I heard nothing without hearing it, and felt nothing without feeling it.

Repetition and parallelism, again, are calls to attention.

It looked from every star, it smiled in every calm, breathed in every wind, and moved in every storm.

This emphasizes those calls to attention: visual and sensory text, repetition, and parallelism.

Source: Narrative of the life of Frederick Douglass, an American slave, written by himself. Boston, MA: Anti-Slavery Office, 1845. (1845)

Movie Review: **Avengers: Age of Ultron** *(Excerpt)*

By Cary Darling

It's perhaps appropriate that the summer movie season kicks off with *Avengers: Age of Ultron*. It checks all the right boxes: It's long, loud, larded with effects and sporadically witty, and it sets up events for yet another sequel. What it doesn't have is any sense of going above and beyond. Unlike some other entries in the Marvel universe—the first *Iron Man, Captain America: The Winter Soldier, Guardians of the Galaxy*, or even the original *Avengers*—it doesn't transcend its boundaries. Fans of the franchise will be pleased, but those looking in from the outside of comic-book culture may find themselves also looking at their watches.

Source: Darling, C. (2015, April 29). Movie review: "Avengers: Age of Ultron." *Star-Telegram*. Retrieved from http://www.star-telegram.com/entertainment/arts-culture/article19881744.html

Available for download at **http://resources.corwin.com/divingdeep-nonfiction**

Harriet Tubman: Conductor on the Underground Railroad and *Narrative of the Life of Frederick Douglass, an American Slave, Written by Himself* (Excerpts)

Excerpt 1

From *Harriet Tubman: Conductor on the Underground Railroad*, Chapter 3: "Six Years Old"

By the time Harriet Ross was six years old, she had unconsciously absorbed many kinds of knowledge, almost with the air she breathed. She could not, for example, have said how or at what moment she learned that she was a slave. She knew that her brothers and sisters, her father and mother, and all the other people who lived in the quarter, men, women and children, were slaves. She had been taught to say, "Yes, Missus," "No, Missus," to white women, "Yes, Mas'r," "No, Mas'r," to white men. Or, "Yes, sah," "No, sah." At the same time, someone had taught her where to look for the North Star, the star that stayed constant, not rising in the east and setting in the west as the other stars appeared to do; and told her that anyone walking toward the North could use that star as a guide. She knew about fear, too. Sometimes at night, or during the day, she heard the furious galloping of horses, not just one horse, several horses, thud of the hoofbeats along the road, jingle of harness. She saw the grown folks freeze into stillness, not moving, scarcely breathing, while they listened. She could not remember who first told her that those furious hoofbeats meant the patrollers were going past, in pursuit of a runaway. Only the slaves said patterollers, whispering the word.

Source: Petry, Ann. *Harriet Tubman: Conductor on the Underground Railroad.* New York: HarperCollins, 1983. (1955)

(Continued)

Excerpt 2

From *Narrative of the Life of Frederick Douglass, an American Slave, Written by Himself*

I preferred the condition of the meanest reptile to my own. Any thing, no matter what, to get rid of thinking! It was this everlasting thinking of my condition that tormented me. There was no getting rid of it. It was pressed upon me by every object within sight or hearing, animate or inanimate. The silver trumpet of freedom had roused my soul to eternal wakefulness. Freedom now appeared, to disappear no more forever.

It was heard in every sound, and seen in every thing. It was ever present to torment me with a sense of my wretched condition. I saw nothing without seeing it, I heard nothing without hearing it, and felt nothing without feeling it. It looked from every star, it smiled in every calm, breathed in every wind, and moved in every storm.

Source: Narrative of the life of Frederick Douglass, an American slave, written by himself. Boston, MA: Anti-Slavery Office, 1845. (1845)

Available for download at **http://resources.corwin.com/divingdeep-nonfiction**

Lesson 4

Noticing Key Details
QUESTIONING

Introduction

Helping students to generate their own questions that support independent comprehension and interpretation definitely depends on (and assists with) noticing what is key. When teachers generate and ask the questions, they are the ones doing the noticing and all the work. When we teach students how to ask powerful questions, we must teach them to notice what's important to ask about, and to think about how these key details and moves make meaning and achieve effect. This moves students to greater competence and independence. We teach our students specific questioning strategies and techniques that reinforce and consolidate student independence with the processes for noticing and interpreting.

We want to stress that the whole purpose of questioning is to get students to internalize questioning schemes so that they come to ask their own independent questions of text that guide and monitor their reading now and into the future. We want the questioning schemes to become transferable and unconstrained sets of strategies—threshold procedures to be used and developed throughout a lifetime.

One of our favorite questioning techniques for helping students to generate questions based on noticing both key details and patterns of details is Taffy Raphael's (1982) QAR (Question–Answer Relationship) (see Wilhelm, Baker, & Dube [2001] and Wilhelm [2007] for how we use QAR questions to inquire into how texts work). We put a little tweak on our use of QARs to ensure that the "Right There" questions (described below) are about key details that can be connected to other details and used to generate inferential, crticial, and applied questions. We call our version *cumulative QARs*.

We really like QARs because they mirror the trajectory of inquiry in all disciplines and subject areas (see Wilhelm [2007] for a thorough explanation of how this is the case in science, social sciences, and math). In QARs, there are four different types of questions that help students do different kinds of work:

PURPOSE

- To learn to generate QAR questions that move from the literal to the inferential and then to the interpretive, evaluative, and applied

LENGTH

- Approximately 45–90 minutes (can be split into two 45-minute classes)

MATERIALS NEEDED

- A short, complex nonfiction text

- Right There questions establish the facts/key details.
- Think and Search questions require inferring the patterns of these key details.
- Author and Me questions get after implied meanings that require combining textual information with background knowledge from one's life.
- On Your Own questions critique and apply what has been learned.

QARs also mirror what we understand about expert readers and what they do; that is, we know that expert readers first notice key details and literally comprehend, through what Raphael calls Right There questions, but that this literal comprehension is the springboard for the much more generative activities of inferring and figuring forth by filling in gaps and putting things together to see what patterns of meaning accrue. These are what Raphael calls Think and Search questions/comprehension.

Expert readers then go beyond this to combine these textual meanings with *extra*textual meanings—with personal life knowledge and a personal response—to see further connections and applications and to build evolving theories (through accommodation or assimilation) about how things work in the world. These are what Raphael calls Author and Me questions/comprehension.

We also know that experts engage in all these activities in the context of asking big questions of application about the world that may be informed by the text they are reading but are much bigger than the text and can be addressed without a specific reading. Raphael calls these On Your Own questions/comprehension. These On Your Own questions are, in fact, essential or existential questions that provide an overarching context of use for any reading. This last type of question gets students to consider real-world applications of general principles and problem-solving procedures and to identify situations in which concepts and strategies can be used. This constitutes cultivating the spirit of transfer and future application.

We also love QARs for showing students that while reading does depend on literal comprehension and noticing key details, it is much *much* more than this. This can be threshold learning for many students. Key details, in fact, become significant to the degree that they inform inferring, connecting to the world, and functional applications and problem-solving strategies for big issues and questions. The QAR scheme demonstrates to students that not only is it good to go beyond the literal, but in fact this (threshold learning!) is a necessary move of expert reading.

We put in this twist: asking students to make sure that their Right There question provides a key detail that can be combined in a pattern with other details, leading to a Think and Search question, then to an Author and Me question, and finally to an On Your Own question.

A cumulative QAR builds and consolidates skills in noticing and unpacking, and works coherently to build conceptual knowledge on a textual throughline about a particular focus.

Lesson Steps

Step 1

Introduce the technique of QARs:

- Tell students that they will be generating a series of questions based on a reading. The series of questions is called a **QAR** and includes **four different types of questions** based on three levels of reading.
- Introduce the three levels of reading:
  - **On the lines:** Right There
  - **Between the lines:** Think and Search
  - **Beyond the lines:** Author and You, On Your Own
- Explain the "on the lines" (Right There) reading. This kind of reading focuses on what is "right there" in the text, what is literally and directly expressed.
- Explain "between the lines" (Think and Search) reading. This requires the reader to see throughlines and make connections between various related details that appear in different parts of the text. Note that the connections are typically not explicitly made by the author, so the reader must see the connection and make meaning of it.
- Explain "beyond the lines" (Author and Me, On Your Own) reading. This requires readers to go beyond the text, at both the literal and the inferential level, and to combine the text with information from their own lives (Author and Me) and from the world and then to apply the reading to a real-world problem (On Your Own).

Step 2

Focus students on connecting details to see patterns of meaning and to make inferences:

- Remind students of the importance of making connections across . related details.
- Explain that expert readers make the following types of connections:
  - **Text–Self** (rule of reader's response)
  - **Text–Text** (making intertextual connections, and doing so to notice different turns taken in an ongoing conversation about particular topics)
  - **Text–World** (noticing problems and conversations going on in the disciplines, popular culture, and the world at large)

- Explain that practicing Text–Self connections will help your students ask and answer Author and Me questions and that seeing Text–Text and Text–World connections will help them understand the On Your Own questioning. Encourage them to use what they read to consider real-world problems.

Step 3

Introduce students to the four types of questions they will generate:

- Explain that expert readers use questions to help them do all three levels of reading. The types of questions they will generate fall into four categories:
    - Right There questions, which establish the facts
    - Think and Search questions, which call for inferring patterns
    - Author and Me questions, which imply meanings
    - On Your Own questions, which call for critiquing and applying what has been learned

Step 4

Model how to generate QARs with a reading:

- Demonstrate the questioning scheme with a previously read short nonfiction text. You may wish to have students reread it quickly before you begin. For each question you generate, explain what type of question it is based on and what is required of the reader to answer it.

- As you move on with asking the questions, allow students to try to identify the type of QAR each one is, and justify that identification based on what the reader would have to do to answer it (this is why the scheme is called question–answer *relationships* because the question type relates to what a reader must do to answer it).

- In the example in Figure 3.3, we use Murphy's *The Great Fire*.

Step 5

Review takeaways:

- Note that to make this a *cumulative* QAR, the Right There question in Figure 3.3 highlighted a key detail that could be combined in a pattern with other details, leading to asking and answering a Think and Search (or "between the lines") question, and in turn to Author and Me and On Your Own questions (or "beyond the lines" questions).

- To generate this kind of cumulative QAR, then, we have to read the whole text before generating our QARs. This enables us to see what key details connect and build on each other.

What was Mr. Sullivan's nickname?

A: Peg Leg.

Identification/Justification: This is certainly a **Right There** question because we can point directly to the answer and say, "It's right there." But this is not a key detail question *unless* it can be combined with another detail to create meaning.

What did Mr. Sullivan's nickname reveal about him?

A: He had lost a leg and therefore used a prosthetic wooden peg for a leg.

Identification/Justification: This is a **Think and Search** question because it combines two details very close to each other in the text that the reader must connect and combine.

How did Mr. Sullivan's disability affect his role in the story about the fire?

A: He stopped to adjust his leg, and this is when he saw the fire. If he had not stopped, then he wouldn't have been the first to see it. Then, when he rushed into the barn to let the animals loose, his leg kept him from doing it, getting stuck in the floorboards and then coming loose. This contributed to his narrow escape as he had to use a cow and hop to get out of the barn, and may have contributed to the fire's getting out of hand. Later in the book we learn about the troubles that other people with infirmities (as well as lack of social standing, lack of resources, etc.) had dealing with the fire, so Sullivan's leg provides the initial detail in a larger throughline.

Identification/Justification: This is a **Think and Search** question because his disability, indicated by his nickname, connected to later details and affected the trajectory of the story. These details are further apart in the text so require more attention and connection work.

What different courses of action do you think Mr. Sullivan could have taken, and what might have been the different outcomes of such actions? What might you have done in Mr. Sullivan's shoes (or shoe!)?

A: Answers will vary, depending on the reader.

Identification/Justification: This is an **Author and Me** question because it combines your life knowledge and judgment with the meaning from the text. It is cumulative because it develops from the first two questions that were purely textual. We are now going beyond the text by combining textual details with extratextual data from our lives and experiences.

How can we best deal with trouble and even disaster as it is happening? How can we best deal with potential trouble and even disaster before it happens?

A: Answers will vary, depending on the reader.

Identification/Justification: These are **On Your Own** questions because they are essential/existential inquiry questions this text can be used to address. One does not actually have to have read this particular text to address the question. The questions are cumulative because they expand on and reflect back on the previous questions.

Figure 3.3

Example: Modeling QARs

- A cumulative QAR builds and consolidates skills in noticing, connecting, inferring, and unpacking, and the questions at different levels work together to coherently build conceptual knowledge with a particular focus that is developed throughout the text.

Step 6

Move from modeling to mentoring students to work together with your help to generate their own QARs:

- Ask students to help you create another complete set of QAR questions—with the same text excerpt if that works, or with another one of your choice.
- Gradually release responsibility by asking them to work together in small groups or pairs to help each other create cumulative QARs about new short sections of text.

Extensions

- Create, justify, respond. Have small groups create QAR questions for other students to answer and test out, review, or improve.
- Stage a "QAR challenge."
    - A question is offered by a team.
    - The members of a second team must identify the question type, tell how they know it is that type, and provide an answer for the question.
    - Other teams confirm the responses or revise or add to them using their own justifications.

For specific information on using QARs in the disciplines, visit this book's companion website at **http://resources.corwin.com/divingdeep-nonfiction**.

Lesson 5

Noticing Key Details
WRITING AND RESPONDING

Introduction

In the following lesson, you'll see how students are prompted to use threshold procedures, concepts, and takeaways in their composition of a choral montage.

A choral montage (Wilhelm, 2012c) is a wonderfully easy and fun technique for composing a group poem with key details, key phrases, or crucial ideas and takeaways. First, each student selects a key detail or crucial phrase from a text. Students then read their sentences or phrases aloud, creating a choral montage, and experiment with revising and ordering them for the greatest meaning and effect.

When we introduce choral montage, we start with a simple stem that prompts students to generate ideas related to our inquiry. So, during a civil rights unit, for example, we might ask students to finish a phrase: "Civil rights are . . ." or "Civil rights require . . ." or "Civil rights are violated when . . ." We might ask students to focus on a threshold concept, like a transformative or troublesome insight gleaned from our readings and studies such as the conditions required for successful improvement in civil rights.

We use the prompt stem as the title of our poem, and then everyone reads his or her response aloud as we go around a circle. Then we can decide how to reorder the phrases to create more meaning and maximum effect. We may decide to repeat a certain phrase as a chorus or an ostinato, slightly change or develop a phrase throughout the montage, or revise, delete, or add new phrases. We typically videotape the final revision and then watch it. Students love it.

For a "reader's rules of notice" choral montage, we ask students to choose three of the most important key details, phrases, or ideas from a text. We ask for three so that if someone else has taken their idea, they have two more choices. Of course, repetition works, too—or repetition with slight tweaks or development throughout the poem. These moves to repeat, use parallelism, or slightly rupture previous phrasings

Lesson 5: Day 1

PURPOSE

- To practice using reader's rules of notice to rank the importance of details and ideas

LENGTH

- Approximately 60–90 minutes (can be split into two 45-minute classes)

MATERIALS NEEDED

- An interesting and complex short text or excerpt (we use *The Great Fire* excerpt as the basis for an example provided in this lesson)
- Notecards for all students
- A video recording device

highlight key ideas and demonstrate the various rules of notice for key details, so if we do this in our poem, we are coding our text with the very rules of notice we have been studying and using as readers.

This activity is a version of "mystery pot," a technique involving single lines that have been cut out and separated from a well-structured short piece. In a mystery pot activity, students must reconstruct the piece, putting it into a sensible order—looking at the various options and the differences in meaning and effect for different orderings. This is a powerful way to highlight authorial choices, as the creation of patterns and revision is made visible. Students then have the opportunity to practice justifying these choices in terms of meaning and effect. In a mystery pot, students can compare their versions with the original author's version, consider why certain choices were made, and consider the meanings and effects that followed from different choices.

Our three-part lesson concludes by having students employ procedural feedback. A major goal of our teaching is to assist students to be helpful and even expert peer editors of each other's work. When they can do this, they become self-regulated, metacognitive, and adept editors of their own work, *and* they become people who can notice, unpack, appreciate, and provide procedural descriptions of how an author's specific choices lead to specific meanings and effects.

When students provide procedural feedback, they comment on what the writer did or accomplished in a particular piece of text, what meaning or effect it had, and how the writer did it. Using procedural feedback emphasizes the fact that making other choices would lead to other meanings and effects. This realization promotes agency on the part of the writer and a need to attend and notice on the part of the reader. The process of composing procedural feedback enacts Carol Dweck's (2006) research on promoting the dynamic or growth mindset that we discussed in the introduction.

Lesson Steps: Day 1

Step 1

Define* montage *and set up the purpose and process of composing a choral montage:

- Ask students if they are familiar with the term *montage*. If not, share a visual montage and see if they can define *montage* by looking at an example (see Figure 3.4 as well as other examples available on the book's companion website at **http://resources.corwin.com/divingdeep-nonfiction**).
- Once they understand what a montage is (a dictionary definition could be reviewed as well), inform students that they are going to create what is known as a "choral montage."
- See the sample choral montage in Figure 3.5.

- Ask: *How might a choral montage be different from a visual montage?*
- Tell students that they are going to find the most powerful key details, phrases, images, or ideas from a text by using the rules of notice for key details. Explain that they will then use these details and phrases to create a piece of poetry—a choral montage—based on their reading of *The Great Fire* (or any other piece your class is reading).

Step 2

Prompt students for their thoughts about the most crucial details from a text:

- On a notecard, ask each student to individually identify the three most important phrases, sentences, images, or ideas from the text (or selected excerpt).
- On the back of their sticky note or notecard, ask students to jot down what rules of notice they used to identify each of their key details.

Step 3

Create a first-draft choral montage in a "whip-around" circle:

- Once students have selected their most crucial details, arrange the class into a circle and have them read *one* of their three ideas in a whip around the circle, one voice after another.
- Go around again, and have students justify why they thought that their key detail choice was the best one to read. If someone has previously spoken their first choice, encourage students to use their second or third choice.
- Have students write on a slip of paper the one sentence or phrase that they read.
- Post the papers in the classroom in the order they were read.

Step 4

Facilitate a gallery walk and reflection on the montage:

- Have students slowly read the displayed montage.
- Invite students to share in pairs what they notice about the details in the montage. Ask:
    - *How was reading and listening to the montage different? How were rules of notice used in the montage?*
    - *How were details or ideas repeated, patterned, or played off each other?*
- Bring the class together and share thoughts with the large group.

Source: © John Phelan/Wikimedia Commons Creative Commons License

Figure 3.4

Example: Visual Montage

The Great Fire

At first so small, its start unseen

The O'Learys sleeping

Flames smoldering small

Flames licking, then thirstily devouring the straw

Then growing, growing

Bursting out the barn rafters

With no one knowing

Seen first by Peg Leg Sullivan

The cows whining and horses screaming

The O'Learys still sleeping

At first the fire was so small

Spreading to the timothy hay

To the wooden outbuildings and neighbors' houses

At first so small

Seen only by Daniel Peg Leg Sullivan, screaming Fire! Fire! Fire!

Losing his leg in the barn

Others losing their houses and all they owned

Before long, the great fire of Chicago

Spreading throughout the whole of the giant city

Drinking the city dry with its giant thirst

Figure 3.5

Example: Choral Montage Created by Sixth Graders for *The Great Fire*

Step 5

Ask students to work together to revise their choral montage:

- Have students confer in pairs. Ask: *What single line would be best to begin the revised montage? Why?*
- Invite them to share with the larger group. Have them justify their selections.
- Have students return to their pairs. Ask: *What line would be best to conclude it? Why?*
- Then ask what lines might build off or answer the first line in some way, making a strong second line. Entertain various ideas and try them out. Then move on to a potential third line and so on.
- Ask students to share their first few lines with the larger group. Have them justify their selections.
- Explain to students that to compose a full choral montage they would use all the rest of the lines, figuring out what order they would best go in to create meaning and effect. They have already chosen the best key details; now they need to put them in the best order.

Step 6

Create a choral montage:

- Now that students have experienced concrete modeling of the process, put them in groups of five or six to create a complete choral montage using the lines from their notes from Steps 2 and 3, or revisions of these. If they want, individuals can read more than one line.
- As students are working, have them reflect. Ask:
    - *What could be revised?*
    - *What could be moved?*
    - *What could be added?*
    - *What could be deleted?*
- Tell students that they can try different constructions, perform them, and compare them.

Step 7

Perform and record the montages:

- Once a group makes a final decision and rehearses it, take a video of the students in that group performing their montage.

Step 8

View the filmed montages:

- Play the montages back for the whole class.
- Ask the composers to list the rules of notice they used to find their details, and the viewers to identify any rules of notice they noticed in the performance of the montage.

Extensions: Day 1

Combine montage composing with the drama technique of in-role writing:

- Ask students to take on the role of a character (Peg Leg or the O'Learys, the mayor, the fire chief, or another character from *The Great Fire*) and to write a diary entry or letter to another character about their experiences described in the text.
- Have students exchange letters and circle the most poignant and moving details or phrases in their partner's letter by using rules of notice.
- Have students use what they've circled to create the choral montage (see Wilhelm [2016] and [2012b] for more ideas on in-role writing and choral montages). This kind of montage features different voices and perspectives and can take on the form of a conversation or call and response.

Optional: Students can engage in reflective writing about the composing or revision process as it relates to creating the choral montages, and reflect on how their use of various strategies and rules of notice made the piece better. They can also reflect on this activity to consider what threshold learnings emerged regarding the inquiry topic.

Lesson 5: Day 2

PURPOSE

- To compare drafts of choral montages to understand authorial choice

LENGTH

- Approximately 45–60 minutes

MATERIALS NEEDED

- Drafts of students' writing to compare (here, we use drafts of their choral montages, but you can do this with other pieces of writing as well)
- Drafts of a classic text that fits into your current unit (we use the Gettysburg Address; Lincoln's five drafts of this can easily be found online)
- A short mentor text that students can use to practice revising for meaning and effect
- Class set of Handout 3.4, "Mentor Sentences Based on *The Great Fire* (Excerpt)" (optional)

Lesson Steps: Day 2

Step 1

Have students compare their writing:

- Assign student groups to compare drafts of their choral montages and reflect on why they made the changes they did.
- Ask: *What differences did your changes have on meaning and effect for a reader?*
- Invite students in each small group to report to the large group and record the effect of some of the changes.

Step 2

Have students compare drafts of a professionally written text:

- Pass out multiple drafts of a classic text, such as the Gettysburg Address, that fits your current unit.
- Ask students to work in pairs to compare the drafts and explain why they think particular changes were made. For example, for the Gettysburg Address, ask them what Lincoln changed or moved and deleted or added in each draft, and then ask them why he might have done so. What meanings and effects do these changes work toward?

Step 3

Make changes to a mentor text and explore changes in meaning/effect:

- Pass out a mentor text of your choice.
- Ask students to work independently to change, move, delete, or add a word, words, or phrases from the chosen mentor text, particularly at the beginning, ending, climax, or some kind of rupture in the text.
- Have students work in pairs or triads to compare their revisions with the original and explore how particular revisions made particular kinds of differences.

Step 4

Identify and use sentences from the mentor text as mentor sentences:

- Explain that using short text excerpts and even sentences as mentor texts and models for writing is extremely powerful and can help students to learn from expert writers how to compose sentences and short passages more powerfully.

- Ask students to choose a powerful sentence or short excerpt from the mentor text they've been working with and explain why it is so powerful, using rules of notice in their explanation.
- Ask students to "copy change"—that is, keep the major structural words in their chosen sentence or excerpt, while adding some of their own nouns, adjectives, or verbs in place of what the original author placed there (like a Mad Lib).
- If students need examples and practice, use Handout 3.4, "Mentor Sentences Based on *The Great Fire* (Excerpt)."

Extensions: Day 2

- Look at more global structural moves and shifts in the text, like the shift in the opening of *The Great Fire* from narrative to commentary and informational writing.
- Consider as a class why and how this shift was made, and then have students practice that same kind of shift in their own collaborative and then independent writing.
- Compare and contrast students' efforts to those of Jim Murphy.

Handout 3.4

Mentor Sentences Based on *The Great Fire* (Excerpt)

by Jim Murphy

Chicago in 1871 was a city ready to burn. The city boasted having 59,500 buildings, many of them—such as the Courthouse and the *Tribune* Building—large and ornately decorated. The trouble was that about two-thirds of all these structures were made entirely of wood.

Original sentence:

Chicago in 1871 was a city ready to burn.

______________ in ______________ was a ______________ ready to ______________.

New sentence:

The North Junior High basketball team in 2017 was a force ready to be reckoned with!

Original sentence:

The city boasted having 59,500 buildings, many of them—such as the Courthouse and the *Tribune* Building—large and ornately decorated.

The ______________ boasted ______________, many of them—such as ______________ and ______________ and ______________.

New sentence:

The team boasted a star-studded cast of players, many of them—such as Tucker and Will—big guys who could also dribble the ball and shoot the three.

Original sentence:

The trouble was that about two-thirds of all these structures were made entirely of wood.

The ____________ was that about ____________ of ____________ were ____________.

New sentence:

The challenge was that about half of the team were not as gifted, but they were willing to work hard.

Source: Murphy, J. (1995). *The great fire.* New York, NY: Scholastic.

Available for download at **http://resources.corwin.com/divingdeep-nonfiction**

Lesson Steps: Day 3

Step 1

Set the purpose and explain the process for giving procedural feedback:

- Tell students that they will be learning to give authors—including their peers—what is known as *procedural feedback.*
- Emphasize that this is a very powerful way of giving feedback. Explain that procedural feedback is meant to be nonjudgmental and to describe what the writer has done, the moves he or she made, and what followed in terms of meaning and effect.
  - Explain that to start you give a description of what the writer has done.
  - Stress that after the description you explain the meaning or the effect of what was done.
- Note that providing procedural feedback expresses a dynamic/growth mindset because we create meaning through our efforts and use of strategies. This kind of feedback demonstrates that we can always revise and improve anything we do or write through the application of renewed effort and new strategies.

Step 2

Demonstrate how to provide procedural feedback with a previously read text:

- Model an example from a recent assignment. For instance, you could provide feedback to the sample student choral montage on *The Great Fire* by using this frame:
  - "The way you ______________ emphasized ___________."
- For example, say:
  - *The way you began your montage with "At first so small" and then repeated this later in the poem emphasized that even the biggest disasters start small, and also emphasized your takeaway that we need to prepare for disasters before they get started.*
- Or model feedback to author Jim Murphy. Say:
  - *The way you began with a story about real people who were so deeply affected by the fire helped to hook me into the book, and made me more deeply experience how real human beings are affected by disasters such as this.*
- Or model feedback to a student argument. Say:
  - *Your use of specific evidence from several different cited and authoritative sources convinced me that you have a point worth considering, even though I initially disagreed with you quite strongly.*

Lesson 5: Day 3

PURPOSE

- To notice what authors do to load their text with meaning, especially through rules of notice, and to describe the meaning and effect of using rules of notice strategically

LENGTH

- Approximately 45–60 minutes

MATERIALS NEEDED

- Class sets of several excerpts of professional pieces of writing; a short piece of student writing; a short piece of your own writing, if possible
- Paper to make an anchor chart

Step 3

Use sentence frames to assist students to generate procedural feedback:

- Provide sentence frames to students, or develop frames with them for providing this kind of feedback.
  - *The way you/the author* ____________ *led me to* ______________.
  - *The use of* ______________ *had the consequence of* ____________.
  - *When you/the author* __________________, *it had the effect of* ________________.
  - *The move you/the author made to* __________________________
    - *resulted in* ____.
    - *should lead to* ______________________________________.
    - *exhibited the principle of* ______________________________.
  - ____________________ *helped me see/notice/feel/think/consider/rethink* ____________________ *because* ___________________.
- Create an anchor chart that archives different sentence stems for providing procedural feedback and ask students to keep thinking about how to add to the chart by experimenting with different phrasings as you go through the day!

Step 4

Use the sentence frames to provide procedural feedback to authors:

- Practice with students using the sentence frames to provide feedback to the author of a text the class has just read. Have them use the stems on the anchor chart as a guide.
- Mentor the whole class in doing one or two together, then involve students in doing some together in pairs or triads.
- Share examples with the large group and discuss how procedural feedback requires noticing, and requires unpacking how texts work to create meaning and effect.

Step 5

Practice "feeding forward" to develop students' repertoire of problem-solving moves in their writing:

- Explain that in peer editing and self-editing it is important to provide feedforward, and to consider one's agency and repertoire in terms of where one can go next—what one has not done *yet* but could one day do after continuing to extend, revise, and improve one's work.
- Provide models of how to provide feedforward for future directions with a piece of your own writing (particularly powerful), a draft of professional writing, or student writing. For example:

- *I wonder what would happen if ____________ [you/I/the author] ______________ [made a specific move/tried a strategy] in order to ______________ [the meaning and effect that you think might accrue from this move].*

- Note to students that the *in order to* is essential because it explains what the move is designed to do.
- Add this sentence stem to the class anchor chart.

Step 6

Practice phrasing feedforwards in pairs or triads:

- Give students a new excerpt from a professional writer or peer. Have students practice in pairs or triads providing procedural feedback and feedforwards on the piece. Encourage them to use the sentence stems you used in your modeling or to create their own.
- When students are done, have them reflect on what rules of notice they used in the feedback, how composing the feedback went, any experiences of productive challenge, and how they navigated—or could navigate—those challenges.
- Have students share other stems they might have come up with for procedural feedback and feeding forward and put these on the anchor chart for reference.

Step 7

Provide independent practice with procedural feedback and feedforward:

- Have students practice more independently giving procedural feedback to the author of another piece of writing, like a reading assignment for the next day.
- Have them cite the rules of notice they used to decide what to describe in their feedback.

Step 8

Share students' procedural feedback in pairs or triads, then the larger group:

- Have students share their procedural feedback from the previous step in pairs or triads, then to the whole class in a charette (a meeting in which all stakeholders in a project attempt to resolve conflicts and map solutions, an idea from architecture).
- Reflect together on how the process works and how to navigate problems.

- Discuss in what immediate and future situations this kind of feedback and feedforward would be powerful to use. Add a list of situations to your anchor chart.
- Emphasize with students that these kinds of feedback and feedforward leave the authority and decision making to the author, but they are specific in suggesting a move or strategy that the author might want to try.
- Highlight that providing this kind of response requires expert readerly and writerly thinking. It requires having a toolbox or repertoire of expert strategies and procedures for solving problems in our writing, and it asks students to go back to the strategies that they have been taught in the context of this unit and consider how they can be applied.

Lesson
6

Noticing Key Details
SEARCH AND FIND

Introduction

Once the tools for noticing key details are consolidated, we ask students to transfer their noticing to a wide variety of texts in real life through the "search and find" technique—our students like to call it "seek and destroy" or "bring 'em back alive." This strategy promotes *transfer* by asking students to consider how texts are present throughout their everyday lives, and how these texts—whether written or multimodal; whether informal like conversation or ads, or formal like school assignments—use rules of notice to cue readers and listeners to navigate and make meaning of the text.

Lesson Steps

Step 1

Share models of found texts using rules of notice:

- Show the PowerPoint models of found texts (or some of your own) and ask students to identify the rules of notice in play. For example:
  - *Street signs like "Share the road" and "Please drive slowly" are direct statements of a generalization, principle, or value.*
- Note that the visuals are calls to attention and provide more information about why it is important to drive slowly.
- Display the water billboard. Point out that it uses three of the rules:
  - There is a direct statement.
  - The visual is both a call to attention and a rupture since the earth is not really ensconced in a water droplet.
  - The visual and the allusions to *The Little Mermaid* and "Part of Your World" are also calls to attention.
- Continue modeling with these kinds of texts until students are ready to proceed on their own.

PURPOSE

- To recognize how the rules for noticing key details work for all kinds of texts and utterances

LENGTH

- Approximately 20–45 minutes

MATERIALS NEEDED

- Students' examples of "found" texts that use rules of notice (see Figure 3.6)
- PowerPoint slides that show "Found Texts" (these can be accessed on this book's companion website at **http://resources.corwin.com/divingdeep-nonfiction**)

PRIOR TO THIS LESSON

- Ask students to look in everyday life for texts that use the rules of notice you've discussed and practiced together. Places to look include
  - Everyday conversation and interactions
  - Billboards
  - Ads or other popular culture texts
  - YouTube
  - Free reading
- Have students bring in examples to share on the day of this lesson whether through photos, the artifact itself, or notes

Found Text	Speaker/Object	Reader's Rule of Notice
Exit Now!	Billboard	Direct statement: command, imperative
Now listen up!	Mom	Direct statement: direction and immediacy ("*now* do this")
Stop learning and listen to me!	Mr. Wilhelm	Rupture: *stop learning* (ironic)
The three major things to remember are . . .	Mr. Smith	Direct statement: explicit ordering, list
The Holy Bible: Inspired. Absolute. Final.	Billboard	Calls to attention: capitalization, colon. The list and parallel structure are for effect. Seems to build over time to a climax.
Last Chance for Gas!	Billboard	Direct statement: ultimatum, warning Reader's response: You certainly don't want all the irritation caused by running out of gas!
Porsche: Strong German Engineering	Advertisement	Direct statement of a general principle
Onboard devices can keep engineers awake: (1), (2), (3)—	From crawler below TV news story on train wreck	Direct statement; calls to attention: colon, list of devices in order of effectiveness

Figure 3.6

Examples: Found Texts and Reader's Rules of Notice

Step 2

Students share their artifacts that exemplify the rules of notice:

- Have students bring in their artifacts and share in triads or quads.
- Then have them share with the larger group through a roundtable, sharing and reading
  - What they found
  - Where they found it
  - The rule of notice that is exemplified
  - How they know it is that rule of notice and how they know it is doing its work to create meaning and effect
- Have students post their examples around the classroom with captions explaining the rule of notice used and how it works.

Extension

Ask students to use the comment function in Microsoft Word to explain how they employed rules of notice in creating one of their own short texts.

Noticing Key Details
PUTTING IT ALL TOGETHER

PURPOSE

- To color code all of the rules of notice for key details to reveal how the rules of notice work together throughout a text to create meaning and effect

LENGTH

- Approximately 60–120 minutes (can be split into multiple classes)

MATERIALS NEEDED

- Hard copies of a complex nonfiction text (e.g., "I Have a Dream")
- A device for projecting "I Have a Dream" and a way to highlight the text using that device (e.g., an ELMO document camera, Google Docs and a computer highlighter tool, or some other technique)
- Multiple sets of colored pencils, markers or highlighters, or another tool
- A Google Docs version of the text for students to work on and a computer's highlighter function to color code the text
- A rules of notice bookmark for each student (you can make these using the template found at the companion website, **http://resources.corwin.com/divingdeep-nonfiction**)

Introduction

What's the ultimate point of all the modeling—all the structured and mentored practice—using the rules of notice? It's to lead our students to independence with a generative tool that they can continue to use strategically throughout their lifetimes.

As we noted in Chapter 1, the real proof of effective teaching and learning is in students' transferring what they've learned to new situations. If we have enacted all the principles of transfer (see page 4) in our previous six lessons and given them enough practice, then they should be able to do it, and their doing so will be a profound achievement to be celebrated and then built upon further.

When it comes to the end of a unit and all that practice, we tell our students that they've had the great luck to be coached throughout the unit. They've gotten nothing but help and productive practice. But now, we tell them, the worm has turned! The time has come for them to show their stuff in actual accomplishment, to pull together all of the strategies they have practiced and orchestrate their use independently.

We typically use shorter anchor texts for a final practice run; following this, we ask students to independently apply their strategies to a more extended anchor text. These anchor texts typically serve as mentor texts for future reading, but also for writing.

The lesson below is inspired by the poet John Ciardi's colored chalk method of analyzing poetry. We assign each rule of notice a different color and take one pass through part of the excerpt while color coding/highlighting each example of that rule. Then we move to another rule and another color, taking one pass with each rule. Sometimes we have students work in pairs; each pair highlights one rule and then jigsaws with another pair who highlighted a different rule. Other times, we assign more specific rules of each type, like allusions or figurative language, or other particular calls to attention that are salient in the mentor text. Often, a phrase might represent more than one rule of notice, so on the second pass, we have students underline the phrase in the new color.

When done, we often do a mop-up pass identifying any other specific rules of notice that come up. This process demonstrates how richly textured texts can be with codes of meaning. Students find it fun, and they get a visual of how codes repeat and relate.

For our civil rights unit, we often use Martin Luther King Jr.'s "I Have a Dream" speech with this technique. It is short, tightly structured, and richly coded, and both requires and rewards using various rules of notice.

- Note: Remind students that you are working with what is known as a "concentrated sample" (i.e., a very dense text that uses the rules of notice over and over again). Remind students that most texts, particularly extended ones, do not make such dense use of the rules. You can also remind students that even expert readers may catch only half of what authors might want them to notice. But you do have to notice some of the rules of notice to be an effective reader!
- Note: For an example of the "I Have a Dream" speech that has been color coded to reflect the rules of notice for key details, see Figure 3.7.

Lesson Steps

Step 1

Hand out rules of notice bookmarks and give directions:

- Ensure all students have a rules of notice bookmark and explain that they will now be using all these rules independently with a famous speech by Martin Luther King Jr., "I Have a Dream."

Step 2

Direct students to work in pairs and triads to activate background knowledge and prepare for success:

- Ask the students in each pair or triad to brainstorm all they know about Martin Luther King Jr. and the "I Have a Dream" speech.
- Allow them to use the Internet to access information as needed.
- Have students share what they know or found out with the larger group.
- Fill in gaps in background knowledge as needed.

Step 3

Explain the color-coding task:

- Tell students they will be using the rules of notice for key details while doing several passes of a reading of "I Have a Dream."
- Explain that they will use different-colored highlighters to mark the text for different rules of notice and to show how these codes of meaning are related and used throughout the text.

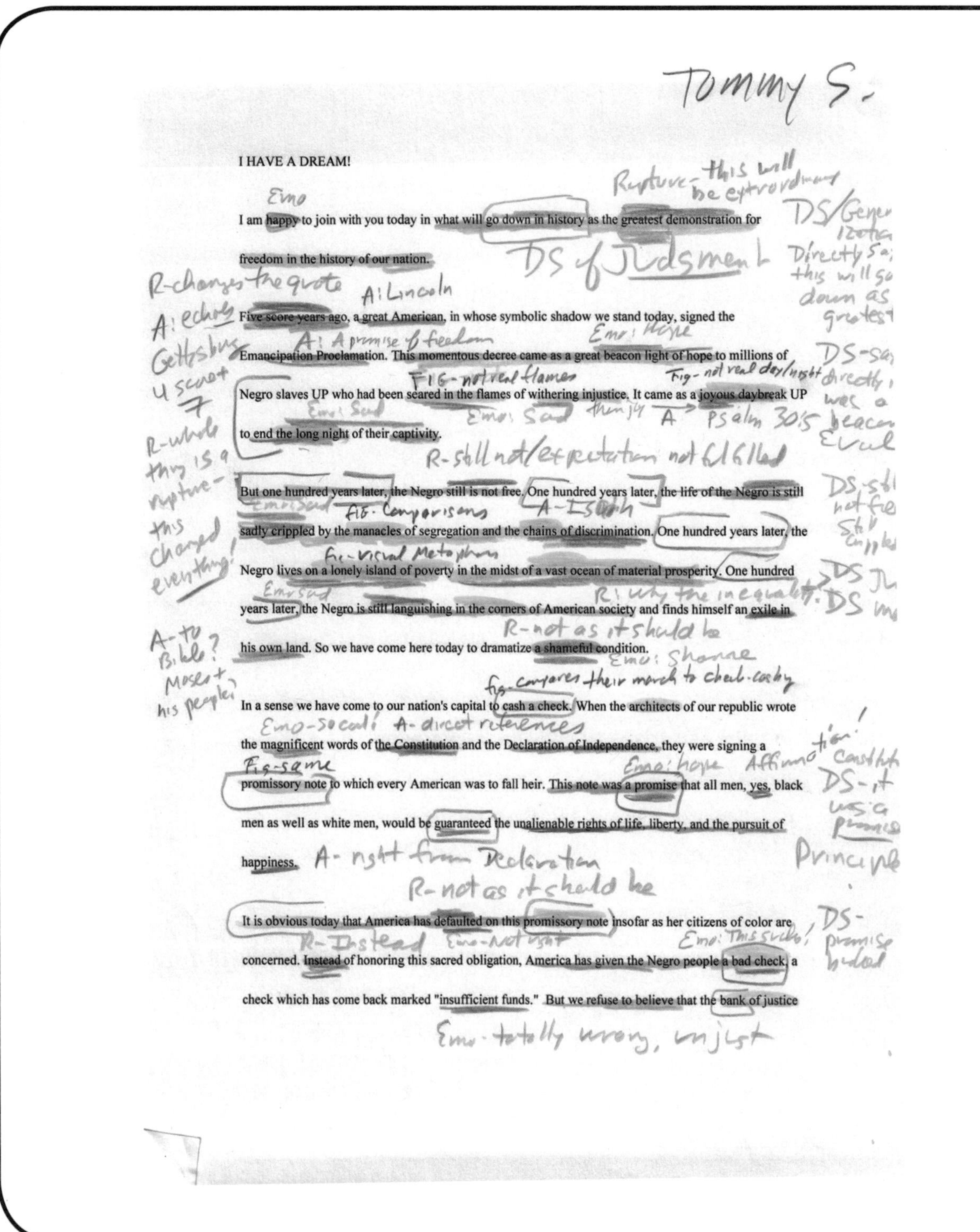

I HAVE A DREAM!

I am happy to join with you today in what will go down in history as the greatest demonstration for freedom in the history of our nation.

Five score years ago, a great American, in whose symbolic shadow we stand today, signed the Emancipation Proclamation. This momentous decree came as a great beacon light of hope to millions of Negro slaves UP who had been seared in the flames of withering injustice. It came as a joyous daybreak UP to end the long night of their captivity.

But one hundred years later, the Negro still is not free. One hundred years later, the life of the Negro is still sadly crippled by the manacles of segregation and the chains of discrimination. One hundred years later, the Negro lives on a lonely island of poverty in the midst of a vast ocean of material prosperity. One hundred years later, the Negro is still languishing in the corners of American society and finds himself an exile in his own land. So we have come here today to dramatize a shameful condition.

In a sense we have come to our nation's capital to cash a check. When the architects of our republic wrote the magnificent words of the Constitution and the Declaration of Independence, they were signing a promissory note to which every American was to fall heir. This note was a promise that all men, yes, black men as well as white men, would be guaranteed the unalienable rights of life, liberty, and the pursuit of happiness.

It is obvious today that America has defaulted on this promissory note insofar as her citizens of color are concerned. Instead of honoring this sacred obligation, America has given the Negro people a bad check, a check which has come back marked "insufficient funds." But we refuse to believe that the bank of justice

Figure 3.7

Example: Color-Coded Rules of Notice for Key Details

is bankrupt. We refuse to believe that there are insufficient funds in the great vaults of opportunity of this nation. So we have come to cash this check -- a check that will give us upon demand the riches of freedom and the security of justice. We have also come to this hallowed spot to remind America of the fierce urgency of now. This is no time to engage in the luxury of cooling off or to take the tranquilizing drug of gradualism. Now is the time to make real the promises of democracy. Now is the time to rise from the dark and desolate valley of segregation to the sunlit path of racial justice. Now is the time to lift our nation from the quick sands of racial injustice to the solid rock of brotherhood. Now is the time to make justice a reality for all of God's children.

It would be fatal for the nation to overlook the urgency of the moment. This sweltering summer of the Negro's legitimate discontent will not pass until there is an invigorating autumn of freedom and equality. Nineteen sixty-three is not an end, but a beginning. Those who hope that the Negro needed to blow off steam and will now be content will have a rude awakening if the nation returns to business as usual. There will be neither rest nor tranquility in America until the Negro is granted his citizenship rights. The whirlwinds of revolt will continue to shake the foundations of our nation until the bright day of justice emerges.

But there is something that I must say to my people who stand on the warm threshold which leads into the palace of justice. In the process of gaining our rightful place we must not be guilty of wrongful deeds. Let us not seek to satisfy our thirst for freedom by drinking from the cup of bitterness and hatred.

We must forever conduct our struggle on the high plane of dignity and discipline. We must not allow our creative protest to degenerate into physical violence. Again and again we must rise to the majestic heights of meeting physical force with soul force. The marvelous new militancy which has engulfed the

Step 4

First pass. Model the task using a green highlighter/colored pencil to mark direct statements, projecting your highlighting of the text onto a screen:

- For the first reading, tell students they will practice coding using a green highlighter to mark direct statements and generalizations. Model highlighting this example on the projected text:
  - "what will go down in history as the greatest demonstration for freedom in the history of our nation"
- Explain how this is a direct statement of generalization and how it works to foreground the importance of the speech.

Step 5

Have students use green highlighters/colored pencils to mark additional direct statements, then share, compare, and look for patterns:

- Invite students to work together to find other direct statements of generalization, principle, or value on the first page of the speech and highlight them in green.
- If students need more help or struggle, you can model one or two more direct statements for the whole class, or just for a smaller group that wants more assistance.
- When finished, do a class think-aloud to see what direct statements or generalizations were found and highlighted.
- As you go, work with students to unpack and explain why King used these direct statements and how they work to create meaning and effect.

Step 6

Second pass. Model the task using a blue highlighter to mark allusions, a particular kind of call to attention:

- Have students use a blue highlighter to mark any allusions in the text. Remind them that this is one kind of call to attention.
- Ask students if they understand what constitutes an allusion and if they can explain it to others.
- If they cannot, review the term until they are comfortable identifying and explaining an allusion.
- Model identifying an allusion by highlighting this example on the projected text:
  - "Five score years ago . . ."
- Explain this is both a rupture and an allusion to "Four score and seven years ago," the beginning of Abraham Lincoln's Gettysburg Address.

- Explain that invoking Gettysburg summons Lincoln's vision of emancipating all slaves through victory in the Civil War.

Step 7

Extending the pass, have students mark allusions with a blue highlighter, then share, compare, and look for patterns in the allusions:

- Have students work together in pairs or triads to identify more allusions on the first page and highlight them in blue.
- Again, if they struggle or want more help, you can provide more assistance to the whole class or a smaller group. For example, you might have students read some short excerpts from the Declaration of Independence or the Bible (e.g., Psalm 30:5, Matthew 5:44) or a song like "All God's Chillun Have Wings" and ask students to do a scavenger hunt, looking for echoes of these text excerpts on their own or in pairs, or as you read the speech together. Note, too, that many phrases or moves might involve more than one rule of notice, just as a figure of speech might make use of more than one literary move or device.

  You can also use this and other online sources if students need another level of assistance: www.bessettepitney.net/2013/08/references-and-allusions-in-i-have.html.
- When finished, do a class think-aloud to see what allusions were found and highlighted.
- Unpack and work together to explain why King used these allusions and how they work to create meaning and effect.

Step 8

Third pass. Model the task using a yellow highlighter to mark figurative language, a call to attention:

- Ask students if they understand figurative language and if they can explain it to others.
  - If they cannot, review this concept with them.
- Once they are comfortable identifying and explaining figurative language, have students use a yellow highlighter to mark any figurative language they find in the text.
- Remind students that figurative language is one kind of call to attention.
- Model identifying figurative language by highlighting in yellow these examples on the projected text:
  - "great beacon light of hope"
  - "seared in the flames of withering justice"

- Share how this language is figurative and how we can use it to visualize meaning in our minds.

Step 9

Extend the pass, having students mark additional examples of figurative language, share, compare, and look for patterns:

- Have students work together in pairs or triads to identify more figurative language on the first page and highlight these uses in yellow.
- When finished, do a whole-class think-aloud to see what figurative language was found and highlighted.
- Unpack and explain why King used figurative language and how it works to create meaning and effect.

Step 10

Use additional colors to highlight ruptures, emotive language, or other salient features in this text:

- As time allows, have the class continue to use this same method on the first page for the following. A jigsaw could be used in which small groups divide up the task and report back on particular techniques:
    - Orange highlighter for ruptures
    - Pink highlighter for emotive language ("withering justice")—call to attention/reader's response
    - For an extension, red highlighter/colored pencil for other literary devices like repetition (see Figure 3.7), parallelism, idioms, rhetorical questions, symbolism, or any other technique you want to reinforce in student reading and writing
- Pick another color if students notice other specific rules of notice.
- Discuss any phrases that are connected by multiple rules of notice. This will become apparent through the color coding.

Step 11

Have students work in pairs or independently:

- Invite students to work on the next two pages of the text in pairs or independently.

Step 12

Have students share completed color-coded texts, discussing patterns noticed:

- Ask students to share final highlights in pairs or triads.

- Together as a class, have them reflect on how the author of the speech used rules of notice to create meaning and effect. What did they learn about using rules of notice to unveil the complexity of a text and how it works for meaning and effect?

Step 13

Model the use of, then invite students to use, circles and arrows to delineate repetitions and connections:

- With your highlighted text visible on the projector, show your students how to use circles and arrows to delineate repetitions and connections.
- Explain the nature of the different connections and how the details work together.
- In their groups, have students circle and use arrows to note additional repetitions or connections on their copies of the text.

Step 14

Have students share the results of their complete annotations:

- Note direct statements:
    - ". . . if America is to be a great nation this must become true."
- Note allusions
    - To the Bible, particularly Isaiah
    - To patriotic songs like "My Country, 'Tis of Thee"
    - To the spiritual "Free at Last" (www.negrospirituals.com/songs/free_at_last_from.htm)
    - If you wish, have students look these up.
- Lead a whole-class discussion on the effect of King's techniques. Ask: *Which moves worked most powerfully for you? How? What makes you say so?*

Extensions

- Show students a video of the speech and ask them to note reader's rules of notice through audience reactions to the speech. Also have them note how the delivery provides rules of notice, as when King pauses, uses voice inflection for emphasis as a call to attention, and so on.
- Have students mark a fresh copy of the text with a highlighter whenever the audience reacts to King's speech.

Chapter 4

Noticing Varied Nonfiction Genres

Jeff recently returned from rafting with friends through the Desolation Gray Canyons of the Green River in Utah, one of the wildest and most untouched stretches of whitewater in the lower forty-eight states. A thousand years ago, give or take, the Fremont Indians lived in these canyons and left impressive numbers of elaborate petroglyphs (pictures carved into stone) engraved in the canyon rocks.

Early in their trip, Jeff's group hiked into a side canyon to view some of the glyphs. Group members pointed out a few details on one of them—a squiggly line running through the other images and branching off in several directions; mountain sheep and goats; deer; what looked like dwellings. They began speculating about the purpose and topic of the petroglyph and concluded that it fit the genre of a *map*—more precisely a hunting map. Getting a sense of the genre was the turning point in the conversation, leading them to consider how this particular text was structured. They interpreted the squiggly lines as the river and side creeks and the humps as mountain peaks. Someone pulled out a map to test this theory, and it was accurate. Then the conversation really took off, people excitedly interpreting or reinterpreting other images in this light. Knowing the topic and understanding the genre, they were able to identify details and decide which were most important.

Two days later, the group visited Flat Canyon and hiked to the petroglyphs there. They first noticed that the same giant figure, seemingly dressed in ceremonial clothing, appeared three times across the rock face, each time accompanied by what appeared to be a female figure wearing a headdress. Smaller figures engaged in various activities encircled them in each iteration. Hovering above each group of figures was a disc they thought might represent the sun; it was lower in each glyph moving left to right across the rock. They decided the pattern most likely represented a narrative chronology moving from summer to winter as the sun appeared lower in the sky. Again, noticing the genre was the breakthrough. The group then interpreted the glyphs as depicting ritual ceremonies throughout the year, the embedded structure being their sequence within the natural calendar. This helped them interpret a small figure above the celebrants as a shaman directing the rituals.

In both instances, the group noticed a few details, inferred a genre that helped them see those details in a new light, noticed additional details, and then inferred patterns that helped them see the relationships among details. This process allowed them to understand how the whole was structured for meaning and effect. Noticing and interpreting topics, details, genres, and structures didn't happen linearly; each kind of noticing worked reciprocally to reinforce the other kinds. The group approached the petroglyphs like expert readers approach a complex text.

What's true for the petroglyphs and other visual or multimodal texts is also true for written ones. Imagine finding a piece of paper with writing on it. Reading it, the first thing you ask yourself is, "What kind of text is this?" Your answer determines what you do with the piece of paper. If it's, "Oh, it's just an advertisement," you probably toss it into a recycling bin. If it's, "It seems to be part of a research paper," perhaps you think of a student in the neighborhood who might have written the paper and let him or her know you've found a page. If it's the signature page of a contract, you might post a notice on the neighborhood listserv. What we do with a text depends in large measure on how we categorize it. As Peter Rabinowitz (Rabinowitz & Smith, 1998) explains, one of the first things we do when we read is determine what it is we're reading. Making that determination helps us know what to expect and the kind of strategies we'll need to employ.

Research supports the notion that determining genre dictates what readers do when they read. Duke and Roberts (2010) point out a variety of think-aloud studies demonstrating that we read different kinds of texts in different ways. If you're reading a recipe for the first time, you might attend carefully to the ingredients to see whether the dish is something you'd like to eat before zeroing in on the amount of each ingredient. If you're using a medicine for the first time, you might attend very carefully to the amount you're supposed to take, perhaps ignoring the list of ingredients completely.

Recognizing Essential Features of Various Nonfiction Genres

The lessons in this chapter help students recognize the essential features of various nonfiction genres and use this information to aid their comprehension. We think that recognizing genres and how the recognition of genre informs reading is threshold knowledge into the world of expert readers.

Our approach is substantially different from the way genre is typically taught. Too often in school and in textbooks, we use the umbrella classification *nonfiction* or informational text. This is problematic on two levels.

First, nonfiction is far too broad a classification to help you know what to notice and how to interpret what you notice. It doesn't indicate anything about how the text is structured and works, and therefore how it is to be approached.

Second, students have many misconceptions about nonfiction. When Jeff asks his ninth graders the difference between fiction and nonfiction, they enthusiastically call out variations of "Fiction is false, and nonfiction is true!" When Jeff incredulously denounced this misconception at a family dinner one night, his adult daughter Jasmine, a passionate reader, said, "Whoa, Dad, that's what they taught us in school!" However, most nonfiction, like fiction, is written from a particular perspective by someone trying to manipulate you (for good or ill) into believing, knowing, or doing something. We certainly don't want our students to read ads, editorials, opinion pieces, profiles, and the like believing that it's all true because it can be called nonfiction.

The problem with the multiplicity of nonfiction genres is figuring out how we can teach them all. Genres can easily become the foundation of the curriculum. Primary schools in South Australia, for example, teach eight nonfiction genres: recount, narrative, procedure, information report, explanation, argument, discussion, and review. Secondary schools add five more. We take a different tack. Rather than investigate the details of a wide variety of genres, we help students understand what a genre is and how recognizing the genre of a text helps a reader understand it.

Rules of Notice in the Content Areas

Video 4.1

http://resources.corwin.com/divingdeep-nonfiction

Noticing Different Genres

Video 4.2

http://resources.corwin.com/divingdeep-nonfiction

Lesson 1

Noticing Varied Nonfiction Genres
READING VISUAL TEXTS

Introduction

Threshold knowledge is foundational concepts and strategies that allow people to learn other concepts and processes. Meyer and Land (2003) put it this way:

> A threshold concept can be considered as akin to a portal, opening up a new and previously inaccessible way of thinking about something. It represents a transformed way of understanding, or interpreting, or viewing something without which the learner cannot progress. (p. 1)

The threshold knowledge that we focus on in this chapter is that texts are patterned, that these patterns are called genres, and that noticing and using these patterns aids comprehension, and helps us to navigate, interpret, and make meaning as we read.

Most students already have a tacit understanding of genre. They know, for example, that role-playing video games work differently than simulations or sports games do. They know that alternative rock sounds different and explores different topics in different ways than does heavy metal. But they don't apply this understanding to their reading. These lessons help them do so.

PURPOSE

- To learn to notice the features of particular genres and to understand why that noticing is important for understanding and producing texts

LENGTH

- Approximately 90 minutes (can be split into two 45-minute classes)

MATERIALS NEEDED

- Internet access, a computer, and a projection device
- A class set of Handout 4.1, "Thinking About Photographic Portrait Genres"
- Paper to make an anchor chart
- A cell phone or other device equipped with a camera (for one student in each small group)

Lesson Steps

Step 1

Introduce the lesson and its purpose:

- Explain that groups of texts that work in similar ways can be called *genres*, and knowing this helps you to read and understand these texts.
- Tell students that this set of lessons focuses on thinking about how to group texts into genres and why that grouping matters.

- Explain that before we work with written texts, we'll be thinking about genre using visual texts.

Step 2

Lead a whole-class discussion using portraits to get started with the notion of genre:

- Ask:
  - *How many of you have taken a selfie?*
  - *How do selfies differ from other kinds of photographic portraits, like school photos?*

Step 3

Note that there are different kinds of photographic portraits:

- Explain to students that school yearbook photos are just one kind of *photographic portrait*—a photo that shows the likeness of a person in order to archive that person's image for classmates.
- Explain that there are other types of photographic portraits. Tell students that, in fact, LearnMyShot.com (http://learnmyshot.com/9-fundamental-styles-of-portrait-photography) identifies eight distinct kinds of photographic portraits.

Step 4

Provide practice using classification to understand genre:

- Divide students into groups of four or five.
  - Say: *I'm going to project examples of several kinds of portraits. With the other members of your group, identify the essential features of each kind—what makes one similar to others like it, and what makes one different from others?*
  - Distribute a copy of Handout 4.1, "Thinking About Photographic Portrait Genres," to each group.

Step 5

Differentiate groups or classes of portraits:

- Project examples of each genre of portrait. (Note that we got the following list from LearnMyShot.com. However, we realize that websites change quickly. If the LearnMyShot.com website is no longer live, simply Google each kind of portrait—e.g., "environmental portrait photography"—and you'll get multiple examples.)
  1. Traditional
  2. Environmental

3. Candid
4. Glamour
5. Lifestyle
6. Surreal
7. Conceptual
8. Abstract

- Tell students that for the purposes of this activity you are going to use these categories. In the future, they will engage in activities where they come up with categories of their own.
- Give student groups a few minutes to discuss each set of examples and complete the handout. Circulate among the groups, pushing them to differentiate each type of photo from the others, to define and explain each category.

Step 6

Lead a whole-class discussion to share discoveries and hypotheses about genre criteria:

- Discuss what students discovered. Answers will vary, but students should recognize that while the groups of photos are all similar, they have specific differences as well. See the sample exchange in the "Voices From the Classroom" box that follows.
- Record their thoughts about the different genres of portraits on an anchor chart. For a sample anchor chart, see Figure 4.1.
- Explain that the groups of photos with similar characteristics can be thought of as *genres*.

Step 7

Group students to create a portrait that fits a particular genre's characteristics:

- Explain that recognizing a genre, its characteristics, what it does, and how it creates meaning and effect helps us understand not only that genre but others that work differently.
- Ask each group to work together to create a portrait in any of the above genres except the traditional/posed portrait (with which they are already familiar). Remind them to use the anchor chart to incorporate the characteristics of their selected genre in their photos.

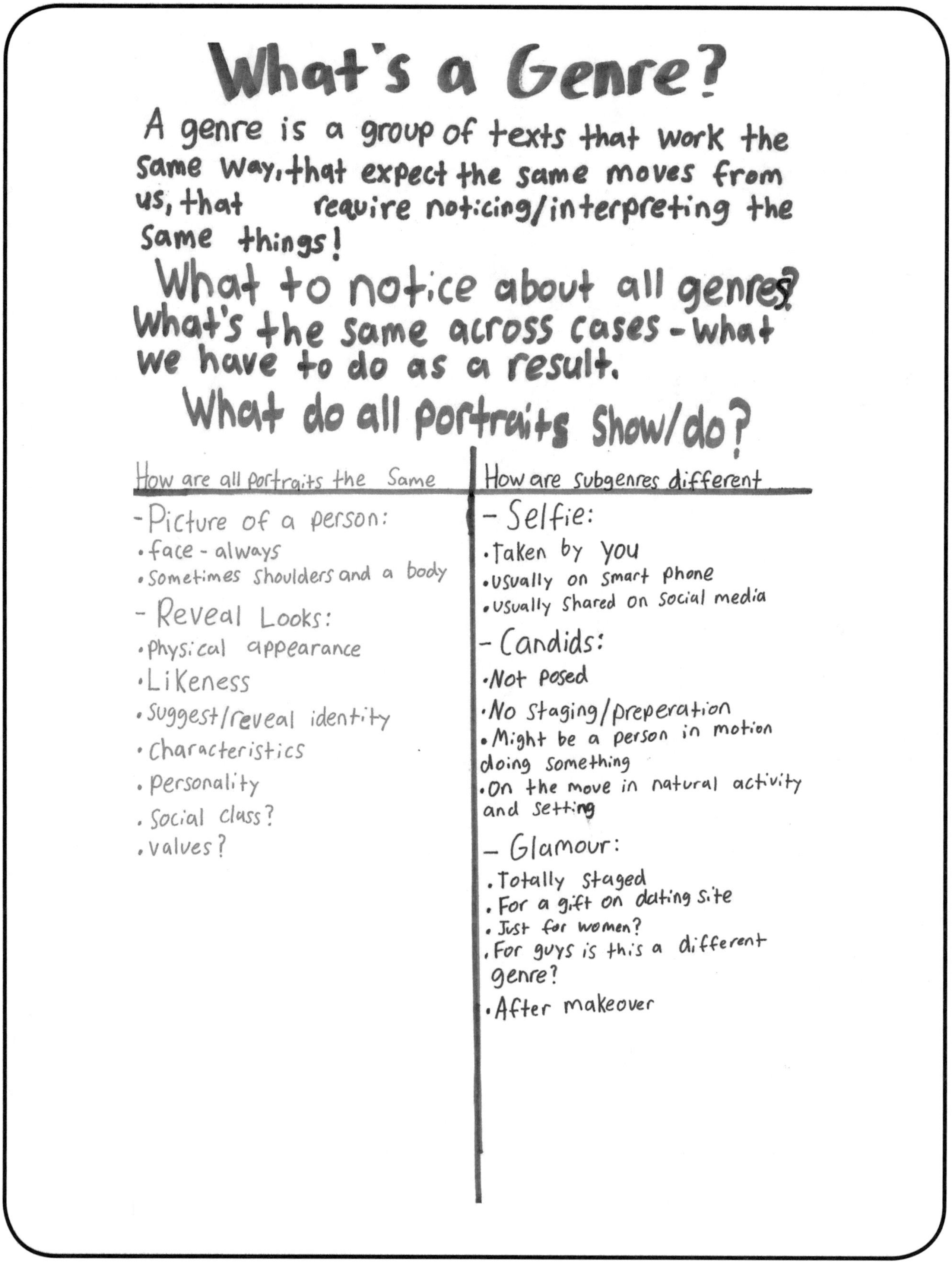

What's a Genre?

A genre is a group of texts that work the same way, that expect the same moves from us, that require noticing/interpreting the same things!

What to notice about all genres?

What's the same across cases - what we have to do as a result.

What do all portraits show/do?

How are all portraits the Same

- Picture of a person:
  - face - always
  - Sometimes shoulders and a body
- Reveal Looks:
  - physical appearance
  - Likeness
  - Suggest/reveal identity
  - characteristics
  - personality
  - Social class?
  - values?

How are subgenres different

- Selfie:
  - Taken by you
  - usually on smart phone
  - usually shared on social media
- Candids:
  - Not posed
  - No staging/preperation
  - Might be a person in motion doing something
  - On the move in natural activity and setting
- Glamour:
  - Totally staged
  - For a gift on dating site
  - Just for women?
  - For guys is this a different genre?
  - After makeover

Figure 4.1

Anchor Chart: Noticing Varied Nonfiction Genres

Voices From the Classroom

WHAT STUDENTS SAID ABOUT
Conceptual Portraits

TEACHER: Let's talk about conceptual portraits. What did you find out? How are they similar to and different from the other kinds of portraits we've discussed?

STUDENT: Well, obviously they're similar because they're a picture of someone.

STUDENT: But they're mostly different.

TEACHER: In what ways?

STUDENT: Well, it seems to me that in traditional photos, for example, the person whose picture is being taken is kind of in charge. Like school photos. I wear what I want to wear to create the look that I want people to see.

TEACHER: And in conceptual photos?

STUDENT: The photographer's in charge. It's the photographer's ideas that are important, not the person's.

TEACHER: Anybody else? Let's think some more about this.

Step 8

Conclude the lesson by sharing students' portraits, defining and justifying their genre:

- Have groups share their photos and tell the class
  - Why they chose the portrait genre they did
  - Using the anchor chart, how their photo displays that genre's essential characteristics
  - How their genre works in a unique and different way from the other portrait genres
- Explain to students that they'll be considering how understanding genre aids comprehension in the next several lessons.

Extension

Have students work individually to create additional portraits of different genres and to write a commentary on each.

Handout 4.1

Thinking About Photographic Portrait Genres

After looking at the images, answer the following questions as a group:

What are the essential features of this kind of photograph?

How is this type of portrait similar to and different from other photographic portraits?

Who would take such a photo? Under what circumstances? For what purpose?

Available for download at **http://resources.corwin.com/divingdeep-nonfiction**

Lesson 2

Noticing Varied Nonfiction Genres
THINKING ALOUD

Introduction

This lesson uses an abstract a middle school student wrote about a science project. Why use an abstract? We think there are a number of good answers to this question:

1. Many state standards emphasize having students read complex texts. Long, hard texts are death in the classroom; short, hard texts are manageable, and they are immediately useful especially if they relate to the inquiry the class is pursuing.
2. If we want to prepare students for college, we need to acquaint them with the kind of disciplinary research they will be expected to read. An abstract is a low-cost way (in terms of classroom time and student effort) to do so.
3. If students understand how abstracts work, they'll read them as they conduct research, not skip over them.
4. Using abstracts focuses students' attention on summary and why it's important. Summarizing is one of the most neglected skills in school because of the mistaken belief that it's easy; it isn't. We struggle with it ourselves.

Why use an abstract from a middle schooler? In our experience, students seldom read research reports, so they aren't familiar with the genre of an abstract. Abstracts from published research articles are difficult, so we like to start with an easier one, written by one of their peers. With that preparation, they will be better able to tackle an abstract related to the inquiry the class is pursuing, if need be.

PURPOSE

- To get more practice both recognizing the features of a genre (in this case, the abstract) and using them to guide understanding

LENGTH

- Approximately 30 minutes

MATERIALS NEEDED

- A class set of Handout 4.2, "Sample Abstract: 'Which AA Battery Maintains Its Voltage for the Longest Period of Time?'" (or one of your own choosing)
- A class set of an additional abstract
- Different-colored pencils or highlighters
- Paper to create an anchor chart

Lesson Steps

Step 1

Introduce the lesson with the definition of a research report and a whole-class discussion around how students have conducted research in the past:

- Ask:
  - *How many of you have conducted research on the Internet before?*
  - *What process do you use to find what is going to be useful to you?*
  - *How do you figure out that it will be worth the time and effort to read an article, especially a really long one?*
- Introduce the *research abstract* as a genre. Explain that it is a summary of a larger report that briefly introduces the author's objective, the method he or she employed, and the major findings.
- Ask: *Before we even start reading, based on this definition, what do you think we should look for in this kind of text?* As the students answer, begin an anchor chart of rules of notice for abstracts.

Step 2

Introduce a think-aloud of genre features, modeling how to do so:

- Say:
  - *I am going to read through this abstract with you and think aloud about what I am noticing. As I read, I will name the rules of notice that tipped me off about what to look for. Use your highlighters to mark the different rules of notice I identify:*

    Direct statements — *Calls to attention*
    Ruptures — *Reader's response*

Step 3

Model noticing genre features:

- Hand out copies of Handout 4.2, "Sample Abstract: 'Which AA Battery Maintains Its Voltage for the Longest Period of Time?'" so that students can follow along.
- Model your thinking (see the sample think-aloud that follows).

Step 4

Update the anchor chart to reflect and articulate what is being learned:

- Add to the class anchor chart for abstracts on the basis of your thinking aloud. Ask students: *What were some things you noticed?* Look for them to note that abstracts explain the problem or issue, how the problem was studied, and what the main findings were. They should also note that direct statements are especially common in abstracts.
- Ask students what they annotated as you read: *Are there other things you noticed that we should add to the chart?*

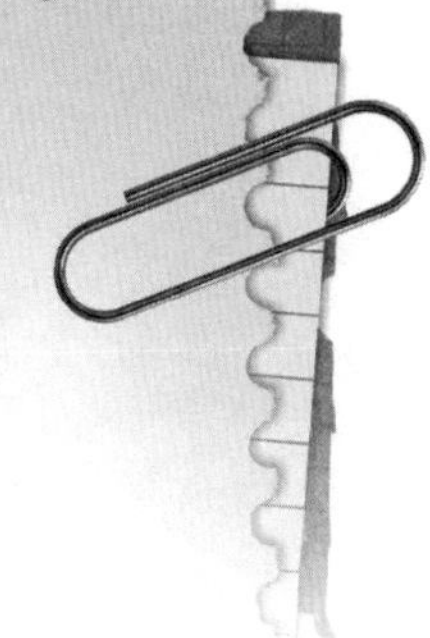

SAMPLE THINK-ALOUD

Lesson 2. Noticing Varied Nonfiction Genres: Thinking Aloud

Sample Abstract: "Which AA Battery Maintains Its Voltage for the Longest Period of Time?"

By Student Author

OK, titles are a call to attention. And questions are too. So I know I have to pay special attention to this. The question tells me that the study is about what batteries last the longest.

Advertisers are always touting more powerful and longer lasting batteries, but which batteries really do last longer, and is battery life impacted by the speed of the current drain?

The sentence is kind of a rupture. The author is saying that advertisers always brag about their batteries, but this sentence suggests that they don't really know.

Pause and make sure students underline and label this rupture. Do the same with other rules of notice as you go.

This project looks at which AA battery maintains its voltage for the longest period of time in low, medium, and high current drain devices.

OK, lists are a call to attention. So the author thinks that the different conditions must be important. Also, I know that abstracts are supposed to explain the method of a study, so the method must have been to do three tests.

The batteries were tested in a CD player (low drain device), a flashlight (medium drain device), and a camera flash (high drain device) by measuring the battery voltage (dependent variable) at different time intervals (independent variable) for each of the battery types in each of the devices.

Technical terms are another call to attention. I know this was written by a kid who probably doesn't use language like "dependent variable" very much. So I guess it's kind of a rupture too.

My hypothesis

Another technical term.

was that Energizer

This is the kind of battery I use. So this is the rule of the reader's response for me.

would last the longest in all of the devices tested. The experimental results supported my hypothesis by showing that the Energizer

(Continued)

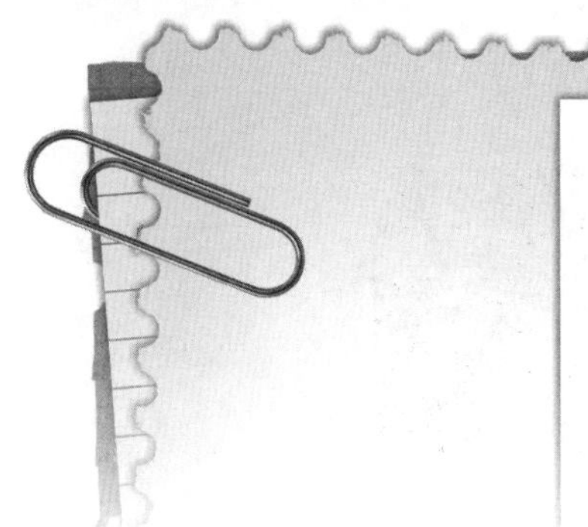

SAMPLE THINK-ALOUD
(CONT.)

performs with increasing superiority, the higher the current drain of the device.

> *Abstracts are summaries of the research. So this one sentence is the main finding. It's a direct statement, and I know I better pay attention to those.*

The experiment also showed that the heavy-duty non-alkaline batteries do not maintain their voltage as long as either alkaline battery at any level of current drain.

> *That's a rupture, because you'd think "heavy-duty" would mean "longest lasting." But wait a minute. The author just named Energizer. What's the other one? This is kind of a rupture too. I need to find out what the other one was.*

Source: Science Buddies. (2016). *Sample abstract.* Retrieved from http://www.sciencebuddies.org/science-fair-projects/project_sample_abstract.shtml

Step 5

Do a second read-aloud, slowly, this time with students contributing what they notice (see the companion website at **http://resources.corwin.com/divingdeep-nonfiction** for a model think-aloud using published research):

- Pass out a new abstract that you've selected.
- Tell students you are going to begin a read-aloud on this second abstract.
- As you read, encourage students to raise their hands if they spot a rule of notice! When they notice one, have them underline the related text and record the name of the rule.
- Read aloud through half of a different abstract you select. You can find one to use by Googling "middle school abstracts" or "high school abstracts" or by selecting an abstract from a study relevant to the inquiry the class is pursuing. As you read, stop to prompt students to say what they notice and to name what the author is doing. Remind them to pay attention to the items on the anchor chart.
- Update the anchor chart for research abstracts with what the class noticed. Ask: *How can abstracts help when you are researching a topic?*

Step 6

Provide independent practice:

- Have students finish the think-aloud in pairs, with one student reading a sentence and the other thinking aloud about the sentence. Have them alternate roles. Remind them to pay special attention to features of the abstract as a genre.
- Remind students to apply the strategies whenever they read.

Extensions

- Challenge students to write abstracts for texts they read on their own, their own compositions, or the compositions of peers.
- Have students jigsaw-read various texts and then compose abstracts to share what they learned with the rest of the class.
- Group students to compose abstracts using Google Docs and share them with the class.
- Visit the companion website at **http://resources.corwin.com/divingdeep-nonfiction** for a more complex supplementary think-aloud using an abstract from a published research report.

Handout 4.2

Sample Abstract: "Which AA Battery Maintains Its Voltage for the Longest Period of Time?"

By Student Author

Advertisers are always touting more powerful and longer lasting batteries, but which batteries really do last longer, and is battery life impacted by the speed of the current drain? This project looks at which AA battery maintains its voltage for the longest period of time in low, medium, and high current drain devices. The batteries were tested in a CD player (low drain device), a flashlight (medium drain device), and a camera flash (high drain device) by measuring the battery voltage (dependent variable) at different time intervals (independent variable) for each of the battery types in each of the devices. My hypothesis was that Energizer would last the longest in all of the devices tested. The experimental results supported my hypothesis by showing that the Energizer performs with increasing superiority, the higher the current drain of the device. The experiment also showed that the heavy-duty non-alkaline batteries do not maintain their voltage as long as either alkaline battery at any level of current drain.

Source: Science Buddies. (2016). *Sample abstract.* Retrieved from http://www.sciencebuddies.org/science-fair-projects/project_sample_abstract.shtml

Available for download at **http://resources.corwin.com/divingdeep-nonfiction**

Lesson
3

Noticing Varied Nonfiction Genres
PRACTICE IN MINIATURE

Introduction

If learners are to transfer what they've learned to new situations, they must have a deep understanding of what they are transferring and plenty of practice doing so. In this lesson, students extend the work they did categorizing photographic portraits into various subgenres (Lesson 1) and discovering how the essential features of a genre help a reader. To do so, they identify different categories of comics and think about how readers ought to engage with these categories of comics in different ways.

PURPOSE

- To learn how to categorize texts into genres and to notice how different genres require different things of readers

LENGTH

- Approximately 45 minutes

MATERIALS NEEDED

- Copies of the comics section of the nearest large city's daily newspaper for each small group
- If these are not easily available, adjust the lesson to project comic strips from a computer with a projection device or have students call them up on their individual computers

Lesson Steps

Step 1

Introduce the lesson and set the stage for classifying comics into genres:

- Explain the purpose of the lesson.
- Remind students that in a previous lesson they placed visual texts into genres someone else had identified and learned how the essential features of a genre help a reader.
- Say:
    - *In this lesson, you'll identify your own genre categories and think about how recognizing them helps you as a reader.*
    - *Comics have been a regular feature in newspapers since 1897, and over the years, different kinds of comics have come along. Sort these examples of comics from our local newspaper into at least three genres. For each genre,*

      Name the genre of comic
      Determine the essential features of this kind of comic
      Explain how this genre of comics is similar to and different from other genres of comics
      Explain how the differences affect how readers read these kinds of comics

- Note that the fourth bullet is the most complex, so be prepared with an illustration like the following:
    - *For example, in the environmental portraits we examined earlier, the viewer needs to pay attention to the surroundings almost as much as the figure. In conceptual portraits, the viewer needs to think about the idea the photographer is trying to communicate rather than what can be learned about the person in the photo. In the comics, what is the creator of a particular genre asking the reader to focus on, notice, and do?*

Step 2

Provide independent practice and direct students to classify comics into genres:

- Divide the class into groups of three or four.
- Give each group at least one comics section.
- As groups are working, circulate, probing them to think especially about how the differences affect how readers read these kinds of comics. Ask questions like these:
    - *Are we supposed to read each strip separately or over a series of days?*
    - *How does the creator want us to feel about the characters in the strip?*

Step 3

Lead a whole-class discussion and prompt students to think about genre expectations:

- Have groups report on what they discovered. Expect that the groups will come up with different genre groupings and labels. The important thing is that they have thought about the distinctions among the various genres and what they mean for readers. See the sample exchange in the "Voices From the Classroom" section that follows.
- Create an anchor chart. If groups come up with similar genres, group them together. How did the distinctive features they noticed compare?
- Remind students that they should be alert to the essential features of each particular genre they identify as they read.

Extension

Have students write instructions to prospective comic strip creators about what they must do to write a particular genre of comic.

WHAT STUDENTS SAID ABOUT
Comic Strip Genres

TEACHER: So who wants to share?

STUDENT: One type of comic we called "lifestyle comics." They're the ones that make jokes by showing or exaggerating what life is really like. Our favorite is *Zits*.

STUDENT: Yeah, we had the same thing. But we also had one we called "weird sarcasm." Like *WuMo*.

TEACHER: What are the features of that kind of strip?

STUDENT: They're bizarre. Like it's a joke or something.

TEACHER: So do you read them the same way as you do lifestyle comics?

STUDENT: No! In lifestyle ones, I think you're supposed to see connections to your life. Not in the weird sarcasm ones. Those you kind of have to figure out.

STUDENT: We had animal strips as one.

STUDENT: We started with that but then changed. Like *Mutts* is so different from *Sherman's Lagoon* and even more different from *Pearls Before Swine*.

TEACHER: So are animal strips sufficiently similar that seeing them as a genre helps us know how to read them?

Lesson 4

Noticing Varied Nonfiction Genres

QUESTIONING

PURPOSE

- To understand and be able to use the KEEP questions independently

LENGTH

- Approximately 90 minutes, over two days

MATERIALS NEEDED

- Class sets of three handouts:
    - Handout 4.3, "Letters to the Editor"
    - Handout 4.4, "Letters of Recommendation"
    - Handout 4.5, "Using Genre Knowledge to Evaluate a Text"
- Large paper for an anchor chart

Introduction

Teaching students a set of questions that prompt them to attend carefully to any kind of text is one way to help them recognize the importance of determining what they are reading. This lesson introduces a set of four questions that students can remember through the acronym KEEP:

- What **kind** of text is this?
- What are the **essential** features of this kind of text?
- How did the author **employ** these features?
- What was the author's **purpose** in employing this genre and the features of this genre in that way? What meaning and effect did the author want to achieve through her choice of genre and use of genre features?

We use letters to the editor and letters of recommendation in this two-day lesson because students are likely familiar with these texts. The most valuable resource we have as teachers is what our students already know. We need to move from the known to the new whenever possible.

Lesson Steps: Day 1

Step 1

Introduce the purpose of the lesson and the KEEP questions:

- Say:
    - *Recognizing how different kinds of texts work in different ways helps us anticipate and understand what we'll be reading.*
    - *We're going to practice this kind of thinking by examining the three texts on the handout I'm about to distribute and answering four questions:*

*What **kind** of text is this?*
*What are the **essential** features of this kind of text?*
*How did the author **employ** these features?*
*What was the author's **purpose** in employing them that way? What meaning and effect did the author want to achieve?*

Step 2

Provide independent practice and set up groups to work on the handout:

- Distribute Handout 4.3, "Letters to the Editor."
- Divide students into groups of four or five to work on it together.
- As groups are working, circulate and assess how they are doing.

Step 3

Lead a whole-class discussion to share and test ideas; create an anchor chart:

- Have groups report to the class. Students will quickly name the genre as letter to the editor. Help them develop a list of essential features, which might include
    - Salutation
    - Reference to the article being commented on
    - Identifying/authorizing who they are
    - Argument
    - Brevity
- Discuss how the writers employed these essential features in different ways (for example, how the nutritionist used his or her position differently than the veteran did).
- Encourage them to consider what meaning and effect the authors wanted to achieve.

Step 4

Set students up for the task:

- Say: *Tomorrow you'll apply the same set of questions to a related but different kind of text.*

Handout 4.3

Letters to the Editor

Please read the three texts below and then answer these four questions:

- What **kind** of text is this?
- What are the **essential** features of this kind of text? (Identify at least four.)
- How did the author **employ** these features?
- What was the author's **purpose** in employing them that way? What meaning and effect did the author want to achieve?

Your answers to the first and second questions will be the same for all three texts, but your answers to the third and fourth questions will vary.

Text 1

Dear Editor,

I am a WWII veteran. Your article about school lunches in America described people being upset by the "healthy changes," and I too think they have a right to be. We have a right to make choices for ourselves in this country. It's not for someone else to decide what we can or cannot eat. People should be free to decide the best portion size for them. I'm not against efforts to correct childhood obesity, but ultimately it should be the parent's decision, not the government's. When we start forcing small, unpalatable meals on kids, they're just going to bring extra food with them to school and ultimately increase childhood obesity. What kids are being served in schools now is garbage. If you want people to choose school lunch, then make it something people will choose!

Text 2

Dear Editor,

In your recent school lunch article I read that kids are still hungry after eating the new healthier school lunches. Several high school students are quoted in the article as saying the new food is not only unappetizing, but also served in too small portions. As someone with a school-age

(Continued)

child, I agree that making school lunches healthy is important, but it doesn't help when the food is inedible or there is not enough of it. Contrary to what schools may think, reducing portion size is not the miracle fix for childhood obesity. Let's not overlook the side effects of reducing portion sizes. The article reports teachers are complaining about students falling asleep and getting distracted in class. I hope the voices of experts and concerned parents like myself will result in permanent, sustainable changes to school lunches—healthy AND adequate; healthy AND tasty!

Text 3

To the Editor:

I have been a nutritionist for twenty-nine years. I can't believe the furor caused and letters to the editor generated by reporting on the new healthier school lunches! In an article published in the *Baltimore Sun* on September 8, 2014, I read this: "Traditionally, the USDA had used the National School Lunch Program as a dumping ground for surplus meat and dairy commodities. Children consumed animal fat and sugary drinks, to the point where one-third have become overweight or obese. These early dietary flaws became lifelong addictions, raising the risk of diabetes, heart disease, and stroke."

I am here to tell you that the new healthy school lunch initiative is a good one! Parents should work with school cafeteria managers to encourage consumption of healthy foods. Initiatives could include student recipe or poster contests, a student garden, and "Meatless Mondays." This will be better for learning in the short term and better for health in the long term.

Lesson Steps: Day 2

Step 1

Make a connection to the previous day's work:

- Say:
  - *Yesterday you learned four questions to help you focus on determining the kind of texts you are reading:*

    *What **kind** of text is this?*

    *What are the **essential** features of this kind of text?*

    *How did the author **employ** these features?*

    *What was the author's **purpose** in employing them that way? What meaning and effect did the author want to achieve?*
  - *You used these questions to help you understand and evaluate three letters to the editor.*
  - *Today you'll apply them to the letters on a new handout.*

Step 2

Provide independent practice asking the KEEP questions:

- Distribute Handout 4.4, "Letters of Recommendation."
- Divide students into groups and have them read the letters and answer the four KEEP questions.

Step 3

Lead a whole-class discussion consolidating what's been learned:

- Ask groups to report on what they discovered, focusing especially on the second question. Students' answers may include
  - A description of the relationship between the recommender and the applicant
  - A description of the record of the applicant
  - Some evaluation or comparison of traits and accomplishments of the applicant
  - A statement of the recommender's credentials

Step 4

Provide additional practice noticing genre features for letters of recommendation:

- Distribute Handout 4.5, "Using Genre Knowledge to Evaluate a Text," and read the letter aloud.
- Discuss as a class. Ask:
  - *On the basis of your analysis of the essential features of this kind of letter, what do you make of the letter?*
  - *Do you think it fits the genre requirements?*

- *Pretend you were considering hiring Dr. Gray. Would you consider the letter? Why or why not? If so, how would this letter affect your decision?*

- Ask students whether they think the letter is sexist; have them explain how their analysis of the essential features of this kind of text influenced their opinion.

Step 5

Consolidate learning and look forward:

- Remind the class how important it is to think hard about the kind of text we're reading at any given time because it helps us anticipate what's to come and to evaluate how the writers use the essential features of the text to achieve their purposes.
- Remind students that another word for a group of texts that have similar features and expect similar kinds of noticing from the reader is *genre*.
- Tell students that the KEEP strategy is a tool to help them understand any genre they read and that will guide them as they write that kind of genre.

Extension

Have students apply the KEEP questions to another class of letters—for example, letters of application or "Dear John" letters. Or have students examine collections of letters (you can find them online or in books) and sort them into genres before applying the KEEP questions.

Handout 4.4

Letters of Recommendation

Please read the two texts on this handout and answer these four questions:

- What **kind** of text is this?
- What are the **essential** features of this kind of text? (Identify at least three.)
- How did the author **employ** these features?
- What was the author's **purpose** in employing them that way? What meaning and effect did the author want to achieve?

Your answers to the first and second questions will be the same for both texts, but your answers to the third and fourth questions will vary.

Text 1

Dear Dr. Koop:

I am writing to support Dr. Harvey's appointment as Clinical Assistant Professor of Medicine. Dr. Harvey did his fellowship here and I got to know him well. I consider him highly intelligent, highly motivated, and highly productive (he wrote an extraordinary number of papers for a fellow). He has a thorough knowledge of medicine. He is excellent with patients and is exceptionally pleasant without a shred of egotism, and was highly admired, liked, and respected by his colleagues. I recommend him highly.

Sincerely,
Dr. Charles Lewis, MD
Director, Cancer Center

(Continued)

Text 2

Dear Dr. Koop:

I am pleased to recommend Dr. Sarah Gray for faculty appointment as Clinical Assistant Professor. I have known Dr. Gray for eight years. She worked in research with me for one year and was a fellow in our training program for two years. She is a very good internist and endocrinologist. She is honest and reliable and of highest moral quality. She has good judgment in patient care and is very thoughtful and considerate toward those she is caring for. She is a good clinical teacher and should serve the department well in the capacity of instructing students and residents.

Sincerely,
Dr. Charles Lewis, MD
Director, Cancer Center

Source: Adapted from F. Trix and C. Psenka, "Exploring the Color of Glass: Letters of Recommendation for Female and Male Medical Faculty," *Discourse & Society*, 2003, 191–220.

Available for download at **http://resources.corwin.com/divingdeep-nonfiction**

Handout 4.5

Using Genre Knowledge to Evaluate a Text

On the basis of your analysis of the essential features of a letter of recommendation, what do you make of the one below? Pretend you are considering hiring Dr. Gray. How would this letter affect your decision?

Dear Alfred:

It is a pleasure to write a letter in support of Sarah Gray, MD, one of our urologists who is leaving St. Louis and would join your program. I have known Sarah for approximately four years, becoming socially friendly with her and her husband, particularly over the past year and a half. Sarah is quite close to my wife, and they frequently seek out each other's company. Sarah is a very committed physician who has very good clinical skills, ambition, and a desire to participate actively in the care of children with urologic problems. I get a sense that she is looking to develop a clinical program now that she has chosen to leave the laboratory and concentrate exclusively on clinical medicine.

Although I can't comment specifically on Dr. Gray's clinical skills, I have been impressed with her care of patients with whom we are mutually involved. I believe she is a concerned and interested clinician who offers excellent care and tries hard to communicate with the patients and with the physicians. She is more academic than most clinical physicians and this should be a resource as she becomes involved in her own programs. Although we will miss Sarah, we are sure she will be a great asset to your program and, therefore, we wish her well.

If there are further questions which I can answer regarding Dr. Gray please do not hesitate to call.

Yours sincerely,
Charles Lewis, MD, Professor of Pediatrics
Chief, Division of Urology

Source: Adapted from F. Trix and C. Psenka, "Exploring the Color of Glass: Letters of Recommendation for Female and Male Medical Faculty," *Discourse & Society*, 2003, 191–220.

Lesson 5

Noticing Varied Nonfiction Genres
WRITING AND RESPONDING

Introduction

Time is a zero-sum game: Any minute we spend in class doing one thing is a minute we can't spend doing something else. Therefore, many teachers may see reading and writing as being in competition. One way to address this is to use writing instruction in service of reading instruction (and vice versa). This lesson accomplishes this reciprocity through the use of procedural feedback.

PURPOSE

- To learn to articulate and apply critical standards about the features and demands of composing in a particular genre

LENGTH

- Approximately 60–90 minutes (can be split into two 45-minute classes)

MATERIALS NEEDED

- Short examples or excerpts of a particular genre, both professionally written and student authored:
  - One sample to teach the whole class
  - Several more short examples—enough to assign a different example to each small group in your class
  - Note that the genre is up to you. Based on the preceding lessons, we would use an abstract, a letter to the editor, or a letter of recommendation, but you can use any genre that your class is reading in your current unit. Just make sure that what students learn about genre will be required and rewarded immediately in the context of how the unit proceeds. The lesson will be most efficient if the examples are short.

(Continued)

Lesson Steps

Step 1

Introduce the lesson and tell students they will be taking on the mantle of the expert (Wilhelm, 2012b) to advise other writers:

- Say: *Now that you are experts in understanding the essential features of different genres and how writers employ those essential features to achieve their purposes, I'm going to ask you to offer advice—first to published writers and then to student writers—using procedural feedback.*

Step 2

Model providing advice to a writer using procedural feedback:

- Project a short piece of writing so that everyone can see it.
- Remind students that you'll be using *procedural feedback*, which describes what the writer has done, the moves he or she made, and what followed in terms of meaning and effect. Remember to give a description of what the writer has done, then explain its meaning or effect.
- Using the projected piece of writing, model giving feedback. For example, if you are using letters to the editor, describe how the author starts the letter and how this works as an essential

(Continued)

- A document camera or other way of projecting a piece of writing that you can mark up in front of the class

feature of the genre. If it doesn't, provide a suggestion to the author for moving forward to improve that feature. For example, say:
  - *The way you begin the letter by saying you are a World War II veteran shows you understand that it can be helpful to introduce and authorize yourself at the beginning of a letter to the editor, but I wonder what would happen if you more clearly connected this authority to the concern you express.*
- Or:
  - *When you cite your position in the second sentence and then provide specific data from a credible source to support it, it lets me clearly know where you stand and convinces me that you have done your homework and should be listened to.*

Step 3

Provide independent practice using the KEEP questions to generate material for procedural feedback:

- Divide students into groups of four or five.
- Distribute a packet of published examples (as many examples as there are groups) of a particular genre. Assign each group a different example from the packet.
- Have each group of students read the examples and apply the KEEP questions.
- Tell students they will now collaboratively provide procedural feedback to the authors of the examples.
- Review the critical standards for procedural feedback, perhaps providing prompts or sentence frames as models:
  - *The way you* _______________ *has the effect of* _______________.
  - *When you* _______________, *it allows/lets me* _______________.
  - *I wonder what would happen if* _______________________________.
- Encourage students to refer to the class anchor charts that list the essential features of the genre they are reading.
- See the sample exchange in the "Voices From the Classroom" box that follows.

Voices From the Classroom

WHAT STUDENTS SAID ABOUT

Providing Procedural Feedback to Authors of Public Service Announcements (Watching the Famous "This Is Your Brain on Drugs" PSA)

STUDENT: Wow—that twang of dark music at the beginning tips you off that something bad is going to happen.

STUDENT: And the way the movie designer then focuses on the boiling oil gives me this totally frenetic feel.

STUDENT: Yeah, that music and boiling oil had the effect of drawing me in.

STUDENT: And the way the videographer just said "This boiling oil in a pan is your brain, and this egg is your brain on drugs," without any explanation means you have to figure out how they are the same.

STUDENT: And the way it ends with "Any questions?" makes me feel like if you have any, then you are an idiot.

STUDENT: The way the whole thing is designed makes me, or anyone watching it, I think, do the work of making the connection. That's what I think is so good about it!

Step 4

Invite groups to share their findings:

- Have each group share and compare their feedback with another group.

Step 5

Have the whole class report their findings:

- Ask students to summarize the essential features of the genre they highlighted in the feedback they gave.
- Record any effective feedback or phrasing on an anchor chart students can refer to. Pay special attention to any feedback highlighting essential features of the genre.

Step 6

Have students write and share their own model examples of the genre:

- Ask students to write an example of the genre being considered.
- When they are done, have students, in pairs, provide procedural feedback to each other in the same way they did to the published authors.
- Ask them to record how they notice the essential features, standards, and demands of the genre and then interpret the text on the basis of what they notice.
- If time permits, have students share their examples with the class.

Extension

Challenge students to alter or revise examples—add, move, delete, or change particular details—for different effects. For example, they could change the title or move the first sentence and then, collaboratively, provide procedural feedback about how the revision changes the meaning and effect of the piece and genre.

Lesson 6

Noticing Varied Nonfiction Genres
SEARCH AND FIND

Introduction

In our study into the literate lives of boys reported in *"Reading Don't Fix No Chevys"* (Smith & Wilhelm, 2002), one of our most salient findings was that students want to be able to use what they've learned, and use it immediately out in the world. They want what they learn to matter—and not just in school.

Searching for and finding actual examples reminds students that the rules of notice we are teaching them—in this case about genre and genre construction—abound in the world around them, and that literacy—in this specific case, genre—matters in the real world.

PURPOSE

- To consolidate students' capacity to notice the tip-offs of a genre and how genres are constructed and expressed through all kinds of speech, communication, and texts

LENGTH

- After initial homework, 50 minutes

MATERIALS NEEDED

- Large paper and markers for small groups so that they can create an anchor chart
- Nonfiction texts students encounter in the real world; have them collect these as a homework assignment, and say:
    - *The work we've been doing in class applies in the larger world as well. I want you to analyze genres you encounter outside school. Start with a big category, like billboards, automobile ads, songs, or sitcoms, and break it into specific genres. Find examples over the next day or two, jotting down answers to the KEEP questions for each one.*

Lesson Steps

Step 1

Have students share their homework:

- Have each student, in small groups of three or four, share the different genres of text he or she found in the outside world, discussing specifically how each example asks to be read and what features ask to be noticed (refer to the KEEP questions).
- Ask students who chose the same genre to work together in groups.
- Have groups create an anchor chart of the features of their particular genre.
- Have groups do a cross-case analysis focusing especially on how they noticed how different genres work, and what these genres therefore require readers to notice about them. For example, they might say that information-based car ads ask readers to pay attention to written details in a way that more visual car ads do not. Or they might say that episodic sitcoms like *Life in Pieces* don't ask viewers to put things together in the same way that full-episode sitcoms do.

Step 2

Lead a whole-class discussion of students' cross-case analyses:

- Have groups report the results of their cross-case analyses.
- Ask: *How did you go about making the groupings that you did? How does each subgenre ask you to read, notice, and interpret in slightly different ways?*

Extension

Have students practice transfer using memes. Ask them to apply the rules of notice to a genre that intrigues them and share their idea by way of a meme. Sites for creating memes include the following:

- https://imgflip.com/memegenerator
- www.mememaker.net
- www.quickmeme.com/caption

Once students have created and shared their memes, ask them to sort memes into categories and apply the KEEP questions to those categories.

Lesson 7

Noticing Varied Nonfiction Genres
PUTTING IT ALL TOGETHER

Introduction

For students to put everything they've learned thus far into practice, they need both support and the opportunity for independent application. This involves doing work *for* them (modeling); then doing work *with* them (mentoring—helping them develop the wide-awake metacognitive strategies of expert readers and thinkers); and finally having them do work *by themselves*, in small groups and individually (so we can monitor their growth and continue to assist them as needed). This kind of deep teaching helps students develop transferable knowledge, skills, and strategies they can apply here and now and in the future (see Smith, Appleman, & Wilhelm, 2014; Wilhelm, Baker, & Dube, 2001).

While we suggest asking a few questions, the majority of the lesson is driven by students' applying the understandings they have gained. An overemphasis on text-dependent questions fosters students' dependence on us. To prepare students for the future, we have to prepare them to do work without us.

PURPOSE

- To apply what students have learned about noticing genre, as well as noticing the conversation and key details, to the reading of two complete texts

LENGTH

- Approximately 90 minutes (can be split into two 45-minute classes if needed)

MATERIALS NEEDED

- Class sets of the following handouts (or another pair of texts appropriate for your unit and students):
    - Handout 4.6, "Lincoln's Second Inaugural Address"
    - Handout 4.7, "Kennedy's Inaugural Address"
- A YouTube video of Kennedy delivering his inaugural address
- Large paper for an anchor chart
- A computer with a projection device

Lesson Steps

Step 1

Introduce the lesson and its purpose in bringing various strategies for noticing together:

- Say: *Today you'll apply everything you've learned in the previous lessons on noticing genre to two very famous speeches: Lincoln's second inaugural address and Kennedy's inaugural address. I'll first model what I want you to do.*
- Ask: *What do you know about inaugural addresses?*
- Record the students' answers on chart paper.

Step 2

Model the think-aloud process:

- Distribute copies of Handout 4.6, "Lincoln's Second Inaugural Address."
- Say: *Read along while I'm thinking aloud, marking where I stop and jotting down any rules of notice you see that I don't comment on.*
- Think aloud as you read Lincoln's speech (remember that these are suggestions, not a script). See the sample think-aloud that follows.

Step 3

Lead a whole-class discussion:

- Distribute Handout 4.7, "Kennedy's Inaugural Address."
- Ask students to discuss what they've learned about inaugural addresses and what that makes them think this one will be like.
- Record their answers on an anchor chart.
- Say: *We'll begin reading Kennedy's speech together. Then I'll let you work on your own.*
- Read the first paragraph of the inaugural address:
    - "We observe today not a victory of party, but a celebration of freedom—symbolizing an end, as well as a beginning—signifying renewal, as well as change. For I have sworn before you and Almighty God the same solemn oath our forebears prescribed nearly a century and three-quarters ago."
- Say: *OK, we know that beginnings are important. What do you notice about this beginning?* See the sample exchange in the "Voices From the Classroom" box that follows.
- Read the second paragraph:
    - "The world is very different now. For man holds in his mortal hands the power to abolish all forms of human poverty and all forms of human life. And yet the same revolutionary beliefs for which our forebears fought are still at issue around the globe—the belief that the rights of man come not from the generosity of the state, but from the hand of God."
- Say: *Remember that a rupture is a rule of notice. What word signals a rupture most clearly?*
- Look for students to notice how the word *yet* signals the unexpected. They might say, "People have this huge power, but still Kennedy says that rights come not from people or governments but from God."

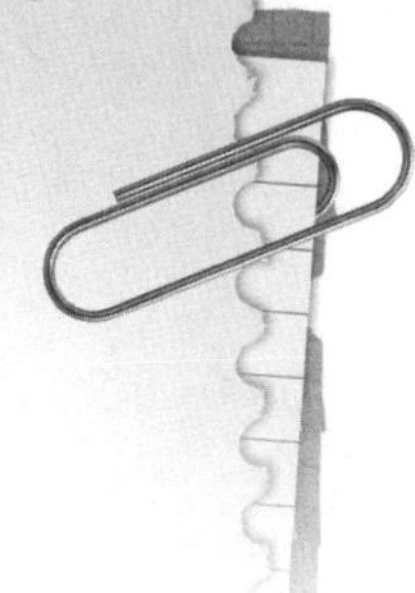

SAMPLE THINK-ALOUD

Lesson 7. Noticing Varied Nonfiction Genres: Putting It All Together

Lincoln's Second Inaugural Address

Before I start, what do I know about inaugural addresses?

Add to students' list of what they know on chart paper, capturing what they did not say.

They're important speeches, because they kick off a presidency. I don't have much experience reading or hearing them, but they probably deliver the big picture about whatever is being kicked off—the challenges being faced and an agenda for addressing the challenges.

The few I've watched on television got the audience emotionally involved. Let's see what Lincoln does.

OK, I immediately see a rule of notice as I look at this: a genre marker. Inaugural addresses typically are not titled except for "inaugural." So I know that this is an address given on the occasion of his second inauguration. I expect he'll reflect back on his first four years as president and ahead to the next four.

Fellow-Countrymen:

This is a call to attention. Beginnings are always important, and anytime someone or some group is addressed directly I have to pay attention. So he's talking to everyone. That's pretty common, I guess, but during the Civil War maybe not. I wonder if he is addressing Southerners too when he says "Fellow-Countrymen" or whether he is just addressing Northerners who elected him.

At this second appearing to take the oath of the Presidential office there is less occasion for an extended address than there was at the first. Then a statement somewhat in detail of a course to be pursued seemed fitting and proper.

Another call to attention. One of the things I have to pay attention to is when the speaker or author refers to another text. Here he's referring to his first inaugural address. Last time he talked about the course to take in the face of Southern secession. Maybe this one will be about unity in some way or another.

Now, at the expiration of four years, during which public declarations have been constantly called forth on every point and phase of the great contest which still absorbs the attention and engrosses the energies of the nation, little that is new could be presented.

He's reflecting back on history and then moving on to the challenges of the current moment. Inaugural speeches are about the future and not the past, so I expect he'll be moving on.

(Continued)

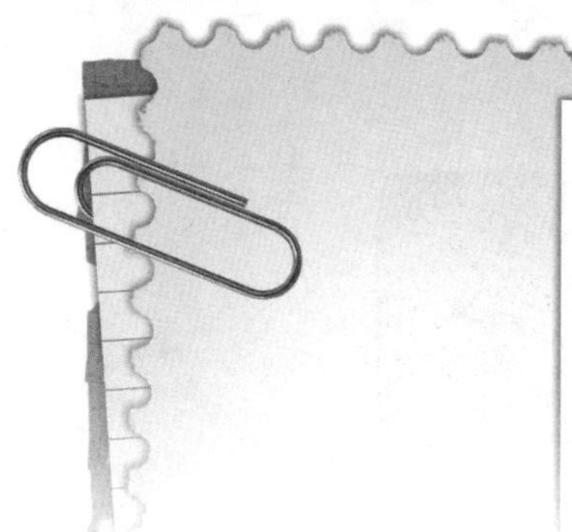

SAMPLE THINK-ALOUD
(CONT.)

The progress of our arms, upon which all else chiefly depends, is as well known to the public as to myself, and it is, I trust, reasonably satisfactory and encouraging to all. With high hope for the future, no prediction in regard to it is ventured.

This is a direct statement of importance. Winning the war is what is most important. But I also notice the rule of rupture: Lincoln says he won't report on the war, but he does so—it's going well. He says he is making no predictions, but he kind of does.

On the occasion corresponding to this four years ago all thoughts were anxiously directed to an impending civil war. All dreaded it, all sought to avert it.

Repetitions are an example of a call to attention.

While the inaugural address was being delivered from this place, devoted altogether to *saving* the Union without war, insurgent agents were in the city seeking to *destroy* it without war—seeking to dissolve the Union and divide effects by negotiation. Both parties deprecated war, but one of them would *make* war rather than let the nation survive, and the other would *accept* war rather than let it perish, and the war came.

Here is the rule of the reader's response. This is pretty emotionally charged language. Lincoln blames the South for causing the war.

One-eighth of the whole population were colored slaves, not distributed generally over the Union, but localized in the southern part of it. These slaves constituted a peculiar and powerful interest.

A direct statement of importance.

All knew that this interest was somehow the cause of the war.

Another direct statement of importance.

To strengthen, perpetuate, and extend this interest was the object for which the insurgents would rend the Union even by war, while the Government claimed no right to do more than to restrict the territorial enlargement of it. Neither party expected for the war the magnitude or the duration which it has already attained. Neither anticipated that the cause of the conflict might cease with or even before the conflict itself should cease.

This is a call to attention. In my experience, presidents often use figurative language and rhetorical devices to make their speeches

(Continued)

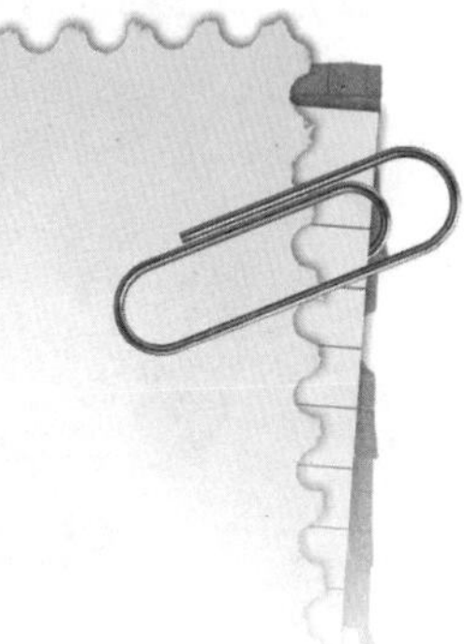

SAMPLE THINK-ALOUD
(CONT.)

memorable. He repeats "neither" to show that the war was not what either side would have predicted. He refers to prior policy that appeased the South and allowed slavery while trying to restrict its growth, and to the Emancipation Proclamation that freed the slaves.

Each looked for an easier triumph, and a result less fundamental and astounding. Both read the same Bible and pray to the same God, and each invokes His aid against the other. It may seem strange that any men should dare to ask a just God's assistance in wringing their bread from the sweat of other men's faces, but let us judge not, that we be not judged. The prayers of both could not be answered. That of neither has been answered fully. The Almighty has His own purposes. "Woe unto the world because of offenses; for it must needs be that offenses come, but woe to that man by whom the offense cometh." If we shall suppose that American slavery is one of those offenses which, in the providence of God, must needs come, but which, having continued through His appointed time, He now wills to remove, and that He gives to both North and South this terrible war as the woe due to those by whom the offense came, shall we discern therein any departure from those divine attributes which the believers in a living God always ascribe to Him? Fondly do we hope, fervently do we pray, that this mighty scourge of war may speedily pass away. Yet, if God wills that it continue until all the wealth piled by the bondsman's two hundred and fifty years of unrequited toil shall be sunk, and until every drop of blood drawn with the lash shall be paid by another drawn with the sword, as was said three thousand years ago, so still it must be said "the judgments of the Lord are true and righteous altogether."

Referring to God and the Bible here is for sure a call to attention.

With malice toward none, with charity for all, with firmness in the right as God gives us to see the right, let us strive on to finish the work we are in, to bind up the nation's wounds, to care for him who shall have borne the battle and for his widow and his orphan, to do all which may achieve and cherish a just and lasting peace among ourselves and with all nations.

Here I notice the rule of the reader's response. Look at the use of "us" and "we" in this final paragraph. I think Lincoln really wanted to end by getting everybody emotionally involved.

Source: Lincoln, A. (1865, March 4). *Second inaugural address.* Retrieved from http://avalon.law.yale.edu/19th_century/lincoln2.asp

Voices From the Classroom

WHAT STUDENTS SAID ABOUT **Kennedy's Inaugural Address**

TEACHER: OK, we know that beginnings are important. What do you notice about this beginning?

STUDENT: He starts out with "we."

TEACHER: So? What made you notice that?

STUDENT: So it's like Lincoln. "Fellow-Countrymen."

TEACHER: What rule of notice might you call that?

STUDENT: Maybe reader's response. 'Cause he wants to get everyone on his side.

TEACHER: Why is it important to get everyone on his side? What do we know about inaugurals that could explain why he started that way?

STUDENT: Like we said before. These speeches are about what the president wants for the future.

TEACHER: So?

STUDENT: So he wants everybody on board.

Step 4

Provide background knowledge to prepare students for success:

- Show the YouTube video of Kennedy delivering his speech. Tell students to follow along and make annotations as they listen.

Step 5

Provide independent practice:

- Divide students into five groups.
- Pass out Handout 4.7, "Kennedy's Inaugural Address." Assign each group a segment of the speech on which to focus.
- As groups are working, circulate and monitor their progress.
- Be prepared to direct them to notice the conversation, to notice key details, and to notice genre markers.

Step 6

Lead a whole-class discussion:

- Have groups report their discoveries to the whole class, jigsaw fashion—that is, by having the groups present in the order their section appeared in the speech.
- Ask: *What did the genre of the inaugural speech allow Kennedy to do? What did it keep him from doing?*
- Record students' comments on the anchor chart.

Extensions

- Have students record a think-aloud for another inaugural address.
- Have students use the KEEP questions on another genre of presidential speeches, for example, a State of the Union address.

Lincoln's Second Inaugural Address

Fellow-Countrymen:

At this second appearing to take the oath of the Presidential office there is less occasion for an extended address than there was at the first. Then a statement somewhat in detail of a course to be pursued seemed fitting and proper. Now, at the expiration of four years, during which public declarations have been constantly called forth on every point and phase of the great contest which still absorbs the attention and engrosses the energies of the nation, little that is new could be presented. The progress of our arms, upon which all else chiefly depends, is as well known to the public as to myself, and it is, I trust, reasonably satisfactory and encouraging to all. With high hope for the future, no prediction in regard to it is ventured.

On the occasion corresponding to this four years ago all thoughts were anxiously directed to an impending civil war. All dreaded it, all sought to avert it. While the inaugural address was being delivered from this place, devoted altogether to *saving* the Union without war, insurgent agents were in the city seeking to *destroy* it without war—seeking to dissolve the Union and divide effects by negotiation. Both parties deprecated war, but one of them would *make* war rather than let the nation survive, and the other would *accept* war rather than let it perish, and the war came.

One-eighth of the whole population were colored slaves, not distributed generally over the Union, but localized in the southern part of it. These slaves constituted a peculiar and powerful interest. All knew that this interest was somehow the cause of the war. To strengthen, perpetuate, and extend this interest was the object for which the insurgents would rend the Union even by war, while the Government claimed no right to do more than to restrict the territorial enlargement of it. Neither party expected for the war the magnitude or the duration which it has already attained. Neither anticipated that the *cause* of the conflict might

(Continued)

cease with or even before the conflict itself should cease. Each looked for an easier triumph, and a result less fundamental and astounding. Both read the same Bible and pray to the same God, and each invokes His aid against the other. It may seem strange that any men should dare to ask a just God's assistance in wringing their bread from the sweat of other men's faces, but let us judge not, that we be not judged. The prayers of both could not be answered. That of neither has been answered fully. The Almighty has His own purposes. "Woe unto the world because of offenses; for it must needs be that offenses come, but woe to that man by whom the offense cometh." If we shall suppose that American slavery is one of those offenses which, in the providence of God, must needs come, but which, having continued through His appointed time, He now wills to remove, and that He gives to both North and South this terrible war as the woe due to those by whom the offense came, shall we discern therein any departure from those divine attributes which the believers in a living God always ascribe to Him? Fondly do we hope, fervently do we pray, that this mighty scourge of war may speedily pass away. Yet, if God wills that it continue until all the wealth piled by the bondsman's two hundred and fifty years of unrequited toil shall be sunk, and until every drop of blood drawn with the lash shall be paid by another drawn with the sword, as was said three thousand years ago, so still it must be said "the judgments of the Lord are true and righteous altogether."

With malice toward none, with charity for all, with firmness in the right as God gives us to see the right, let us strive on to finish the work we are in, to bind up the nation's wounds, to care for him who shall have borne the battle and for his widow and his orphan, to do all which may achieve and cherish a just and lasting peace among ourselves and with all nations.

Source: Lincoln, A. (1865, March 4). *Second inaugural address.* Retrieved from http://avalon.law.yale.edu/19th_century/lincoln2.asp

Handout 4.7

Kennedy's Inaugural Address

Segment 1

We dare not forget today that we are the heirs of that first revolution. Let the word go forth from this time and place, to friend and foe alike, that the torch has been passed to a new generation of Americans—born in this century, tempered by war, disciplined by a hard and bitter peace, proud of our ancient heritage, and unwilling to witness or permit the slow undoing of those human rights to which this nation has always been committed, and to which we are committed today at home and around the world.

Let every nation know, whether it wishes us well or ill, that we shall pay any price, bear any burden, meet any hardship, support any friend, oppose any foe, to assure the survival and the success of liberty.

This much we pledge—and more.

Segment 2

To those old allies whose cultural and spiritual origins we share, we pledge the loyalty of faithful friends. United there is little we cannot do in a host of cooperative ventures. Divided there is little we can do—for we dare not meet a powerful challenge at odds and split asunder.

To those new states whom we welcome to the ranks of the free, we pledge our word that one form of colonial control shall not have passed away merely to be replaced by a far more iron tyranny. We shall not always expect to find them supporting our view. But we shall always hope to find them strongly supporting their own freedom—and to remember that, in the past, those who foolishly sought power by riding the back of the tiger ended up inside.

To those people in the huts and villages of half the globe struggling to break the bonds of mass misery, we pledge our best efforts to help them help themselves, for whatever period is required—not

(Continued)

because the Communists may be doing it, not because we seek their votes, but because it is right. If a free society cannot help the many who are poor, it cannot save the few who are rich.

To our sister republics south of our border, we offer a special pledge: to convert our good words into good deeds, in a new alliance for progress, to assist free men and free governments in casting off the chains of poverty. But this peaceful revolution of hope cannot become the prey of hostile powers. Let all our neighbors know that we shall join with them to oppose aggression or subversion anywhere in the Americas. And let every other power know that this hemisphere intends to remain the master of its own house.

To that world assembly of sovereign states, the United Nations, our last best hope in an age where the instruments of war have far outpaced the instruments of peace, we renew our pledge of support—to prevent it from becoming merely a forum for invective, to strengthen its shield of the new and the weak, and to enlarge the area in which its writ may run.

Finally, to those nations who would make themselves our adversary, we offer not a pledge but a request: that both sides begin anew the quest for peace, before the dark powers of destruction unleashed by science engulf all humanity in planned or accidental self-destruction.

Segment 3

We dare not tempt them with weakness. For only when our arms are sufficient beyond doubt can we be certain beyond doubt that they will never be employed.

But neither can two great and powerful groups of nations take comfort from our present course—both sides overburdened by the cost of modern weapons, both rightly alarmed by the steady spread of the deadly atom, yet both racing to alter that uncertain balance of terror that stays the hand of mankind's final war.

(Continued)

So let us begin anew—remembering on both sides that civility is not a sign of weakness, and sincerity is always subject to proof. Let us never negotiate out of fear, but let us never fear to negotiate.

Let both sides explore what problems unite us instead of belaboring those problems which divide us.

Let both sides, for the first time, formulate serious and precise proposals for the inspection and control of arms, and bring the absolute power to destroy other nations under the absolute control of all nations.

Let both sides seek to invoke the wonders of science instead of its terrors. Together let us explore the stars, conquer the deserts, eradicate disease, tap the ocean depths, and encourage the arts and commerce.

Let both sides unite to heed, in all corners of the earth, the command of Isaiah—to "undo the heavy burdens, and [to] let the oppressed go free."[1]

And, if a beachhead of cooperation may push back the jungle of suspicion, let both sides join in creating a new endeavor—not a new balance of power, but a new world of law—where the strong are just, and the weak secure, and the peace preserved.

Segment 4

All this will not be finished in the first one hundred days. Nor will it be finished in the first one thousand days; nor in the life of this Administration; nor even perhaps in our lifetime on this planet. But let us begin.

In your hands, my fellow citizens, more than mine, will rest the final success or failure of our course. Since this country was founded, each generation of Americans has been summoned to give testimony to its national loyalty. The graves of young Americans who answered the call to service surround the globe.

Now the trumpet summons us again—not as a call to bear arms, though arms we need—not as a

(Continued)

call to battle, though embattled we are—but a call to bear the burden of a long twilight struggle, year in and year out, "rejoicing in hope; patient in tribulation,"[2] a struggle against the common enemies of man: tyranny, poverty, disease, and war itself.

Can we forge against these enemies a grand and global alliance, North and South, East and West, that can assure a more fruitful life for all mankind? Will you join in that historic effort?

Segment 5

In the long history of the world, only a few generations have been granted the role of defending freedom in its hour of maximum danger. I do not shrink from this responsibility—I welcome it. I do not believe that any of us would exchange places with any other people or any other generation. The energy, the faith, the devotion which we bring to this endeavor will light our country and all who serve it. And the glow from that fire can truly light the world.

And so, my fellow Americans, ask not what your country can do for you; ask what you can do for your country.

My fellow citizens of the world, ask not what America will do for you, but what together we can do for the freedom of man.

Finally, whether you are citizens of America or citizens of the world, ask of us here the same high standards of strength and sacrifice which we ask of you. With a good conscience our only sure reward, with history the final judge of our deeds, let us go forth to lead the land we love, asking His blessing and His help, but knowing that here on earth God's work must truly be our own.

1. Isaiah 58:6
2. Romans 12:12

Source: Kennedy, J. F. (1961, January 20). *Inaugural address.* Retrieved from http://avalon.law.yale.edu/20th_century/kennedy.asp

Available for download at **http://resources.corwin.com/divingdeep-nonfiction**

Chapter 5

Noticing the Text Structures in Nonfiction Texts

In Chapter 4, we explored how understanding genres can help readers comprehend texts. Genres, as you recall, are groups of texts that operate in very similar ways, which includes using similar features and conventions and placing similar demands on readers.

In this final set of lessons, we share our ideas about how to help students notice more local structures. Text structures, which can also be thought of as thought patterns, are different from genres. **Text structures express patterns of thought.** Perhaps the two most common are comparison and classification (Bruner, 1986; Wilhelm, Smith, & Fredricksen, 2013).

Genres deploy text structures in service of doing their work, and they do so in different ways in different situations. Think, for example, of the nature of description in a scientific report or medical diagnosis as opposed to a movie review or feature article, or the nature of comparison for comparison shopping in *Consumer Reports* versus the ranking of teams in *Sports Illustrated.* Expert readers understand how genres work to guide reading, and they also understand how recognizing the text structures within genres is useful in their efforts to navigate a text to make meaning.

How Text Structures Work

Bruner (1986) has helped us understand that informational text structures are basically different ways of categorizing data. He argues that "to perceive is to categorize, to conceptualize is to categorize, to learn is to form categories, to make decisions is to categorize." Each informational text structure requires a different and very specific kind of thinking and problem solving through the use of categories. In turn, this means that teaching students how to comprehend, compose, and use informational text structures means that we are teaching them how to think with these different categorical patterning tools.

A Hierarchy of Text Structures

Let's take a look at the informational text structures cited in the Common Core State Standards (CCSS). We have put them into a hierarchy from simplest to most complex, and will show how one text structure informs the basis for the next category. (The following is adapted from Wilhelm et al., 2013.)

Naming

Naming is a powerful intellectual act. Naming gives us an enhanced awareness of something, imbuing it with meaning and allowing us to both think about and use that meaning. **Labeling** is another way to think of naming. Cognitive scientists use the motto "Name it to tame it." Naming gives us conscious power over the named and allows us to think with it and manipulate it.

Let's say you are sending a family member to the grocery store. You'll want to be very precise in naming what you want purchased, or there may be mistakes. You wouldn't say "Pick up some greens" if you really wanted lettuce, and if you wanted romaine, you'd specify that because otherwise you might get something else like iceberg. Writers often employ naming in their writing. The most obvious example is employing neologisms. Researchers often invent names for new concepts and findings. As Thomas Jefferson put it, "Necessity obliges us to neologize." If there aren't names for what we want to say, we have to invent them.

Listing

Lists are categories of names compiled for some purpose. Listing allows us to place what we've named into a category of similar things so they can be remembered and used more easily. Naming and listing seem to us to be prerequisite to all other kinds of informational patterns and text structures and to all forms of Bruner's (1986) notion of categorization (see Wilhelm et al., 2013).

When you send your family member to the grocery store, you're likely to provide a list, and that list is likely to be divided into categories of food like fresh vegetables, canned goods, and dairy products. The more organized the list, the easier it will be to follow and use. The same is true for reading nonfiction. Lots of nonfiction texts embed bulleted lists, sometimes as an introduction to describing or explaining the listed elements. Researchers often use lists to orient the reader to major ideas and their relationships. Organized lists are known as *significant lists*. The more organized the list, say from least to most important, the more helpful it will be in organizing one's thinking and subsequent reading of the text.

Summarizing

A summary is a quick and highly focused statement that includes only the most essential details of an extended data set or text in some organized and connected way. Summaries build on the bulleting of lists by connecting the elements and reflecting the structure of what is being summarized.

If you trust the family member going to the store, you can just say, "Remember that we need a fruit salad for dessert, and get some cheese that goes with it!" Likewise, reading the abstract of a research article can help you decide if you want to read the article, and if you do, it provides a map of what you can expect to find out, in what order, as you go through the text.

Descriptions

Descriptions provide details about an object, element, place, or process so that it can be understood, categorized, and generalized from ("Make sure to buy the gluten-free pancake mix. It's right next to the regular mixes, but in a smaller box. The box is orange, and it's got a GF label on it"). A description expands on summary to flesh out the basic details, give them life and sensory expression, and demonstrate relationships between them. Descriptions allow us to understand something deeply, including how that object, event, or being is patterned. Research articles, for example, often give rich descriptions of the informants and their backgrounds or of the data collection methods used, and these descriptions enrich our understanding of the research process and findings.

Process Descriptions

Process descriptions in the CCSS are also referred to as *how-tos* or *recipes*. This text structure allows us to prepare and rehearse a specific activity; to direct, monitor, and correct our activity while we are doing it; and to evaluate, reflect, and plan after an activity or for the repetition of that activity.

You might tell your family member, "First go around the outside of the grocery store to get all of the produce and dairy, then just dip in to the baking aisle to get the pancake mix and the maple syrup. If you go through that aisle, you'll come out by the registers and be done." Recipes are an obvious example of process descriptions, as are other kinds of directions. Research articles describe the processes of selecting informants and collecting data, and often the implications and process of applying findings in the real world.

Definitions

Definitions are employed to categorize a term or concept and to differentiate it from other similar categories. Think, for example, of the various meanings *organic* can have. A definition explains the meaning of a term or concept and its limits. There are two kinds of definitions: short definitions of the sort one might see in a dictionary, and extended definitions. We regularly make use of dictionary-style definitions in our daily conversations or reading. Think, for example, of teaching someone how to play a new game. You can't learn how to play bridge unless you know the definition of *trump*. If a concept introduced in a text is fairly complex or arcane, a definition is usually provided.

Extended definitions are very important when exploring conceptual terms in the disciplines, such as *exponent* or *invertebrate* or even *courage* or *hero*. Extended definitions are essential to classification, often used in research findings. You can't place something into a class unless you understand the definition of the class. Extended definitions typically require writers to enumerate criteria, characteristics, or subclasses and to differentiate the defined term from related concepts.

Comparisons

Comparisons are clearly forms of categorization ("You'll find it in the baking aisle not with the other pancake mixes but with the organic and natural nonwheat flours"). Comparisons depend on identifying salient similarities and differences and then putting that identification to use. This identification stems from definition. Typically, comparisons are used in one of three ways, all widely used in various kinds of texts including argument and research writing:

- To reason by **analogy** (these things are sufficiently similar that what you have learned about one can be applied to the other; or although these things appear similar, they are in fact different, so what you learn about one can't be applied to the other)
- To **evaluate** (this thing is better or more efficient, etc., than the other)
- To **interpret** (by looking at X and Y we can learn about Z; for example, looking at the Vietnam and Iraq wars provides insight into why public opinion is so important for policy makers to consider)

Teaching Compare and Contrast With Think-Aloud in Science

Video 5.1

http://resources.corwin.com/divingdeep-nonfiction

Classifications

Classifications group multiple elements of a specific topical universe. This obviously involves comparing and contrasting the definitions of group membership. The most famous classification scheme is Linnaean or biological classification, developed by Carl Linnaeus to group life according to physical characteristics, and later under the influence of Darwin, according to common descent. This kind of classification proceeds from life to domain, kingdom, phylum, class, order, family, and genus to the individual example of life: species. Classifications proceed from the topical universe (in this case, life) and the most general subordinating categories to the specific individual example of the topical universe (in this case, species). Classification builds on comparison, and obviously does tremendous amounts of work in helping researchers and inquirers analyze data, allowing them to see and explain relationships. Think of a grocery store or library where the items were not classified. You'd never be able to find anything.

Cause and Effect

Cause-and-effect structures are an effort to link categories of causes to resulting categories of effects

("Gluten has been causing some bowel and digestive problems for me, so gluten-free is easier on my stomach and aids my digestion"). Cause-and-effect structures explain the relationship between an impetus or set of causes and their consequences (at least for events that have already occurred—anything predictive seems to us to clearly be a cause-and-effect argument). When we talk about the *possible* effects of particular ways of being—like resilience—or of actions—like risky behaviors—we name the possible implications, and this becomes an argument. These implications might just be effects, but they might also become additional problems, and they are worth thinking about when taking risks. Cause and effect involves defining, comparing, and classifying the causes and effects, which are usually multiple.

Causality is considered to be fundamental to all natural science, especially physics. It is also important to logic and argumentation and all research, as well as much of philosophy, computer science, statistics, and other fields. In everyday life, we all have a fundamental interest in our surroundings and how to shape and control our lives and events in these situations. Causality is essential to narrative; without it we could not use narrative to make sense of human experience. Cause and effect can easily be confused with simple correlations (experiences or events that have occurred in tandem but without causing each other). But if causality can be determined, then not only is understanding achieved, but new ways of solving problems can be found.

Problem/Solution

Problem/solution structures are likewise an attempt to link categories of problems to categories of potential solutions. Inquiry, the search for understanding, is based on framing a topic as a problem to be solved. When we inquire, we search first for understanding of the problem (which involves causality and often many of the previously cited thought patterns), and next for possible solutions to the problem. This is what professionals do, from medicine (What is the health problem? How can we solve it?) to education (What is the learning challenge? How can we most positively and proactively help students meet it?). Research leading to policy proposals necessarily uses this thought pattern. Professional practice and knowledge making in any discipline are based on inquiry and therefore on problem/solution. This involves explaining the nature of a problem and relating the causes of the problem to the effects of a solution.

Rules of Notice for Text Structure

Once again, we will focus on the four rules of notice to help students recognize and make meaning with text structures:

- Direct statements
- Ruptures
- Calls to attention
- Reader's response

Direct Statements

Sometimes authors explicitly announce a text structure with a direct statement. For example, in an accreditation report, Michael wrote: "We define professionalism not only as knowing and meeting school and district procedures for attendance, punctuality, dress, demeanor, and the like, but also as demonstrating awareness of individual and cultural diversity, employing the best technological tools available to teachers and students." Sometimes a direct statement announces a move required by a text structure, such as articulating characteristics in a definition: "The most significant features of megafauna are . . ."

Ruptures

Ruptures are shifts from one text structure to another. For example, an argument trying to establish that states should have stricter laws against cell phone use in cars might include a list of states that have strict laws and then a comparison of traffic fatalities in states with strict laws and those in states with less strict laws.

Calls to Attention

Calls to attention include text features—for example, a process description set off in a text box or bulleted list. Authors also may explicitly indicate that something is worthy of special attention (e.g., "Examining what happened in other states sheds light on why this is so important").

Reader's Response

As always, readers should pay attention to any part of a text, including structural moves, that evokes a particularly strong response. It might be a definition of an abstract term that results in their reconsidering a previous understanding or a solution to a problem that the reader finds especially noteworthy.

Teaching students how to notice and use embedded text structures as thought patterns can be very rewarding and generative, helping to achieve threshold knowledge and assisting students to use these powerful strategies for categorical thinking throughout a lifetime.

In the rest of this section, we highlight the teaching of text structures as thought patterns, with a focus on comparison. We hope this will provide a generative model for you to use in teaching *any* text structure important to you and your students during a unit of study. We focus on comparison and contrast because we think it is essential to the work we do in school and in life on a daily basis. This structure is often explicitly embedded in argument, equally often (though sometimes implicitly) in narrative, and always in definition and classification. Comparison also makes use of text structures mentioned earlier in our hierarchy, and it lays the foundation for later ones like classification, problem/solution, and cause and effect.

Teaching Three Rules of Structure: Martin Luther King Jr.'s "I Have a Dream" Speech

Video 5.2

http://resources.corwin.com/divingdeep-nonfiction

Noticing Patterns: Martin Luther King Jr.'s "I Have a Dream" Speech

Video 5.3

http://resources.corwin.com/divingdeep-nonfiction

Lesson 1

Noticing the Text Structures in Nonfiction Texts

READING VISUAL TEXTS

Lesson 1: Day 1

PURPOSE

- To recognize how the rules of notice play out in highlighting comparison in visual texts

LENGTH

- This lesson is designed to be taught over two to three days. The lesson in Day 1 can be split into two parts if need be.
  - Day 1: 60–75 minutes
  - Day 2: 30–45 minutes

MATERIALS NEEDED

- Chart paper or board space and a marker
- A way to display Will Eisner's spread "Prisons" from *New York: The Big City*
- We found it by searching online for *Eisner + prisons + big city* (you can also try www.wizards-keep.com/index.asp-Q-Page-E-will-eisner--32917422)

Introduction

Paintings, photographs, graphic novels, and other visual or multimodal texts can provide wonderful introductions to text structures. Paintings, for instance, often operate as a kind of summary—a snapshot in time of essential elements of a situation, relationship, or some other topic. They obviously provide visual descriptions using the most telling details.

Visual artwork also often calls for comparison, sometimes explicitly as in *Beer Street* and *Gin Lane*, and sometimes less so, as in the comparison a viewer would make between the man and the woman in *American Gothic*. Sometimes artists imply comparisons, counting on viewers to relate the work in front of them to another they have seen, as both paintings may be part of the same conversation and about the same topic. As we noted in each preceding set of lessons, visual texts are a great way to involve students in understanding the rules of notice they apply when they read.

Lesson Steps: Day 1

Step 1

Introduce the purpose of the lesson and the first activity of seeing and naming rules of notice:

- Recall for students that they just finished discussing *genres*, groups of texts that share significant similarities in how they operate.
- Note that texts also employ smaller structures that direct our noticing and interpreting of details, and that one of the most important is comparison. Point out that comparisons appear in many of the genres they just looked at—for example, the writer of a letter of recommendation comparing the person he or she is recommending to others, or an inaugural address comparing how things are to how they used to be.
- Explain that you'll be focusing on how authors cue readers to make comparisons and how they use comparisons to create meaning and effect.

- Project the image "Prisons" from *New York: The Big City* by Will Eisner. *Do not* tell students the name of the illustration. Ask them to individually jot down what they notice—what jumps out at them—and why.

Step 2

Invite students to study the illustration and note potential rules of notice:

- Ask students to study the spread in pairs or triads, making note especially of how it calls for readers to make comparisons and of the rules of notice they apply to do so.
- Ask students to share their thinking with the class. On an anchor chart, keep notes on the rules of notice students employ. See Figure 5.1 for an example.
- Probe for how the spread invites comparisons by noting the different people in different situations, both inside and outside.

Step 3

Have students look at the individual pictures for rules of notice:

- Ask students to study individually each of the four pictures within the larger picture. If you can, project the image in these quadrants one at a time.
- Tell students to develop an interpretation of the meaning and effect of the whole spread based on their reading of each picture and how each individual picture compares to the others in terms of similarities and differences.

Step 4

Have students share in pairs or triads, then in the larger group:

- Group students in pairs or triads to share their ideas. As students work, circulate. Note especially interesting ideas and tell students to be prepared to share them.
- Have the pairs or triads share. Probe for the rules of notice the students applied. Track their findings on the anchor chart.
- See the sample exchange in the "Voices From the Classroom" box on page 176.

Step 5

Encourage students to look for commonalities across all of the pictures and consider the topic and comment being made:

- Ask students in pairs or triads:
    - *What do all the pictures have in common? How do they differ?*
    - *What is the topic and the possible comment on the topic being made through this combination of pictures?*
    - *What title would you give the illustration on the basis of your analysis?*

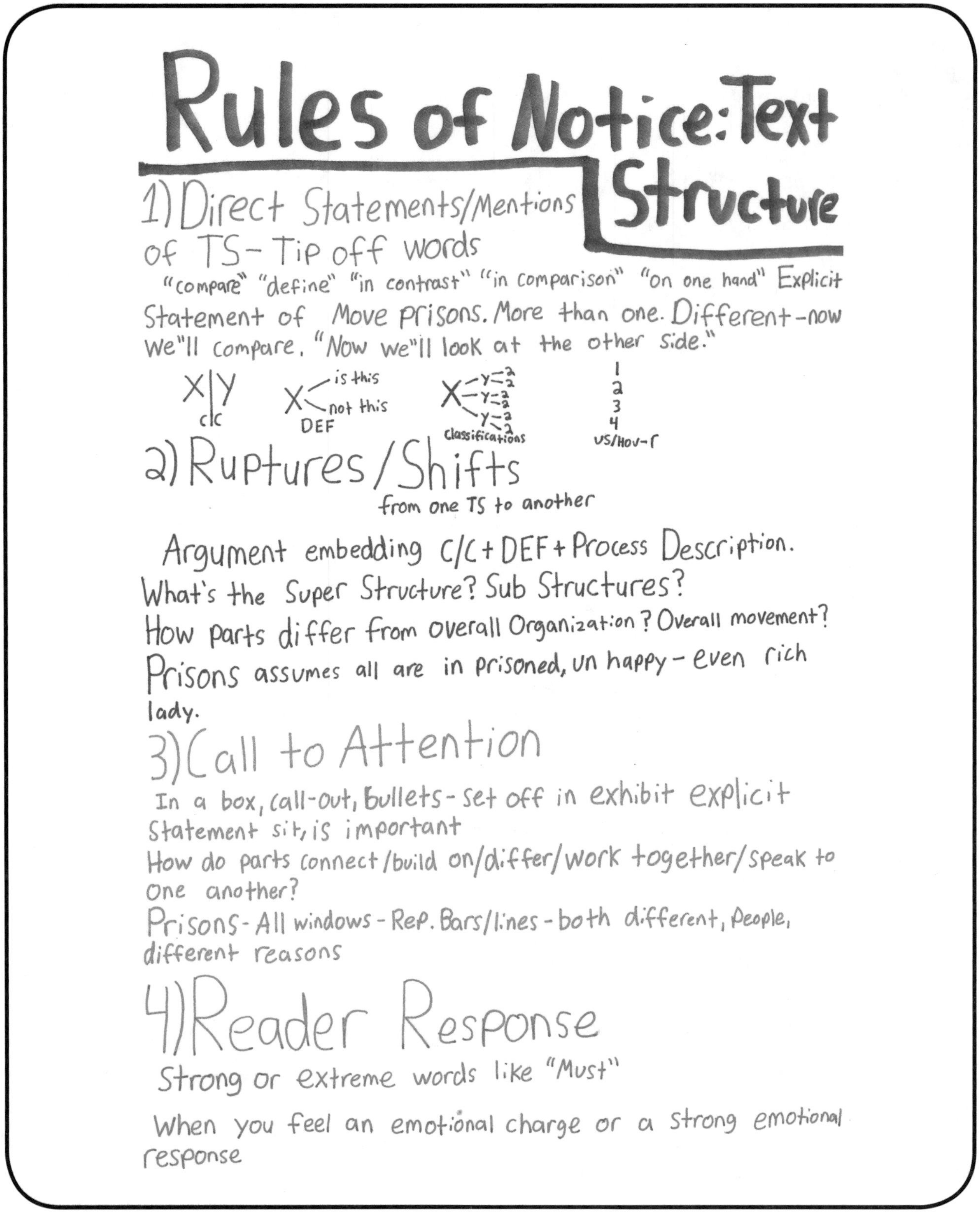

Rules of Notice: Text Structure

1) Direct Statements/Mentions of TS - Tip off words

"compare" "define" "in contrast" "in comparison" "on one hand" Explicit Statement of Move prisons. More than one. Different-now we'll compare. "Now we'll look at the other side."

X|Y C|C; X < is this / not this DEF; X < Y < 2 2 ... Classifications; 1 2 3 4 US/Hov-r

2) Ruptures/Shifts from one TS to another

Argument embedding C/C + DEF + Process Description.

What's the Super Structure? Sub Structures?

How parts differ from overall Organization? Overall movement?

Prisons assumes all are in prisoned, un happy - even rich lady.

3) Call to Attention

In a box, call-out, bullets - set off in exhibit explicit statement sit, is important

How do parts connect/build on/differ/work together/speak to one another?

Prisons - All windows - Rep. Bars/lines - both different, people, different reasons

4) Reader Response

Strong or extreme words like "Must"

When you feel an emotional charge or a strong emotional response

Figure 5.1

Anchor Chart: Noticing the Text Structures in Nonfiction Texts

- Lead a whole-class discussion on the topic, comments, and titles. See the sample exchange in the "Voices From the Classroom" box on page 176.

Step 6

Have students compare their titles to Eisner's:

- After students have shared their topic–comment responses (this strategy is introduced in Chapter 2, Lesson 4, page 41), share that Eisner's title for this spread is "Prisons."
- Ask students to compare their topics and titles to Eisner's. Ask: *How does each picture relate to a prison or being imprisoned?*
- Share that Eisner has said that the theme (topic–comment) he was striving for is that modern urban life is intensely isolating.
- Ask students to discuss their own interpretations versus Eisner's. Highlight their use of comparisons whenever it occurs in their noticing and interpreting.

Step 7

Reflect on the window to introduce the use of symbols:

- Explain that authors, painters, and other artists expect readers or viewers to identify symbols by noticing repeated images and comparing how they are used (note that this is just one rule of notice for symbolism).
- Ask students to reflect on the use of windows in the spread. On the basis of their comparisons, what do they think the windows represent? See the sample exchange in the "Voices From the Classroom" section that follows.

Step 8

Summarize the process that students went through:

- Remind students of the rules of notice they applied.
- Note that they engaged in a two-step process of comparison:
  - Noticing significant similarities and differences
  - Using those noticings to draw conclusions

Extension: Day 1

Encourage students to follow the same process with another spread (e.g., from a graphic novel or a collage) that uses comparison. Try the very first spread of Nick Bertozzi's *Shackleton* (2014), which uses a chronological narrative but also a comparison of the different Antarctic expeditions and their results, all leading to Ernest Shackleton's 1910 Terra Nova Expedition. Or ask students to find and share such spreads. This will give them continued deliberate practice in noticing and interpreting the comparison text structure.

Voices From the Classroom

WHAT STUDENTS SAID ABOUT
The Bottom-Left Quadrant of "Prisons," From *New York: The Big City* by Will Eisner

TEACHER: OK, super students! Talk with your partner about what details you notice first and what rules of notice help you notice these things. Go! [Waits one minute.] OK, what have you got?

STUDENT: There's a bank worker inside eating lunch while standing and a painter outside eating lunch while sitting on a scaffold.

TEACHER: Rule of notice?

STUDENT: Call to attention through repetition.

STUDENT: Another repetition is they both look pretty preoccupied.

STUDENT: But it's also a kind of rupture. They aren't looking at each other. They are in different jobs, are inside or outside, sitting or standing. Maybe a call to attention through lots of direct contrasts?

TEACHER: But what's it all mean? How can we interpret all these details and what they mean when they work together?

STUDENT: Though they have different jobs, they are in the same situation.

STUDENT: Yeah, they are all trapped by work—or by some kind of role that must be work like the lady—but thinking about something else.

STUDENT: And maybe by how their work is different from their dreams—maybe that is what they are thinking about: what they'd rather be doing, how they want life to be different.

Voices From the Classroom

WHAT STUDENTS SAID ABOUT

"Prisons," From *New York: The Big City* by Will Eisner

TEACHER: All right, you writers in waiting! Time to think like an author. Given the patterns you see across the pictures, what do they all have in common? And what would be a good title that catches the topic of what they have in common? Talk with your partner! Go! [Waits one minute.] Lay it on me!

STUDENT: "Dreaming."

TEACHER: What makes you say so?

STUDENT: They are all looking out their windows and dreaming of something else, something that's outside. The sick boy is dreaming of spring and playing baseball as you can see by the mitt.

STUDENT: I agree. Because of their faces, I think the workers are dreaming of not working.

TEACHER: Wow! The way you supported your assertion about the topic and title and then backed it up with evidence and analysis helps me see your reasoning and tells me that you rock! Who's got a different title?

WHAT STUDENTS SAID ABOUT "Prisons," From *New York: The Big City* by Will Eisner

TEACHER: OK, readers! Talk with your partner about what the windows represent in each case. [Waits 90 seconds.] OK, my peoples, what do you think?

STUDENT: Invisible barriers.

TEACHER: What makes you say so?

STUDENT: A window is kind of invisible, but it still keeps you in or out, and you can see what you are missing out on.

TEACHER: You are applying a definition of a window and applying it to your case here—that's what good reasoners do. Who else has something?

STUDENT: Perspectives. Wait—I got this. Because the window is what they see the world through. Like a pair of glasses. It's their perspective because that's where they are standing and what they see.

TEACHER: Wow! That's just about all that I can say: Wow! What would someone else say about the reasoning just presented? What rules of notice were used in coming up with a title?

Lesson Steps: Day 2

Step 1

Introduce the lesson:

- Remind students that in the previous class they worked to understand a graphic novel spread by making comparisons *within* the text. Explain that sometimes artists and authors expect readers and viewers to make comparisons *across* texts, too. Note that this is especially true in parodies, where authors and artists create a new version of a work that they expect the audience to be familiar with.
- Tell students that as a class they are going to apply what they've learned about comparisons by looking back at a painting they've already studied, Bruegel's *Children's Games*, and then a modern version that parodies that painting.
- Project the original painting; if possible, zoom in on quadrants of the painting one at a time. Or, print an enlarged version of each quadrant for students to look at closely.
- Divide students into groups of four or five. Ask each group to divide a sheet of paper in half. Tell the groups to list what they noticed in the left-hand column and why they noticed it in the right-hand column.
- Ask them to identify and draw on specific examples of the four rules of notice whenever possible.
- Have groups share their results, adding to the anchor chart for rules of notice or naming what was noticed from the anchor chart.

Step 2

Discuss how the details are useful for understanding the topic of a text and the comment being made:

- Remind students that they've already discussed two topics the painting addresses: children and play. Ask them to write out the comment that the artist is making on each topic. Ask students how they used comparison to identify their comments.
- Ask students to share any other possible topics the painting is commenting on, and to justify their topic–comment statements with evidence from the painting. Once again, ask them to explain how they used comparison in making their justifications.

Lesson 1: Day 2

PURPOSE

- To learn how to employ rules of notice to compare

LENGTH

- Approximately 30–45 minutes

MATERIALS NEEDED

- Projector, zoomed in
- Printed copies of Bruegel's *Children's Games* (see Handout 2.2, "Two Views of Children's Play," in Chapter 2 for the image)
- Digital projection or access to Bruce Van Patter's parody: www.brucevanpatter.com/brueghel_painting.html. Note: Mouse over the original, and the parody will appear.

Step 3

Look at a parody in terms of points of comparison and contrast:

- Have students write what they notice individually.
- Ask:
    - *What point is Van Patter making about the difference between today's games and those of the original painting? Between children of the past and today? Between the experience of childhood then and now?*
    - *What is similar and different?*
    - *What does the artist do to let you know that you're supposed to make a comparison?*
    - *What comment is he making about childhood and/or child's play today, and how childhood/childhood play now compares to previous times?*

Extension: Day 2

Have students read short articles about the effects of technology, video games, and not playing outdoors. You can provide them, or you can ask students to find articles on these topics and bring them in to share. Good examples are excerpts from *Last Child in the Woods* by Richard Louv (2008) or from the Kaiser Family Foundation report *Generation* M^2 (Rideout, Foehr, & Roberts, 2009).

Lesson 2

Noticing the Text Structures in Nonfiction Texts

THINKING ALOUD

Introduction

In some think-alouds, we use professional texts that we want our students to be able to read with understanding and appreciation. Sometimes, though, it makes more sense to compose texts to use in the classroom. Following Langer (2001), we call such texts *simulated texts*. Simulated texts are texts designed to provide a particular kind of focused practice. In our experience, it's sometimes easier to write a text that focuses specifically on what we're planning to teach than it is to find one. Each of the three simulated texts in this lesson invites readers to employ one of the three different purposes for comparison we discussed in the introduction to this chapter: reasoning by analogy, evaluating, and interpreting.

Lesson Steps

Step 1

Introduce the lesson and its purpose:

- Recall that the work students did on the visual texts was informed by noticing and interpreting the use of comparisons.
- Explain that today they're going to see how text structure rules of notice operate in written texts.

Step 2

Model how you notice text structure cues:

- Distribute Handout 5.1, "Noticing Comparisons: Camping," to each student.
- Read aloud this text, and think aloud with it, highlighting rules of notice that help you identify the calls to make comparisons. See the sample think-aloud in the box that follows.

PURPOSE

- To see how experienced readers apply text structure rules of notice, and then to apply those same strategies

LENGTH

- 45 minutes

MATERIALS NEEDED

- Class sets of Handouts 5.1, 5.2, and 5.3 (or write and use your own texts):
  - Handout 5.1, "Noticing Comparisons: Camping"
  - Handout 5.2, "Noticing Comparisons: Class Election"
  - Handout 5.3, "Noticing Comparisons: Spring Dance"
- Anchor chart of rules of notice begun in Lesson 1

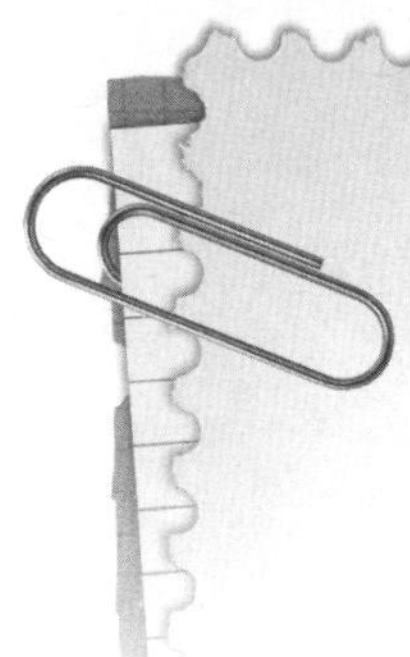

SAMPLE THINK-ALOUD

Lesson 2. Noticing the Text Structures in Nonfiction Texts: Thinking Aloud

Camping

Steve was totally prepared!

That's a direct statement.

This time

"This" is a text structure cue word—compared to a "last" time. The very short sentence is kind of a rupture and implies a comparison between this time and last time.

he had made a camping list for his trip.

So he must not have made a list last time.

He had his friends double-check the list. He rehearsed how he would go through each day and what he would do; considered all the problems that might occur, from waking to eating to hiking to sleeping; and checked his list against the equipment required for each task or problem on his list.

He is listing strategies for making a list. I need to see every item on the list as an implied comparison to what he didn't do last time.

He laid out all the gear and checked it against the list. In contrast

Here he's making a direct statement of comparison.

to the last trip

"Last trip" is another direct statement.

when he forgot several essential items including his tent poles, this time would be better.

Text structure cue words of comparison! So the difference between this time and the last time is pretty clear. I think the author is telling us something about the importance of preparation. And maybe about special cases that require special preparation—like camping—because you can't easily solve problems when they come up.

Step 3

Have students comment on the think-aloud:

- Ask: *What sentence do you think is the strongest signal of the comparison text structure?*
- Note that the think-aloud identifies two topics about which the comparison suggests a comment: preparation and camping. Ask students to explain what comment the text is making on preparing for camping, then what comment it is making on being prepared for other activities.

Step 4

Pair up students to do their own think-alouds:

- Distribute Handout 5.2, "Noticing Comparisons: Class Election," to each pair.
- Have the partners alternate sentences, reading and commenting, as they take over the thinking aloud.

Step 5

Ask students to reflect and write out notes about what comparisons they noticed and how they were tipped off to notice these comparisons.

- For example, ask:
  - *What rules of notice did you use?*

Step 6

Lead a whole-class discussion on the student pairs' think-alouds:

- Ask:
  - *What comparisons did you notice?*
  - *What in the text made you notice those comparisons?*
- Record any new examples of rules of notice on the anchor chart begun in Lesson 1.
- Note that one purpose of comparison is to allow people to evaluate. Ask students how they would advise Fiona to vote.
- Tell students that one topic of the text is high school.
- Ask: *What comment is the text making about high school?*
- Discuss this issue as a whole class. Focus on how the comparisons of the candidates help establish that comment.
- Have students identify other topics (e.g., leadership), the comments on these topics, and how comparisons help to make those comments.

Step 7

Assign students to form new pairs to do another think-aloud:

- Distribute Handout 5.3, "Noticing Comparisons: Spring Dance," to each pair.
- Have student pairs do another think-aloud, alternating reading of each sentence, then reflecting on what they noticed and how they knew to notice it, and how comparisons were part of their noticing.

Step 8

Lead a whole-class discussion on the pairs' think-alouds:

- Ask:
  - *What comparisons did you notice?*
  - *What in the text made you notice those comparisons?*
- Record any new examples of rules of notice on the anchor chart begun in Lesson 1.
- Tell students that one purpose of comparison is to reason by analogy—that is, to draw a conclusion about something based on what happened in a similar situation. Ask students what they think Janine is going to say.
- Ask them what topics this little story is addressing, and what comments it is making on those topics.

Step 9

Review what students learned:

- Review the rules of notice students applied for noticing comparison.
- Note that they used those comparisons for three distinct purposes:
  - To reason by analogy
  - To evaluate
  - To interpret (i.e., to use comparison to understand topics and comments made about something beyond the specifics of the comparison)

Extension

Invite students to record a think-aloud on a text of their own selection that makes uses of comparison to share in pairs.

Noticing Comparisons: Camping

Steve was totally prepared! This time he had made a camping list for his trip.

He had his friends double-check the list. He rehearsed how he would go through each day and what he would do; considered all the problems that might occur, from waking to eating to hiking to sleeping; and checked his list against the equipment required for each task or problem on his list. He laid out all the gear and checked it against the list. In contrast to the last trip when he forgot several essential items including his tent poles, this time would be better.

Available for download at **http://resources.corwin.com/divingdeep-nonfiction**

Handout 5.2

Noticing Comparisons: Class Election

Fiona had a problem: She did not know for whom to vote in the election for class president. Jessica, a cheerleader and one of the most popular kids in the class, was running. Jessica focused her campaign on the importance of building school spirit. In her speech, she talked about why that's important. Fiona had to give it to her. At least she talked about more than football and basketball. Jessica said it was just as important for people to support the Arts Festival and the choir. Fiona wondered how Jessica expected to do that. Fiona was a big ice cream fan, and she found herself often using ice cream metaphors to help her think about situations. So what was Jessica? Straight vanilla.

Skye was running too. She was one of the green kids who were always talking about some environmental issue. Unlike Jessica, she didn't talk about any school activities. Instead, she talked about the importance of recycling. She had really specific ideas about how to reduce waste, like starting a composting initiative. But jeez, she could sure go on and on and on. If Skye were an ice cream cone, she'd be a mint and vanilla swirl, heavy on the mint.

And then there was Jordan. Fiona was really surprised that he decided to run. She always thought Jordan was a burnout who didn't really care. But when she heard his speech, she was a bit surprised. He sure did more campaigning *against* things than *for* them. He wanted to get rid of the need to get passes to go to the restroom. And to abolish weekend homework. And no more rules about wearing hats to class. But he made his arguments in a surprisingly intellectual way. He talked about freedom and how students needed to have the ability to do more than school if they were to flourish. It was pretty interesting, really. Not like Skye who was kind of a one-trick pony and who went on and

(Continued)

on and on about the same stuff. Jordan's speech had given Fiona something new to think about. Jordan's flavor? Maybe one of those that sound really weird but might be really good like bacon and maple.

Handout 5.3

Noticing Comparisons: Spring Dance

It was spring again. And what did spring mean to Devin? Allergies. But something worse than allergies, too: the spring formal. Why that stupid dance was so important was beyond him, but it was. And last year he really got sucked in. Devin was a quiet kid. He didn't have many really good friends in school. He was more interested in stuff outside school than in. Music. Art. He'd go to the city to a gallery or a museum and stay for hours. Most of the kids didn't get it. But they thought it was cool that he knew so much about what was happening. They'd sometimes ask Devin whom he was listening to, and he'd share tracks from the indie bands he'd discovered. Sometimes he'd wear a T-shirt that he made modeled on the work of a favorite artist. Nobody in school dressed like Devin. But he always got a lot of nods when he wore something new. So Devin thought that it wasn't out of the question that he could get a date. But man, asking was hard. It took him until 10 days before the dance last year to ask Maura. He didn't really know her well. They sat at the same table once at lunch and talked a bit. All of the other cheerleaders seemed surprised she sat next to him. But that talk went pretty well. They didn't have much in common, but she seemed interested in what he had to say. So he was really pretty hopeful when he asked. But no luck. She blushed and told him that she had a date. She said she'd been seeing the guy for months. Shot down. And he heard the whispers: "How did he have the nerve to ask Maura?" It shouldn't have bothered him. He really didn't want to go that much. But it seemed like all the other students were able to figure this dating thing out. Devin's mom told him that the spring formal was just an experience. But she said that it was maybe one that he'd want to have.

Devin thought his mom might be right. Especially if he could go with Janine. Janine was a dancer. Devin saw her once at a modern dance show.

(Continued)

Handout 5.3 cont.

And he heard her talking about dance to her friends in their English class. They worked together on a project to make a modern-day version of a scene from Shakespeare. That turned out pretty cool. The teacher liked it anyway. They actually did an animation. Janine waved when she saw him. And he asked around and found out that she didn't have a date. So this time he didn't wait until the last minute to ask. With a month left before the dance, Devin decided to ask Janine.

Lesson 3

Noticing the Text Structures in Nonfiction Texts

PRACTICE IN MINIATURE

PURPOSE

- To apply the rules of notice to more complex texts

LENGTH

- Approximately 45 minutes

MATERIALS NEEDED

- Class sets of Handout 5.4, "Noticing Comparisons: More Practice"
- Anchor chart of rules of notice

Introduction

To get a quick understanding of how important comparison is, take a look at the texts provided in Appendix B of the Common Core State Standards in the section on Informational Texts: Science, Mathematics, and Technical Subjects for Grades 6–8. You'll see that comparisons abound. We've selected three of those texts that call for comparison for our practice in miniature.

Before we present the lesson, we'd like to explain how we sequenced the lessons. As we have shared, we find visual texts to be the most easily accessible, so we started there. The simulated think-aloud texts move students into the realm of written texts; however, they have been designed to highlight comparison in a way that authentic texts do not always do. The texts we use in this lesson should ratchet up the rigor a bit, but because they are so short, we find students are ready to tackle them, as short texts are typically easier to handle than longer ones.

Lesson Steps

Step 1

Introduce the lesson:

- Explain that today students will be applying what they've learned to a new set of texts.
- Note that the texts they'll be working with are excerpts from the kinds of texts they'll be expected to read and understand as they go through school.

Step 2

Engage students in applying what they have learned to a new set of texts:

- Distribute Handout 5.4, "Noticing Comparisons: More Practice," one copy for each student.

- Divide students into groups of four or five.
- Read the excerpt from *The Number Devil: A Mathematical Adventure* by Hans Magnus Enzensberger together.
- Have student groups write their answers to the questions that follow the excerpt.
- Circulate as students work. Note especially interesting ideas and tell students to be prepared to share them.

Step 3

Lead a whole-class discussion on the groups' work:

- Highlight the rules of notice students employed. Add any new examples to the anchor chart.
- Also track on the chart the different topic–comment statements students make. Probe for evidence that supports them. See a sample exchange in the "Voices From the Classroom" box that follows.

Step 4

Provide repeated practice:

- Read the excerpt from "Space Probe" in *Astronomy & Space: From the Big Bang to the Big Crunch*, edited by Phillis Engelbert.
- Have students work together in groups to answer the questions that follow the excerpt.
- Repeat the process used with the previous excerpt by circulating as students work and noting especially interesting ideas. Tell students to be prepared to share them.

Step 5

Lead a whole-class discussion on the groups' work:

- Once again, highlight the rules of notice students employed. Add any new examples to the anchor chart.
- As you did in Step 3, track the different topic–comment statements students make. Probe for evidence that supports them. See the sample exchange in the "Voices From the Classroom" box that follows.

Step 6

Provide additional practice:

- Read the excerpt from "The Evolution of the Grocery Bag" by Henry Petroski.
- In groups, have students work on the questions that follow the excerpt.
- Once again, circulate as students work, noting especially interesting ideas and telling students to prepare to share them.

Voices From the Classroom

WHAT STUDENTS SAID ABOUT *The Number Devil: A Mathematical Adventure* by Hans Magnus Enzensberger

TEACHER: So what's the topic of this piece?

STUDENT: Math.

TEACHER: And what's the comment?

STUDENT: Something about what math is?

TEACHER: So what comparison does the author make to math in order to make the comment?

STUDENT: Sums.

TEACHER: Say some more.

STUDENT: He says most mathematicians are bad at sums.

TEACHER: Why did you notice that?

STUDENT: It's a rupture. Most people think math *is* sums. It also surprised me, so I guess it was a rule of reader's response too.

TEACHER: But what does the author think?

STUDENT: That real math is about much more than sums.

TEACHER: So that's the comment. What does that mean anyway?

Voices From the Classroom

WHAT STUDENTS SAID ABOUT "Space Probe" From *Astronomy & Space: From the Big Bang to the Big Crunch*

TEACHER: So what's the comparison?

STUDENT: Space probes versus planetary probes.

TEACHER: Other groups?

STUDENT: We said that it's *Voyager 1* and *2*.

STUDENT: No, it can't be that. They're too much the same. We thought it was earlier versus later probes.

TEACHER: Three ideas. Which is it?

STUDENT: I think all three work. The comparisons all show that despite all the differences the probes have both been really useful. That was a call to attention to me.

TEACHER: How did you notice that?

Step 7

Lead a whole-class discussion on the groups' work:

- Highlight the rules of notice students employed. Add any new examples to the anchor chart.
- Once again, track the different topic–comment statements students make.
- See the sample exchange in the "Voices From the Classroom" box that follows.

Step 8

Engage students in a comparative analysis of the three excerpts:

- Have students work individually to rank the three excerpts on two dimensions. Ask:
  - *Which excerpt most clearly signaled the comparison?*
  - *In which excerpt was the comparison most important?*
- Lead a whole-class discussion of students' rankings. Create a matrix on the board that looks like the following and tally the results:

	Clarity (1 = most clear, 2 = second clearest, 3 = least clear)	Importance (1 = most important, 2 = second most important, 3 = least important)
Math		
Space Probe		
Paper Bag		

- If students agree, focus on the reasons for their agreement, highlighting mentions of the rules of notice as they appear.
- In the more likely event that students don't agree, focus on the reasons for their disagreement, highlighting mentions of the rules of notice as they appear.

Step 9

Review what students learned:

- Review the rules of notice students applied for noticing comparison.
- Note how important recognizing the comparisons was to understanding the topics and comments the authors were making.

Voices From the Classroom

WHAT STUDENTS SAID ABOUT "The Evolution of the Grocery Bag" by Henry Petroski

TEACHER: OK, how about this one? What's the comparison?

STUDENT: We thought it was about what happened compared to what could have happened.

TEACHER: Can you explain?

STUDENT: Yeah. Imagine not having a bag to put stuff in. Or if what you had was hard to work with. Groceries would just pile up.

TEACHER: What makes you think that's the comparison? What rule of notice did you use?

STUDENT: We mostly used the rule of the reader's response.

TEACHER: Tell me more.

STUDENT: Look at the second paragraph. "Magical." "Fascinated." He's really pushing for an emotional response.

Noticing Comparisons: More Practice

Excerpt 1

From *The Number Devil: A Mathematical Adventure* by Hans Magnus Enzensberger

"I see," said the number devil with a wry smile. "I have nothing against you, Mr. Bockel, but that kind of problem has nothing whatever to do with what I'm interested in. Do you want to know something? Most genuine mathematicians are bad at sums. Besides, they have no time to waste on them. That's what pocket calculators are for. I assume you have one."

"Sure, but we're not allowed to use them in school."

"I see," said the number devil. "That's all right. There's nothing wrong with a little addition and subtraction. You never know when your battery will die on you. But mathematics, my boy, that's something else again! . . .

"The thing that makes numbers so devilish is precisely that they are simple. And you don't need a calculator to prove it. You need one thing and one thing only: one. With one—I am speaking of the numeral of course—you can do almost anything. If you are afraid of large numbers—let's say five million seven hundred and twenty-three thousand eight hundred and twelve—all you have to do is start with

1 + 1

1 + 1 + 1

1 + 1 + 1 + 1

1 + 1 + 1 + 1 + 1

. . . and go on until you come to five million etcetera. You can't tell me that's too complicated for you, can you?"

Source: Enzensberger, H. M. (1997). *The number devil: A mathematical adventure.* New York, NY: Holt.

(Continued)

Questions for Group Discussion

1. What comparison(s) is the author asking you to make?

____

____

2. What rules of notice did you apply in recognizing the importance of the comparison(s)?

____

____

3. What work does the author accomplish through the comparison(s)?

____

____

4. What is the topic and comment being made through the comparison(s)?

____

____

5. How do(es) the comparison(s) help you understand the topic and comment the author is making?

____

____

(Continued)

Excerpt 2

From "Space Probe" in *Astronomy & Space: From the Big Bang to the Big Crunch*, edited by Phillis Engelbert

A space probe is an unpiloted spacecraft that leaves Earth's orbit to explore the Moon, planets, asteroids, comets, or other objects in outer space as directed by onboard computers and/or instructions sent from Earth. The purpose of such missions is to make scientific observations, such as taking pictures, measuring atmospheric conditions, and collecting soil samples, and to bring or report the data back to Earth.

Numerous space probes have been launched since the former Soviet Union first fired *Luna 1* toward the Moon in 1959. Probes have now visited each of the eight planets in the solar system.

In fact, two probes—*Voyager 1* and *Voyager 2*—are approaching the edge of the solar system, for their eventual trip into the interstellar medium. By January 2008 *Voyager 1* was about 9.4 billion miles (15.2 billion kilometers) from the Sun and in May 2008 it entered the heliosheath (the boundary where the solar wind is thought to end), which is the area that roughly divides the solar system from interstellar space. *Voyager 2* is not quite as far as its sister probe. *Voyager 1* is expected to be the first human space probe to leave the solar system. Both *Voyager* probes are still transmitting signals back to Earth. They are expected to help gather further information as to the true boundary of the solar system.

The earliest probes traveled to the closest extraterrestrial target, the Moon. The former Soviet Union launched a series of *Luna* probes that provided humans with first pictures of the far side of the Moon. In 1966, *Luna 9* made the first successful landing on the Moon and sent back television footage from the Moon's surface. The National Aeronautics and Space Administration (NASA) initially made several unsuccessful attempts to send a probe to the Moon. Not until 1964 did a *Ranger* probe reach its mark and send back thousands of pictures. Then, a few months after *Luna 9*, NASA landed *Surveyor* on the Moon.

(Continued)

Handout 5.4 cont.

In the meantime, NASA was moving ahead with the first series of planetary probes, called *Mariner*. *Mariner 2* first reached the planet Venus in 1962. Later *Mariner* spacecrafts flew by Mars in 1964 and 1969, providing detailed images of that planet. In 1971, *Mariner 9* became the first spacecraft to orbit Mars. During its year in orbit, *Mariner 9*'s two television cameras transmitted footage of an intense Martian dust storm, as well as images of 90 percent of the planet's surface and the two Martian natural satellites (moons).

Encounters were also made with Mars in 1976 by the U.S. probes *Viking 1* and *Viking 2*. Each *Viking* spacecraft consisted of both an orbiter and a lander. *Viking 1* made the first successful soft landing on Mars on July 20, 1976. Soon after, *Viking 2* landed on the opposite side of the planet. The *Viking* orbiters made reports on the Martian weather and photographed almost the entire surface of the planet.

Source: Engelbert, P. (Ed.). (1997). *Astronomy & space: From the big bang to the big crunch.* Farmington Hills, MI: Gale.

Questions for Group Discussion

1. What comparison(s) is the author asking you to make?

2. What rules of notice did you apply in recognizing the importance of the comparison(s)?

3. What work does the author accomplish through the comparison(s)? What is the topic and the comment being made?

4. How do(es) the comparison(s) help you understand the topic and comment the author is making?

(Continued)

Excerpt 3

From *"The Evolution of the Grocery Bag"* by Henry Petroski

That much-reviled bottleneck known as the American supermarket checkout lane would be an even greater exercise in frustration were it not for several technological advances. The Universal Product Code and the decoding laser scanner, introduced in 1974, tally a shopper's groceries far more quickly and accurately than the old method of inputting each purchase manually into a cash register. But beeping a large order past the scanner would have led only to a faster pileup of cans and boxes down the line, where the bagger works, had it not been for the introduction, more than a century earlier, of an even greater technological masterpiece: the square-bottomed paper bag.

The geometry of paper bags continues to hold a magical appeal for those of us who are fascinated by how ordinary things are designed and made. Originally, grocery bags were created on demand by storekeepers, who cut, folded, and pasted sheets of paper, making versatile containers into which purchases could be loaded for carrying home. The first paper bags manufactured commercially are said to have been made in Bristol, England, in the 1840s. In 1852, a "Machine for Making Bags of Paper" was patented in America by Francis Wolle, of Bethlehem, Pennsylvania. According to Wolle's own description of the machine's operation, "pieces of paper of suitable length are given out from a roll of the required width, cut off from the roll and otherwise suitably cut to the required shape, folded, their edges pasted and lapped, and formed into complete and perfect bags." The "perfect bags" produced at the rate of eighteen hundred per hour by Wolle's machine were, of course, not perfect, nor was his machine. The history of design has yet to see the development of a perfect object, though it has seen many satisfactory ones and many substantially improved ones. The concept of comparative improvement is embedded in the paradigm for invention, the better

(Continued)

mousetrap. No one is ever likely to lay claim to a "best" mousetrap, for that would preclude the inventor himself from coming up with a still better mousetrap without suffering the embarrassment of having previously declared the search complete. As with the mousetrap, so with the bag.

Source: Petroski, H. (2003). The evolution of the grocery bag. *American Scholar, 72*(4), 99.

Handout 5.4 cont.

Questions for Group Discussion

1. What comparison(s) is the author asking you to make?

2. What rules of notice did you apply in recognizing the importance of the comparison(s)?

3. What work does the author accomplish through the comparison(s)? What is the topic and the comment being made?

4. How do(es) the comparison(s) help you understand the topic and comment the author is making?

Available for download at **http://resources.corwin.com/divingdeep-nonfiction**

Lesson 4

Noticing the Text Structures in Nonfiction Texts

QUESTIONING

PURPOSE

- To learn Hillocks's questioning hierarchy; apply it to notice important literal information, fill textual gaps, and see connections among details; and use what was noticed to make authorial and structural generalizations

LENGTH

- Approximately 90 to 120 minutes (can be split into three class periods if needed)

MATERIALS NEEDED

- Any rich, complex, well-constructed text that students are familiar with. We draw our examples from Jim Murphy's *The Great Fire* (1995)
- Copies of the text for each student
- A document camera or board that all students can see when you write model questions
- Materials to create an anchor chart

Introduction

The power of questioning strategies is actualized when students are able to

- Generate questions
- Apply that strategy to a wide variety of texts
- Use the strategy to help them get at complex levels of textual meaning

Our all-time favorite questioning scheme is George Hillocks's (1980) questioning hierarchy. Hillocks devised his hierarchy to evaluate students' understanding of literature, but we have found it useful for helping students understand almost any carefully constructed text.

The hierarchy consists of a precise set of question types based on the assertion that "before students can deal with abstractions . . . they must be able to deal with the literal and inferential content of the work" (Hillocks, 1980, p. 54). The Hillocks hierarchy uses seven levels of questions to move students from the literal to the inferential, and then to two kinds of generalizations:

- *Authorial generalizations*, or themes about the world expressed in the work, such as the topic–comment structures we've been working with throughout this book
- *Structural generalizations*, or how the author constructed the text to make meaning, express his or her ideas, and affect the reader

In our experience, the hierarchy fosters like no other scheme a level of understanding about how texts are constructed. You'll see how it encompasses but then goes beyond the different kinds of readerly activities required by Question–Answer Relationships (QARs), Question the Author

(QtA), the KEEP questioning scheme (introduced in Chapter 4, Lesson 4, page 138), and other questioning strategies. This is particularly true with Hillocks's Level 7 question on structural generalizations.

Hillocks slices question types more finely than the QAR scheme does to show different kinds of factual (Right There) and inferential (Think and Search) questions that depend on each other. The cumulative QAR from Chapter 3 (see Lesson 4, page 89) provides a great way to practice cuing students in to this interdependence of different details and the interdependence of different reading moves, strategies, and questions, but Hillocks goes further.

Factual questions are divided into three types:

1. Questions that ask for basic stated information
2. Questions that ask for key details
3. Questions that ask for stated relationships between key ideas or events

Inferential questions are divided into two types:

1. Those looking for *simple implied relationships* (a few ideas that the reader must connect that are close to each other)
2. Those looking for *complex implied relationships* (ideas that the reader must connect that can be multiple and stretch throughout a text)

These question types, in turn, provide the basis for understanding authorial and structural generalizations. It is important to remember that this scheme is hierarchical (i.e., the questions on one level are prerequisite to and provide support for answering questions at the next level). In other words, unless students get the facts in order, they cannot make inferences from these facts. If students do not make simple and complex inferences, they cannot infer an author's generalizations. And if they can't identify authorial generalizations, then they cannot figure out how a text was constructed to express those generalizations.

In our own teaching, we've found that some of our students stall out at simple implied relationships, and many of our students stall out at the level of asking and answering complex implied relationship questions. This means that they cannot figure out theme or how texts are constructed to express theme. These generalization strategies are the hallmarks of expert reading in life and necessary to meeting most standards. The unique power of the Hillocks scheme is that it gives students practice with the prerequisite steps to complex inferencing, focuses attention on those steps, and then leads students to generalize about textual meaning and structuring based on their inferencing, making this roadblock easier to overcome.

Lesson Steps

Step 1

Introduce the lesson:

- Tell students that you are going to model a powerful questioning scheme that helps readers move from different layers of literal comprehension to work with inferencing and generalizing that expert readers always do with texts. Emphasize that this is a questioning scheme that readers can use *during* and *after* reading to deepen comprehension, foster inferencing and generalizing, and generally come to appreciate how texts are constructed purposefully and carefully to create specific meanings and effects. This is essential to expert reading, and also to expert composing!
- Explain that the first set of questions are literal and can be classified as "Just the Facts!" questions to help them establish the facts.
- Make sure each student has a copy of the text so that everyone can refer to it and follow your thinking.

Step 2

Model and justify examples of the first set of questions: "Just the Facts!"

- Introduce the first three question types and record them on an anchor chart:
  - Questions that ask for basic stated information
  - Questions that ask for key details
  - Questions that ask for stated relationships between key ideas or events
- Model how you generate questions of each type and how you check that the question is that type.
- Generate a question that asks about really obvious but important *basic stated information* that is repeated and can be found right in the text.
  - For example, ask: *Where did the fire take place?*
- *Check the question type: The rules of notice help students generate questions about details that are absolutely essential to carry forward throughout a reading. For example, this question highlights obvious basic stated information that readers need to know and remember to make sense of many other details like the maps in the book, why the city was so susceptible to fire, and so on. You can check the question type by confirming that the information provided in the answer is important background to carry through a reading.*

- Create a question that asks about a *key detail* that is very important to the plot or trajectory of the text and helps move this plot or movement forward.
    - For example, ask: *Where exactly in the city did the fire start?*
- *Check the question type: This detail is expressed at the beginning of the book and is referred to on occasion throughout the book. It's a key detail because it is important to how and where the fire spread and the blame that was placed on the poor, and what happened as a result in the aftermath of the fire. You can check your question type by confirming that it connects to later details in ways that explain deeper consequences, implications, and meanings.*
- Create a question that focuses attention on a *direct statement* about the relationship between two events or details:
    - For example, ask: *How did the richer and poorer sections of the city compare in their susceptibility to fire?*
- *Check the question type: The author directly states that both the richer and poorer sections of town were built mostly of wood, had buildings crammed together, and had raised wooden sidewalks. Because the comparison is explicitly made and explained, this is a stated relationship question. You can confirm your question by explicitly noting how at least two ideas are related, compared, or contrasted. In this case, the text directly states that the rich and poor sections did not differ very much in the ways that made them susceptible to fire.*

Step 3

Reflect as a class, then ask students to generate their own questions of each type:

- Ask students if they have questions about each question type and how it works.
- Group students in pairs or triads to generate a new question of each type.
- Circulate and help as needed.

Step 4

Invite students to share and justify their new questions:

- Have the pairs or triads share their questions and justify why each is the type of question they identify.
- Identify *productive struggle* (i.e., expending effort with a strategy and learning something new through the struggle) and strategies for getting through this productive struggle successfully. See the sample exchange in the "Voices From the Classroom" box that follows.

Voices From the Classroom

HELPING STUDENTS **Identify Question Types**

Julie and Tanya posed the question, "What was unusual about the weather on October 8?"

Because both the temperature and the wind were unusual, and because the text did not explicitly say that the warmth caused the wind, they were unsure if this was a literal-level question.

TEACHER: Can the question be answered by pointing at literal details?

STUDENTS: Yes.

TEACHER: Since it can, is it a *literal* or *inferential* question?

STUDENTS (quickly): *Literal!*

TEACHER: Are these details important and explanatory of what happens later in the story?

STUDENTS: *Yes!*

TEACHER: You're right—this is in fact a key detail question because even though the answer requires two different details, those are stated together. Remember, you can ask yourselves those same questions to confirm a key detail question:

1. Can I point directly at the answer in the text?
2. Is the detail important and explanatory to what happens later in the text?

- Discuss how and why the question types are important to literal comprehension and how stated relationship questions set readers up for inferring. As Jeff says to his students:
    - *"Expert reading mostly involves making inferences about main ideas and generalizations!"*

Step 5

Model and justify examples of the second set of questions: "Connecting the Dots"

- Tell students you will now demonstrate how to ask *inferential-level questions*, which are much harder but also much more interesting, fun, and expert! Explain that these inferential questions depend on literal comprehension, and that these question types will require students to see connections, fill in gaps, and figure out what these connections mean.
- Explain that inferential questions can be thought of as "Connecting the Dots" questions to help them figure things out. Add this to the anchor chart.
- Explain that there are two types of inferential questions and add them to the anchor chart:
    - Those looking for and explaining *simple implied relationships* (the ideas to be connected are usually few and are close to each other in the text)
    - Those looking for *complex implied relationships* (the ideas to be connected can be multiple and stretch throughout a text)
- Explain that you'll create the first type of simple inferential question. The question should depend on two or three clues that are close together and work together in some way.
- Note that the question should ask the answerer to connect the dots to determine a solution or meaning not stated in the text.
    - For example, ask: *How did Chicago in October of the year of the Great Fire compare to Chicago in previous years?*
- *Check the question type: The author spends some time exploring why the year of the Great Fire was different in terms of weather patterns and human preparedness, but he does not explicitly state how these differences led to the fire. Remember, this kind of question is called a simple implied relationship question because the reader must notice various details close to each other (within a page or so) and explain their connection and relationship.*
- Reinforce that simple implied relationship questions are *not* explicitly answered—the reader has to do the work of connecting the dots. Ask: *What kind of question is it if the relationship is explicitly explained?*
    - Students' answer should be "A stated relationship!"

- Explain that you'll now create the second type of inferential question, a complex implied relationships question. This should be a question that requires the reader to use many details from throughout an extended section or the whole text to arrive at a solution or conclusion that isn't explicitly stated.
    - For example, ask: *What are the three biggest reasons why the poor and immigrants were disproportionately affected during and after the fire?*
    - Follow up by asking: *How are these reasons related? Which reason do you think is most important, and why?*
- *Check the question type: This set of questions requires readers to think about an issue that runs through the text, but is never directly addressed in its entirety. To answer such questions, readers have to make a comparison between the poor and immigrants and all other groups mentioned in the story, and they must do it by finding details spread out through the text and setting up the comparison and its meaning. They also need to know how to rank the importance of ideas on their own since the author does not provide this.*
    - Remember that answering and asking complex implied relationship questions is the hallmark of an expert reader. Understanding complex implied relationships will allow your students to ask and answer generalization questions—which in turn will allow them to understand the deep meanings of texts and how they were created! Totally exciting!

Step 6

Reflect as a class, then ask students to generate their own questions of each type:

- Ask students if they have any questions about either inferential question type and how it works.
- Group students in pairs or triads to generate a question of each type.
- Circulate and coach as needed.

Step 7

Invite students to share and evaluate each other's questions:

- Have students share their new questions and justify why each is the type of question they identify.
- Identify strategies for successfully getting through the productive struggle. See the sample exchange in the "Voices From the Classroom" box that follows.
- Ask students to reflect and name how the two inferential question types help readers see connections, make inferences, and recognize how various parts of the book work together.

HELPING STUDENTS
Identify More Question Types

Julie and Tanya built off their key detail question to ask, "How did the high temperature contribute to the fire and its consequences?"

They wondered whether this was an inferential question because the relationships between heat and drying wood, heat and wind, heat and human lethargy, and many other factors were not directly stated but could be inferred, as well as because the wind and its direction spread the fire.

TEACHER:	What would be required to answer the question?
STUDENTS (talking over each other):	That it was super hot! That everything was wood! Even the sidewalks were wood! The wood was dried out. The heat was making the wind blow! Everybody was tired! The O'Learys went to bed early they were so tired!
TEACHER:	Are these details explicitly connected by the author?
STUDENTS:	*No!*
TEACHER:	This makes the question a complex inferential one. Are the details to answer this question in one specific place, or are they spread throughout the book?
STUDENTS:	Spread throughout the book!
TEACHER:	Yes, there are lots of details spread over long sections. Yet by connecting them we see deeper meanings.

Step 8

Model asking generalization questions: "But What Does It Mean, and How Does It Mean That?"

- Tell students there are two more question types and that these have to do with making generalizations—which is important to taking usable ideas from a text for application in one's life.
  - *Authorial generalizations*, or questions that reveal themes about the world, such as topic–comment structures
  - *Structural generalizations*, or questions that reveal how the author constructed the text to express those ideas—and other effects
- Record the above definitions on the anchor chart.
- Explain that you will now model how to ask the generalization-level questions, and that these are much more challenging than the "Just the Facts!" and even the "Connecting the Dots" questions. These will require the students to see connections, fill in gaps, *and* figure out what these connections mean in terms of real-life takeaways.
- Explain that these types of questions can be classified as "But What Does It Mean?" and "How Does It Mean That?" questions. Create a question about an authorial generalization the text expresses about the world, or about life and how to live.
  - For example, ask: *What statement is the author making about how and what we learn from the past, particularly in terms of disaster preparation?*
- *Check the question type: Answering this question requires inferencing since the question is never directly answered, and requires generalization because it asks readers to take what they have read and generalize from it to actual behaviors and policies that exist in the world.*
- Create a question about a structural generalization that explores how the text was structured to express the authorial generalization.
  - For example, ask: *What does the author accomplish by comparing the stories about less powerful people to those of more powerful people?*
- *Check the question type: This question highlights both the individual stories told and the implicit comparison made between them to get at how the text was structured to express meaning and effect. The author used these comparisons to make a generalization about the effects of the fire on different classes of citizens. So the question focuses on how the author created meaning and effect.*

Step 9

Reflect as a class, ask questions, then generate questions of each type:

- Ask students if they have questions about each question type and how it works.
- Group students in pairs or triads to generate a question of each type.
- Circulate and coach as needed.

Step 10

Invite students to share and justify each other's questions:

- Have students share their new questions and justify why each is the type of question they identify.
- Identify strategies for successfully getting through the productive struggle.
- See the sample exchange in the "Voices From the Classroom" box that follows.
- Discuss how and why the question types are important to generalizing and why generalizing is so important to expert reading—and writing.
- Review how various parts of the book are working together to set readers up for generalizing and how comparison is absolutely essential to creating the meanings and effects the author is trying to achieve.

Extension

Challenge students to work together in pairs or small groups—or alone if they are reading—to write one question of each type for another text, perhaps from their free reading.

HELPING STUDENTS Identify Question Types

Julie and Tanya offered a question that they were not sure was an *authorial generalization question*: "What is the author saying about the role of pure chance in suffering from or avoiding disaster?"

The teacher once again encouraged students to justify their thinking by considering what is required to answer this question, asking, "Does this question require inferencing?"

STUDENTS: *Yes!*

TEACHER: How do you know?

STUDENTS: The answer isn't there! You have to figure it out!

TEACHER: Is the answer to this question a generalization that you could think with and use to think about other disasters?

STUDENTS: Yes!

TEACHER: Who can prove it?

STUDENT, (raising his hand): When we had the wildfires last year, it was just chance where it started and what houses burned down. It depended on the wind and where the firefighters could get to. Just like in Chicago.

TEACHER: So we can apply the generalization to fires in other places, like here in Boise. So it works as a generalization because it works across cases.

For *structural generalization*, Lily and Ave offered, "How does the author use the comparison of different stories to focus the reader on the role of chance?"

TEACHER: Does this question require inferencing?

STUDENTS: Yes!

TEACHER: How do you know?

STUDENTS: The answer isn't there! You have to figure it out!

TEACHER: Does this question focus on what the author did to make one of his points?

STUDENTS: Yes.

TEACHER: How do you know?

STUDENT: They said, "*How* does the author do things like compare stories?" so they are focusing on what the author did to talk about chance. Like comparing how different people had different things happen to them.

Lesson
5

Noticing the Text Structures in Nonfiction Texts

WRITING AND RESPONDING

Introduction

One instructional strategy we use throughout this book is the sentence frame. As you've seen, sentence frames provide students with something akin to a fill-in-the-blank structure so they can practice writing sentences of the sort that experienced writers fluently produce. Although sentence frames resemble traditional fill-in-the-blank exercises, they function quite differently. Whereas traditional fill-in-the-blank exercises are designed to reward simple recall, sentence frames require students to do more complex thinking. Indeed, as they are working with the frames, they must engage in the kind of thinking the targeted thought pattern (text structuring) requires. As Imbrenda (2016a) argues, "Sentence frames strike a careful balance between giving students too much and too little" (p. 65).

Lesson Steps

Step 1

Introduce the lesson:

- Explain that becoming better readers can help students become better writers and that becoming better and more reflective writers can help them become better readers.
- Note that they will be writing sentences designed to make readers notice that they need to make comparisons.

Step 2

Provide model sentences for students to analyze:

- Pass out copies of Handout 5.5, "Cuing Comparisons." Section A provides examples of three similar sentences that cue readers to attend to comparisons.
- Read through the sentences as a class, then ask students to work in pairs or triads to answer the questions at the bottom of Section A.

PURPOSE

- To learn how sentences can reveal the comparison text structure and apply knowledge of sentences that cue comparison to think about structuring texts

LENGTH

- Approximately 45–60 minutes

MATERIALS NEEDED

- Class copies of Handout 5.5, "Cuing Comparisons"
- Enough "mystery pot" sentences (see Chapter 3, page 96) for students to work on in pairs
- Materials to make an anchor chart

- When they are finished, discuss their answers as a whole class. Record the rules of notice they used on an anchor chart.
- Emphasize the use of the semicolon and a *logical linker* (i.e., an adverbial conjunction that provides a logical link between two different ideas) if you have not already done so. (We prefer to use the term *logical linker* since it is more transparent and usable for students than *adverbial conjunction*—see Smith & Wilhelm [2007] for a full explanation.)

Step 3

Invite small groups to compose and then share their own sentence frames using the same structure you used in your models:

- Group students in pairs or triads to write an example sentence using a semicolon and a logical linker to make a comparison or contrast.
- Ask students to share their responses. Add them to the anchor chart.

Step 4

Introduce another possible sentence frame:

- Provide a second example frame for comparison and contrast, such as "X and Y are similar in that they both _____, but X _____ while Y _____."
- Have students write a sentence using this pattern.
- Invite them to share their sentences in pairs or triads and ask each small group to select one sentence to share with the class.

Step 5

Move from writing sentences to structuring text:

- Explain to students that what they learned about individual sentences can help them structure texts.
- Have them look at Section B of Handout 5.5, "Cuing Comparisons."
- Ask students work in pairs or triads to put the sentences into the correct order.
- Explain that they need to explain how they figured the order out by using text structure rules of notice.

Step 6

Reflect as a class:

- Ask students to share:
    - *What sentence did you start with?*
    - *What rules of notice did you use to help make your decision?*

- Continue to ask students for the order of the sentences, once again probing for rules of notice they used.

Step 7

Continue practice using sentence-level cues to structure entire paragraphs:

- Pair up students to put the sentences from Section C of Handout 5.5, "Cuing Comparisons," into the correct order.
- Explain that they need to explain how they figured the order out by using text structure rules of notice.

Step 8

Reflect as a class:

- Once again, ask students to share what sentence they started with. Probe for the rules of notice they used in making their determination.
- Continue to ask students for the order of sentences, probing for rules of notice used.

Step 9

Review what students learned and encourage transfer:

- Note that students worked as writers and readers to signal and recognize comparison.
- Remind them to apply what they have learned in their future reading and writing.

Extension

Challenge students to collect sentences that invite comparisons and write their own examples from the models they collect. Post the examples around the classroom.

If students are up for it, try teaching the lesson with an extended mystery pot text, such as the one provided on the companion website at **http://resources.corwin.com/divingdeep-nonfiction**.

Cuing Comparisons

Section A

1. The teacher loved the writing of T. S. Eliot; however, her students did not see what the fuss was about.
2. The principal wanted the bathrooms to be shiny clean and made many rules to that end; nevertheless, the girls continued to complain that the room was too smoky and dirty to use.
3. At first, the team seemed to be playing well and everything was going in the goal; after that, everything seemed to go awry, and the players couldn't even complete a pass.

Questions for Group Discussion

- What do you notice about the sentences' shape and structure?

  ____

  ____

  ____

  ____

- What's the rule for structuring a sentence this way?

  ____

  ____

  ____

  ____

Section B

Scrambled Sentences: Bulldogs

Put the following sentences into the correct order:

___ 1. They were, however, originally bred to fight bulls (hence their name) and were ferocious and trained to be hardened to pain.

___ 2. Now, in spite of their terrifying looks, they are exceptionally gentle.

___ 3. Although the breed nearly died out when bull-baiting and dogfighting were outlawed in the 19th century, fanciers decided to breed out its savagery.

___ 4. But they are actually among the gentlest of breeds.

___ 5. Bulldogs appear to be quite vicious and mean.

(Continued)

Section C

Scrambled Sentences: Mammals in Winter

Put the following sentences into the correct order:

___ 1. Mammals have special problems staying alive in winter.

___ 2. The most obvious adaptation by animals active in winter is their protection by fur, like that of polar bears, horses, and dogs.

___ 3. Humans, in contrast, have no physical attributes to help them survive winter, so they must be creative in combining strategies like developing clothing, finding shelter and storing food, and migrating somewhere warmer.

___ 4. A final option is to move somewhere warmer: Many birds and other animals like reindeer just migrate to warmer climes.

___ 5. Then there are the bears and raccoons that get fat in summer and then hibernate and slow down their metabolism to get through the winter.

___ 6. Still others store food to get them through, like squirrels.

Handout 5.5 cont.

Available for download at **http://resources.corwin.com/divingdeep-nonfiction**

Lesson 6

Noticing the Text Structures in Nonfiction Texts

SEARCH AND FIND

PURPOSE

- To consolidate expertise with using the rules of notice for text structure

LENGTH

- Approximately 10–20 minutes of class time over two days

MATERIALS NEEDED

- Student-provided examples of found texts that use rules of notice
- Teacher-provided examples of comparison and contrast from billboards, street signs, conversations, and so on

Introduction

As always, we want to reinforce to students that text structures abound in the world and that they help us to make meaning as both readers and composers of any kind of text. They have another benefit as well. In our work as teachers and researchers, we've seen again and again students who read all the time but don't consider themselves readers because they don't read the texts most valued in school. By bringing what students read outside class into the classroom, we help break down the wall between what students do in school and what they do outside.

Lesson Steps: Day 1

Step 1

Direct students to notice text structure cues:

- Ask students to note the rules of notice for comparison that they experience throughout their day and to bring their notes (or artifacts) to class to share in Day 2, Step 2.
- Encourage students to find examples both of texts that make an *internal* comparison and of texts that expect readers or viewers to compare them (or something in the text) with a *different* text.
- Provide a few models of comparison collected from your own life. For example, say: *My friend told me, after dinner at my house, that when she had dinner at another friend's, they had champagne, inviting a comparison between our two dinners, and highlighting that I did not serve any drinks. Rules of notice included the repetition of dinner and the ruptures or differences between the dinner she described and the one she just had. And here is a billboard with a young man in a minivan and that same young man in a sports car, which is an explicit comparison*

of what it looks like and maybe even feels like to drive different kinds of cars, so it's an internal comparison. The differences in color, in his expressions, and in the styles of car are all calls to attention.

Lesson Steps: Day 2

Step 1

Have students share examples in small groups:

- Divide students into groups of three or four.
- Explain that each student should share his or her notes or artifacts from the outside world that exhibit rules of notice for comparison.

Step 2

Have groups share examples with the class:

- Invite students from each group to discuss specifically how the rules of notice play out in what they shared.
- Add or refer to the anchor chart as students explain.

Extension: Day 2

Have students generate their own short multimodal texts that cue comparisons—for example, advertisements, public service announcements, or memes.

For links to model memes, visit the companion website at **http://resources.corwin.com/divingdeep-nonfiction**.

The following three sites will help students create memes:

- Imgflip: https://imgflip.com/memegenerator
- Meme Maker: www.mememaker.net
- Quick Meme: www.quickmeme.com/caption

Lesson 7

Noticing the Text Structures in Nonfiction Texts

PUTTING IT ALL TOGETHER

PURPOSE

- To integrate rules of notice about comparison with other rules of notice

LENGTH

- Approximately 90 minutes (can be split into two 45-minute classes)

MATERIALS NEEDED

- Class copies of Handout 5.6, "'Troposphere' (Excerpt)"
- Class copies of Handout 5.7, "Hillocks Hierarchy Questions"
- Pens, pencils, and highlighters
- A globe
- Plastic wrap
- Anchor chart paper or space on a whiteboard
- Whiteboard markers
- Sticky notes for generalization statements

Introduction

As always, we want to provide students with multiple opportunities to integrate all that they have learned about text structure and how to apply it to extended reading. Remember, transfer doesn't happen automatically. You have to make it happen by providing the opportunity for students to deliberately practice and mindfully apply what they have learned over the course of time.

Lesson Steps

Step 1

Introduce the lesson:

- Remind students that throughout their work with comparison, noticing text structures has helped them more deeply understand texts.
- Note that what's true in reading is true in life as well.
- As a class, discuss recent examples in which comparison helped students do some important thinking. Initiate the discussion by providing an example or two from your own life. For example, Michael might share that in helping his daughter look for an apartment, he has been making many comparisons: cost/square foot, distance to public transportation, size of bedroom, and so on.

Step 2

Start, and have students continue, a think-aloud:

- Pass out copies of Handout 5.6, "'Troposphere' (Excerpt)."

- Model a think-aloud with the first paragraph of the excerpt from "Troposphere," specifically noting
  - Where the author uses comparison
  - The rules of notice you employ
  - How comparison is working to express meaning

Step 3

Use Hillocks's questions to support students' understanding:

- After students complete their think-aloud, pass out copies of Handout 5.7, "Hillocks Hierarchy Questions." Have students verify the questions—that is, justify that each question is of the indicated type—and answer them as they do so.
- Point students to the anchor charts you created in previous lesson steps that will help them verify the questions.
- Tell them that they will use this model to ask their own questions later on as they continue reading in pairs.

Step 4

Create a Venn diagram for making generalizations:

- Ask students to create a Venn diagram that compares and contrasts the first two layers of the atmosphere (troposphere and stratosphere). Have students use their think-alouds and generalization answers to help them make this comparison.
- Invite students to work in pairs to make generalization statements about each layer of the atmosphere. The statements should be supported by key details from the Venn diagram. See Figure 5.2 for an example.
- Ask students to share their generalization statements, and then record them on sticky notes and place them on the appropriate side of the Venn diagram.
- Return students to their pairs to make generalization statements about the whole atmosphere.
- Ask students to share their generalization statements, and then record them on sticky notes and place them on the appropriate side of the Venn diagram.

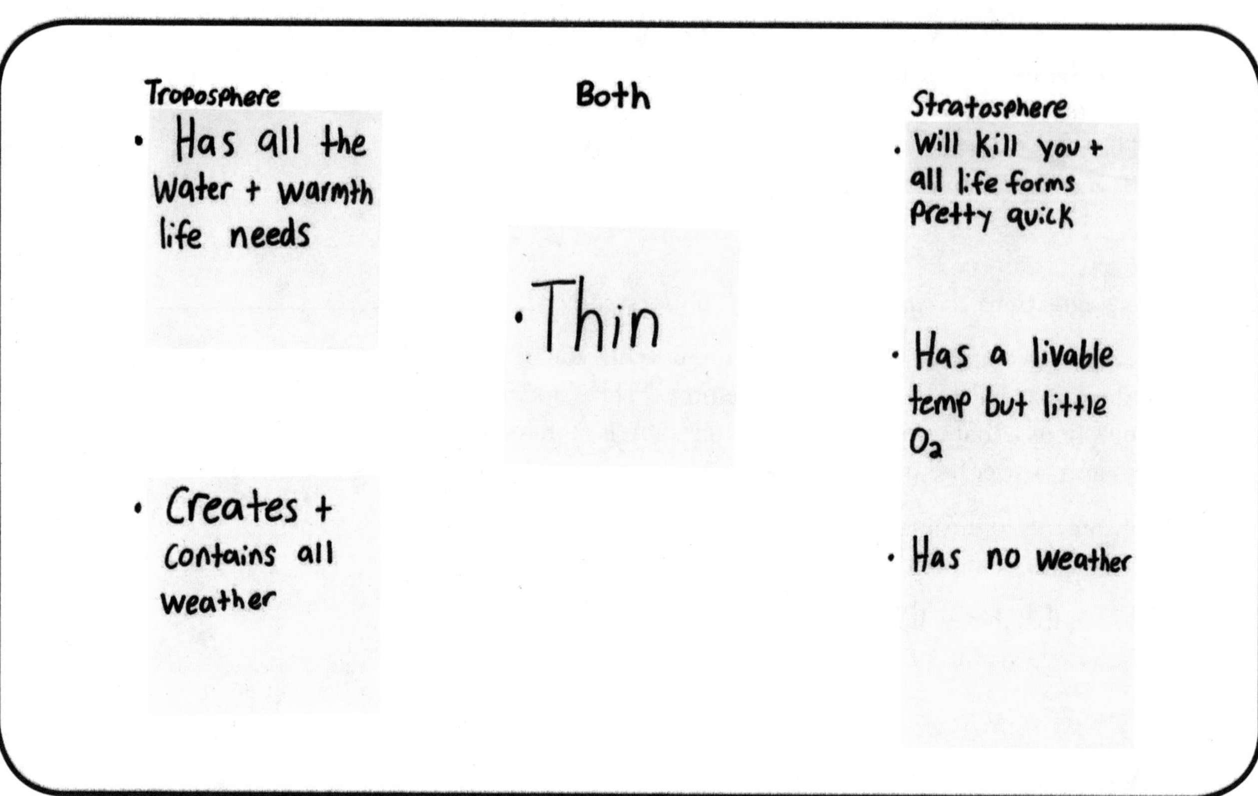

Figure 5.2

Sample Venn Diagram: Noticing Text Structures in "Troposphere"

Step 5

Review what students learned and encourage transfer:

- Note how noticing and making meaning with comparisons is so crucial to understanding a text.
- Encourage students to notice and make meaning with comparisons both in school and out.

Extension

Have students write a dystopian story that portrays what Earth would be like if people didn't care for the atmosphere using implicit or explicit comparisons to what life and Earth were like before the atmosphere was destroyed versus afterward.

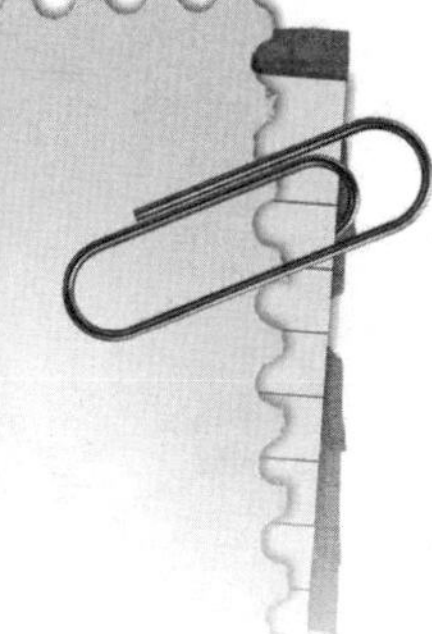

SAMPLE THINK-ALOUD

Lesson 7. Noticing the Text Structures in Nonfiction Texts: Putting It All Together

"Troposphere" (Excerpt) by Bill Bryson

Thank goodness for the atmosphere.

I'm noticing right off the bat that Bryson is making a direct statement of generalization about the world. The text structure makes it sound like a claim in an argument that he is going to have to back up. He is going to explain why *we should be grateful for the atmosphere. This comment also makes me think that the topic of this chapter is going to involve important characteristics about the atmosphere. I'm also noticing calls to attention: beginnings and emotion.*

It keeps us warm.

And just like that, he starts supporting his claim.

Without it, Earth would be a lifeless ball of ice with an average temperature of minus 60 degrees Fahrenheit.

Here is another important detail about what it means to be warm. I'm noticing that the author just compared Earth with an atmosphere to Earth without an atmosphere to help us see why the atmosphere matters. I'm going to be on the lookout for more text structure comparisons like this.

In addition, the atmosphere absorbs or deflects incoming swarms of cosmic rays, charged particles, ultraviolet rays, and the like.

Again, he is supporting his claim or direct statement of generalization with specific details about why we should be grateful to the atmosphere.

Altogether, the gaseous padding of the atmosphere is equivalent to a fifteen-foot thickness of protective concrete,

Oh! Here is another great text structure comparison—invisible air and thick concrete. I can more easily imagine how concrete protects and blocks. I have to remember to notice comparisons and metaphors.

and without it, these invisible visitors from space would slice through us like tiny daggers.

Yikes! He's comparing tiny particles to deadly daggers. That's another metaphoric comparison, and it really drives the point home with its specificity and visual and emotional effect.

Even raindrops would pound us senseless if it weren't for the atmosphere's slowing drag.

(Continued)

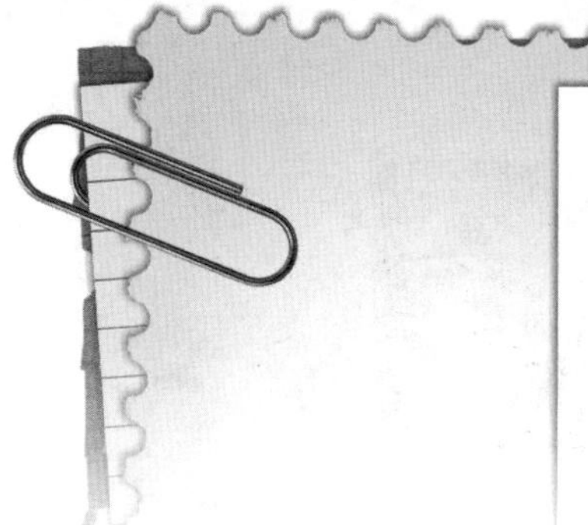

SAMPLE THINK-ALOUD
(CONT.)

Let's put it all together. All the advantages and benefits of the atmosphere are building up in a kind of list. And lists are always a call to attention. This latest element in the list adds an important supporting detail and a comparison about how raindrops would act without the atmosphere versus with the atmosphere. This is another call to attention through exaggeration and the emotional response I have to being pounded senseless.

The most striking thing about our atmosphere is that there isn't very much of it.

Here is a rupture with a movement or shift and a surprise: The atmosphere seems pretty big to me.

It extends upward for about 120 miles,

Hmm. How far is 120 miles? Seems like a lot. That's how far it is from Boise to Twin Falls. This is a bit of a rupture, so it also seems like a key detail that I need to highlight or circle.

which might seem reasonably bounteous when viewed from ground level,

The text structure presents an implied comparison. I notice that Bryson just used some language to make me think he is going to challenge an assumption about the size of the atmosphere—"which might seem." This shows he's going to do a comparison and rupture my assumption.

but if you shrank the Earth to the size of a standard desktop globe, it would only be about the thickness of a couple of coats of varnish.

Oh, I really like what he did here! He made a comparison and scaled Earth and its atmosphere down to a size that we can better understand. He shifted our perspective. He continues the throughline of how little atmosphere we have. In fact, let's take a quick look at this using a globe and some clear plastic wrap.

> *Pause here and use the plastic wrap to cover the globe. Say something like this:*
>
> *"Plastic wrap is the same thickness as varnish, but much easier to work with. Let's tear off four pieces of plastic wrap—to represent the four layers of the atmosphere—and layer them on the globe."*
>
> *When you have finished the globe activity, have students continue the think-aloud of Bryson's text in pairs, alternating sentences.*

Source: Bryson, B. (2003). *A short history of nearly everything.* New York, NY: Broadway Books.

"Troposphere" (Excerpt)

By Bill Bryson

Thank goodness for the atmosphere. It keeps us warm. Without it, Earth would be a lifeless ball of ice with an average temperature of minus 60 degrees Fahrenheit. In addition, the atmosphere absorbs or deflects incoming swarms of cosmic rays, charged particles, ultraviolet rays, and the like. Altogether, the gaseous padding of the atmosphere is equivalent to a fifteen-foot thickness of protective concrete, and without it, these invisible visitors from space would slice through us like tiny daggers. Even raindrops would pound us senseless if it weren't for the atmosphere's slowing drag.

The most striking thing about our atmosphere is that there isn't very much of it. It extends upward for about 120 miles, which might seem reasonably bounteous when viewed from ground level, but if you shrank the Earth to the size of a standard desktop globe, it would only be about the thickness of a couple of coats of varnish.

For scientific convenience, the atmosphere is divided into four unequal layers: troposphere, stratosphere, mesosphere, and ionosphere (now often called the thermosphere). The troposphere is the part that's dear to us. It alone contains enough warmth and oxygen to allow us to function; though even it becomes uncongenial to life as you climb up through it. From ground level to its highest point, the troposphere (or "turning sphere") is about ten miles thick at the equator and no more than six or seven miles high in the temperate latitudes where most of us live. Eighty percent of the atmosphere's mass, virtually all the water, and thus virtually all the weather, are contained within this thin and wispy layer. There really isn't much between you and oblivion. . . .

After you have left the troposphere the temperature soon warms up again, to about 40 degrees Fahrenheit, thanks to the absorptive

(Continued)

effects of ozone . . . It then plunges to as low as −130 degrees Fahrenheit in the mesosphere before skyrocketing to 2,700 degrees Fahrenheit or more in the aptly named but very erratic thermosphere . . .

Temperature is really just a measure of the activity of molecules. At sea level, air molecules are so thick that one molecule can move only the tiniest distance—about three-millionths of an inch, to be precise—before banging into another. Because trillions of molecules are constantly colliding, a lot of heat gets exchanged. But at the height of the thermosphere, at fifty miles or more, the air is so thin that any two molecules will be miles apart and hardly ever come in contact. So although each molecule is very warm, there are few interactions between them and thus little heat transference.

Source: Bryson, B. (2003). *A short history of nearly everything.* New York, NY: Broadway Books.

Hillocks Hierarchy Questions

Directions: Verify that each question is the type indicated and explain how you know. Then answer the questions.

Level 1: Basic stated information

What are the four layers of the atmosphere? How are they layered from the ground up?

Level 2: Key details

Why does Bryson argue that the troposphere is "dear to us" as human beings?

Level 3: Stated relationships (comparison)

What is the relationship between temperature in the atmosphere and molecules in the air?

Level 4: Simple implied relationships

Why aren't all layers of the atmosphere habitable by humans?

(Continued)

Level 5: Complex implied relationships

In what various ways can the atmosphere be considered both thick and thin? Cite some examples of comparisons that Bryson uses. What might be the functional effects of this thinness and thickness?

____

____

____

____

Level 6: Authorial generalization

What might Bryson say about our relationship with, dependence on, and responsibility toward the atmosphere?

____

____

____

____

Level 7: Structural generalization

How does Bryson use comparisons to help the reader understand characteristics of the atmosphere's layers and how dependent we are on the atmosphere?

____

____

____

____

Chapter 6

Why This Method Works

The challenge of improving student motivation, capacity, and performance in reading has long been a topic of both professional and public debate. That it's a challenge to improve student performance is not a surprise. Reading well is a profound achievement and not easily attained. But this does not mean that meaningful improvement in student achievement cannot be achieved. We know it can both from educational research and from personal experience.

Motivating Deep Learning

As Tharp and Gallimore (1990) argue, if students perceive a clear and significant purpose and receive sustained assistance and practice over time in a meaningful context of use, they can learn and master complex literacy skills, and their abilities can develop dramatically.

In this book, we've articulated a clear purpose: to help students become more metacognitive and competent readers. We've also provided clearly articulated instruction and relevant practice over time that can be immediately applied to the reading and writing of new texts. According to Tharp and Gallimore's research into general principles of literacy learning with struggling students, and our own research into the specific methods shared here, this instruction will lead to reading expertise.

Several other conditions for motivation and deep learning supported by research are met in this book:

- **Correspondence.** Studies in cognitive science (Bereiter, 2004) show that instruction must correspond to actual expertise as practiced in the world and move students toward that expertise. That is our project here: practicing the kinds of noticing and interpreting that expert readers employ.
- **Situated Cognition.** People learn best and most deeply in a context that requires and rewards their learning by providing a meaningful situation for applying what has been learned. The instruction here is provided in the context of actual reading and meaningful inquiry.
- **A Dynamic Mindset.** The research of Carol Dweck (2006), Peter Johnston (2012), and others demonstrates that students can and will learn if they attribute learning to effort and the use of strategies. Our method promotes and leverages this mindset.
- **Competence.** In our research on the literate lives of young men (Smith & Wilhelm, 2002, 2006), we found that competence was the linchpin of motivation. When students discover and hone a new strategy, they want to keep developing it. Our instruction here articulates what competent readers do, helps students do it, and gives them ways to practice and develop this competence independently over time.

- **Shared Secrets.** In a wonderful turn of phrase, Margaret Meek (1983) summarizes what we see as the central job of a teacher of reading: sharing the "list of secret things that all accomplished readers know, yet never talk about" (cited in Thomson, 1987, p. 109). This book shares the secrets of accomplished readers by naming the rules of notice that will help students recognize conversational topics, key details, genres, and text structures, and then use what they've noticed to understand how authors have created meaning and effect. The rules of notice lead to threshold learning—they reorient students to reading in a more powerful, proactive way and allow them to develop as readers and writers with more conscious competence. In so doing, our method helps students name themselves as people with potential, as readers and writers who can develop throughout a lifetime. That's a threshold we want all of our students to cross: the threshold to the dynamic mindset.

Developing Cultural, Critical, and Identity Literacies

In current academic conversations, it's widely accepted that rather than speaking of literacy, singular, it's more accurate to speak of literacies, plural (Street, 1995). Literacy plays out in various ways and in various contexts, serving many different combinations of ends. Our noticing and unpacking approach powerfully promotes three different but intersecting notions of literacy.

The first is the notion of *cultural literacy* introduced into popular consciousness by E. D. Hirsch Jr. (1988) as the understanding of "the basic information needed to thrive in the modern world" (p. xiii). Being literate is embedded in a cultural context and constitutes successfully mastering information central to a culture (or to a specific discipline). This database of essential information is cultural in two ways: (1) The information needed to thrive is specific to a culture (academic disciplines also being considered cultures) and therefore different in different cultural contexts, and (2) such information, although useful and necessary to cultural participation in the present moment, is nevertheless anchored to the historical past of a cultural community.

Readers must have a basic understanding of this core knowledge because communicators within any culture assume and take for granted that this background knowledge is part of the communal background. It is therefore often left out of the explicit articulations of texts (remaining part of what we call the *pretext*) on the assumption that readers will bring the necessary background to bear by activating it when they comprehend the topic (i.e., reading across the intertextual grid) and inferring to fill gaps in the text (i.e., reading along indices).

We tell our students: *There is always a pretext. Authors expect you to know certain things and bring them to the game of reading. This means you have to activate background and fill in gaps left for you in the text. You have to summon the pretext and help co-create the text itself before you decide where to go with it. You also have to know cultural conventions and agreements for reading. That's what the rules of notice are: articulations of the implicit agreements between writers and readers.*

To summarize the thrust of cultural literacy: "Thriving within a community is the end goal, and understanding is the means. To understand, one needs to have the background knowledge that is taken for granted and understand it in a culturally appropriate manner" (Schachter & Galili-Schacter, 2012).

This has everything to do with noticing a conversation, respecting the content of that conversation, and accessing or building background knowledge necessary to understand and participate in the conversation.

Our method achieves cultural literacy by helping students consciously understand how texts work and what authors expect of readers. This in turn allows students to more fully and deeply understand the cultural knowledge and disciplinary concepts expressed by texts.

The second notion of literacy is that of *critical literacy* rooted in the work of educator Paulo Freire and philosophers of the Frankfurt School (Freire, 1970; Kincheloe, 2008). The central principle here is that literacy extends far beyond the ability to decode written text and comprehend content to the capacity to evaluate and relate to text critically—to recognize any text as authored, politically motivated, and claiming authority in the guise of neutrality.

We say to our students: *Every text, from a poem to an advertisement, was composed by somebody wanting to manipulate you to know, believe, or do something. So you need to ask who wrote this text, why they want to manipulate you, how they are manipulating you, and whether you want to go along.*

When students understand that texts are constructed by other human beings in particular ways to inform, influence, and even manipulate them, they have achieved threshold learning that is a gateway to critical literacy.

Critical literacy entails knowing who stands to benefit and who loses from accepting certain propositions and worldviews. Expert readers understand that knowledge and discourse about knowledge is social capital (Gee, 1990) and that mastery of cultural knowledge and approved ways of doing things yields power. A major critique of cultural literacy is that Hirsch's notion reproduces and perpetuates rather than transforms social structures and material conditions by privileging groups who traditionally control and produce socially accepted processes and knowledge (Giroux, 2002). Critical literacy interrogates how texts work and seeks to consciously align, resist, or revise them for social ends.

Critical literacy is based on a deep understanding that knowledge is constructed and expressed by human beings. It depends on deep understanding of texts, what they mean, and how they are constructed for meaning and effect. It is only with such deep understanding that one knows enough not only to understand but to consciously resist—to see other possibilities and revise, put one's own oar into the conversation, and provide a unique turn in that conversation.

Our instruction introduces students to critical literacy by helping them develop a conscious awareness of how texts are constructed to achieve particular purposes, meanings, and effects.

A third view of literacy is *identity literacy*, defined as

> readers' proficiency in the practice of engaging the meaning systems embedded within texts, considering while doing so whether to adopt, adapt, or reject these as part of their own personal meaning systems. A personal meaning system is a semiotic system (socioculturally based, but personally adapted) with which individuals make sense of themselves, the world they are in, and their relation to it. (Valsiner, 2007)

In other words, as they engage texts, expert readers are developing their personal identity (Schachter & Galili-Schacter, 2012).

Our notion of identity is based on the work of Erik Erikson (1968), in which identity is a dynamic psychological structure providing "a subjective sense of an invigorating sameness and continuity" (p. 19). Erikson's concept focuses on how one's self-understanding in relation to groups and ideas organizes one's various roles and self-perceptions, thus enabling meaningful, proactive, self-directed participation in society (Côté & Levine, 2002; Schwartz, 2001). Precisely because individuals operate in many contexts and enact different local identities, Erikson theorized that they have a need for a core executive function that provides sameness and continuity—and identity serves this purpose (Schachter & Galili-Schachter, 2012). In this model, identity—including a sense of who one is, who one wants to be, and how to become that—is co-constructed with others in the cultural context, including characters and authors, through processes of *identification*, *exploration*, and *commitment*.

One *identifies* with roles, ideas, role models, heroes, and a variety of other significant individuals and communities as one decides who one is and who one wants to become. One then *explores* available roles, beliefs and ideologies, partners, groups, communities, and worldviews as one considers how they speak to one's rehearsals for being and might be rejected, assimilated, or accommodated in this light. Eventually one *commits* to pursue specific self-chosen social roles, beliefs and ideologies, relationships, groups and communities, and worldviews, persevering in the actions needed to actualize them (see Schachter & Galili-Schachter, 2012, for a full account).

We tell our students: *Reading provides "imaginative rehearsals for living"* (George Santayana, cited in Booth, 1983, p. 212), *and if you are not rehearsing what you want to be and how you want to think, believe, and act as you read, rejecting and accepting visions of being that are presented, then you are not really reading* (Wilhelm & Novak, 2011).

Only when students comprehend what an author is selling and how he or she is selling it can they apply that text to their pursuit of identity. Our approach therefore provides a gateway into identity literacy.

To be competent readers, students need to possess, activate, and know how to build the background required to comprehend particular texts, and they need to know how to attend to those texts to understand them as they were written to be understood (cultural literacy). But competent readers also need actively to consider the political implications of the claims texts make and the way they position readers and those affected by their views, and this they can only do if they understand how texts influence readers (critical literacy). Finally, competent readers need to be actively and consciously constructing identity in the ways that they accept, reject, and revise the propositions presented by texts (identity literacy).

To integrate these three kinds of literacy, we must actively notice and unpack the codes of texts and know how texts are situated in ongoing cultural conversations with very real consequences for the material circumstances of human beings, social structures, and the wider environment. We need to understand how reader response is part of identity literacy and how reading can help us become something new—a better or even best possible self.

Reader's Rules of Notice: Frequently Asked Questions

Video 6.1

http://resources.corwin.com/divingdeep-nonfiction

This approach allows us to be accountable—to conversations and to authors, to the texts used to express the turns in the conversation, to those people or ideas left out or marginalized by the current trend of the conversation, and to ourselves as evolving human beings.

A Final Word

We argue throughout this book that the central moves of expert reading are noticing and unpacking. These are also the two central moves of procedural feedback:

1. One notices what an author (or learner, composer, or problem solver) has done.
2. One unpacks the meaning and effect of that move.

This process promotes a sense of agency—a feeling that what we *do* as readers and writers (and problem solvers and learners) *matters* and has *consequences*; that we have control over choices, and those choices lead to different meanings and effects. This process also promotes a sense of self-efficacy and a dynamic mindset: With effort and the conscious use of strategies, we can and will improve, and this growth is under our control.

The conscious use of procedural feedback while reading and writing promotes cultural literacy (we understand cultural knowledge and how culture is transmitted) but, more importantly, critical literacy (we see how texts work to communicate and influence, and we come to consciously appreciate how this is done but also decide whether to accept, revise, or resist this influence) and identity literacy (we see how we are actively composing and constructing our own identity through our choices, especially the choices about what texts and beliefs to align ourselves with and against).

Without understanding the conversation a text is part of and the stakes of that conversation, both to disciplinary communities and to the public, but also to other silenced perspectives and to ourselves individually, we cannot be wide-awake, consciously competent readers in control of our reading and being. But with such an understanding, all this is possible.

Making it possible for your students is your responsibility. We hand the baton over to you and wish you the best of luck as you run the race.

Appendix

General Reader's Rules of Notice for Nonfiction

A textual cue can involve more than one rule—cuing both a conversational topic and a key detail, for instance. The specific cues that constitute rules of notice often work across the kinds of labels we've named here. For example, titles are always a call to attention, but they can also make a direct statement and might also make use of a rupture (e.g., *Bomb: The Race to Build—and Steal—the World's Most Dangerous Weapon* by Steve Sheinkin makes a direct statement and uses a rupture in the title, set off by dashes). Or, a title can give the reader a personal emotional charge or intense connection, making it a cue for the rule of the reader's response in addition to other cues used (e.g., *Hitler Youth: Growing Up in Hitler's Shadow* by Susan Campbell Bartoletti gives Jeff a personal charge and personal connections as his Rotary scholarship German host mother was part of this program).

Above all, what's important is to use the cues that follow to notice a detail or authorial move as important—and to then interpret it and fit it into the overall meaning that is being made with a text.

General Rules of Notice

Direct Statements

- Explicit statements of meaning
- Explicit statements of principle

Source: A resource to support Wilhelm and Smith, *Diving Deep Into Nonfiction, Grades 6–12*, Corwin, 2016. These rules of notice are findings from a teacher research study into teaching students to read complex nonfiction texts, conducted by the Boise State Writing Project Teacher Inquiry Group.

Please note that this is an exploratory list of specific examples of rules of notice that represents the work that came out of one particular teacher research study. As such, it is not meant to be comprehensive or conclusive; it was conceived of and classified in a way that worked for the specific teacher research group.

For a more complete list of rules specific to noticing conversations/topics, noticing key details, noticing genre, and noticing text structures, visit the book's companion website at **http://resources.corwin.com/divingdeep-nonfiction**.

- Explicit generalizations
- Explicit judgments or evaluations
- Explicit indications of text structure (e.g., "In comparison . . . ," "Now we'll compare this to . . .")
- Direct statements of theme
- Direct statements of application or of takeaway
- Direct statements of command; imperatives
- Explicit questions—especially bringing the status quo into question
- A definite article and an intensifier or judgment/evaluation (e.g., *The Great Fire*)

Ruptures

Rules of General Surprises/Shifts

- Surprises/shifts in topic
- Surprises/shifts in text structure
- Events or ideas that change relationships
- Events/ideas that offer different perspectives on a topic
- Ruptures of trajectory, continuity, expectations
- Instances when the author uses a specific detail when the reader expected another
- Discoveries and revelations
- Deviations from any norm—cultural, social, individual, textual
- Events that change relationships—between people, ideas, events, and so on
- Emotional charges, outliers, coincidences
- Inappropriate behaviors and responses on the part of characters (especially narrative nonfiction)

Rules of Problems

- Tensions
- Contact zones—points of disagreement; where multiple perspectives meet
- Problems/trouble
- Moral choices

Rules of Stylistic Choices That Surprise or Shock

- Silences—when the reader expects to hear or find out something but doesn't, or expects to hear from a character or perspective but doesn't (especially with narrative nonfiction)

- Exaggeration and understatement
- Blatantly irrelevant/that which is mentioned seems irrelevant or off-point
- Undue attention—what seems like undue attention is given to something, markedly long descriptions
- Plot direction changes (especially with narrative nonfiction)
- Shifts in point of view
- Significant changes in perspective of narrator or character
- Ruptures in time—flashbacks, fastforwards, collapsed or exploded moments, reflections and memories
- Shifts in tone
- Shifts in style
- Shifts in pacing
- Unexpected authorial choices and moves
- Unreliable narrators (especially with narrative nonfiction)
- Irony (especially with narrative nonfiction)

Rules of Wordplay/Sound Devices

- Use of rhyme
- Neologisms
- Wordplay/double entendre—words or phrases with double or multiple meanings
- Sound devices
- Shifts from standard English—foreign words, dialect

Rules of Shifts in Length

- A short paragraph or sentence among longer ones, or vice versa
- Movement from a close-up to a wide-angle lens, or vice versa, giving a new view or angle on the topic
- Exploded moments (long descriptions that may give a sense of undue attention) that are typically about the topic
- Close-ups or wide-angle descriptions that shift focus and pacing

Calls to Attention

Rules of Positioning

- Introductions
- Introductions of new characters (especially when extended, using comparison/contrast, etc.), of new situations, of ideas, of new withheld details, and so on

- Conclusions—of sections, of chapters, of the whole
- Endings as especially important—the difference between the beginning and end is a powerful indicator of theme, of the ultimate conclusion the details add up to
- Titles
- Subtitles
- Headings
- Epigraphs
- Callouts
- Book covers—commentary on back, book flaps

Rules of Print Features

- Illustrations, photos, and graphics
- Bolding, highlights, or italics

Rules of Questions

- Questions in a title, near the beginning or the end of a text or section
- All explicit questions
- Details that implicitly or explicitly address these questions

Rules of Implicit Meaning—Filling the Gaps

- References to pretext—what has happened before, signals of what knowledge readers are expected to bring to the text
- References to the narrator's presence: Who is speaking, and how should we think about him or her? (especially with narrative nonfiction)
- Implied causes and causality
- Any implied connection

Rules of Resonance

- Anything evoking intensity—emotional, visual, physical
- Semantic gestures—*immediately*, *suddenly*, swear words, *realize*
- Syntax for emphasis such as inversions, or for singling out—"*It was the single most spectacular soirée of the season . . .* "
- Immediacy/directness
- Climactic moments/dramatic events
- Details at climactic moments
- Threats/warnings/promises

- Details that follow up on threats/warnings/promises
- Causes and causality—explicit and implicit
- Figurative language
- Special case of symbols or archetypes
- Extended metaphors—connection of very unlike things
- Direct address to readers
- Positioning of reader, reader's stance and purpose (e.g., through specific address, questions, problems, and inquiries)
- Quotes, especially authoritative quotes
- Recognitions—statements highlighting a detail as new, important, or an insight
- A character notices or pays special attention to something ("He read through it again")

Orderings

- Lists
- Numbering
- Rankings
- Process descriptions

Intertextual Cues

- Allusions to other texts of any kind
- Citations—of other works in the conversation
- Connections to intertextual positions—sequels, trilogies, series
- Comparisons to other perspectives, ideas
- Implicit connection: What other texts are like this? Could they be put into a conversation with this text? Do they offer similar or different perspectives and positions to this text?
- Explicit connections, references, and allusions: What other texts are mentioned?
- References to formulas, ideas, and perspectives from other texts
- Connections to intratextual positions/inside the text—connections between beginning, middle, end, *in media res*

Throughlines

- Repetitions and connections
- Repetitions with a twist, tweak or some kind of development: What do all the key details and events comment on? What do they all connect to?

- Details that reflect or refer to the title: What is the connection?
- Parallelisms
- Relationship of introductions and conclusions
- Relationship between headings and other text features

Reader's Response

- Activation of prior knowledge and interests—probably related to the topic
- Intense questions that come up and make the reader stop and pause—usually related to the topic
- Intense intellectual responses to anything in the text—usually related to the central topic
- Any connections the reader makes between the text, the reader's personal lived experience, the world, or current events and the newspaper—probably related to the conversational topic
- Anything that strikes the reader as *totally true*, or that the reader recognizes as a personal idea never quite articulated
- *Super ruptures* in the reader's understanding or way of looking at the world (passing through a threshold)
- Direct address to the reader; or a feeling that one is being directly addressed
- Intense emotional charges to anything in the text—reflect on why
- Intense visualization—scenes that the reader can really see
- Intense response to events, actions, or character decisions—actions that stay with the reader, that the reader thinks about over time, that are disturbing, that the reader might even use as psychic material in daydreaming or dreaming
- Intense satisfactions or dissatisfactions that come from certain character actions, decisions, events, or resolutions
- Intense meanings and takeaways the reader gleans, savors, talks about, and applies from the reading
- Intense reflection upon one's response and attempts to explain it: *Why did I react that way?*

Available for download at **http://resources.corwin.com/divingdeep-nonfiction**

WORKS CITED

Bartoletti, S. C. (2005). *Hitler youth: Growing up in Hitler's shadow*. New York, NY: Scholastic.

Barton, D., Hamilton, M., & Ivanič, R. (2000). *Situated literacies: Reading and writing in context*. New York, NY: Psychology Press.

Beastie Boys. (1994). Sure shot. *Ill Communication*. Los Angeles, CA: Grand Royal, Capital Records.

Beck, I. L., McKeown, M. G., Sandora, C., Kucan, L., & Worthy, J. (1996). Questioning the author: A yearlong classroom implementation to engage students with text. *The Elementary School Journal, 96*(4), 385–414.

Bereiter, C. (1997). Situated cognition and how to overcome it. In D. Kirshner & J. A. Whitson (Eds.), *Situated cognition: Social, semiotic, and psychological perspectives* (pp. 281–300). Hillsdale, NJ: Erlbaum.

Bereiter, C. (2004). Reflections on depth. In K. Leithwood, P. Mcadie, N. Bascia, & A. Rodriguez (Eds.), *Teaching for deep understanding* (pp. 8–12). Toronto, ON: EFTO.

Bertozzi, N. (2014). *Shackleton: Antarctic odyssey*. New York, NY: First Second Books.

Biancarosa, C., & Snow, C. (2006). *Reading next—A vision for action and research in middle and high school literacy: A report to the Carnegie Corporation of New York* (2nd ed.). Washington, DC: Alliance for Excellent Education.

Booth, W. (1983). A new strategy for establishing a truly democratic criticism. *Daedalus, 112*, 193–214.

Bransford, J. D., & Johnson, M. K. (1972). Contextual prerequisites for understanding: Some investigations of comprehension and recall. *Journal of Verbal Learning and Verbal Behavior, 11*, 717–726.

Brown, J., Collins, A., & Duguid, P. (1989). Situated cognition and the culture of learning. *Educational Researcher, 18*(1), 32–42.

Bruner, J. (1986). *Actual minds, possible worlds*. Cambridge, MA: Harvard University Press.

Burke, K. (1941). *The philosophy of literary form: Studies in symbolic action*. Baton Rouge: Louisiana State University Press.

Byrnes, J. P. (2008). *Cognitive development and learning in instructional contexts* (3rd ed.). New York, NY: Allyn & Bacon.

Bryson, B. (2003). *A short history of nearly everything*. New York, NY: Broadway Books.

Casey, M. (2015, August 17). Do violent video games lead to criminal behavior? *CBS News*. Retrieved from http://www.cbsnews.com/news/do-violent-video-games-lead-to-criminal-behavior/

Cazden, C. (1992). *Whole language plus: Essays on literacy in the US and NZ*. New York, NY: Teachers College Press.

Chase, C. (2015, June 17). LeBron James' legacy fades with each NBA Finals loss. *USA Today*. Retrieved from http://ftw.usatoday.com/2015/06/lebron-james-legacy-loser-nba-finals-two-titles-mvp

Churchill, W. (1940, May 13). *Blood, toil, tears and sweat*. The Churchill Centre. Retrieved from http://www.winstonchurchill.org/resources/speeches/1940-the-finest-hour/92-blood-toil-tears-and-sweat

Cianciolo, A., & Sternberg, R. (2004). *Intelligence: A brief history*. Hoboken, NJ: Wiley-Blackwell.

Common Core State Standards Initiative. (2010). *Common Core State Standards for English language arts & literacy in history/social studies, science, and technical subjects: Appendix B*. Retrieved from http://www.corestandards.org/assets/Appendix_B.pdf

Côté, J. E., & Levine, C. G. (2002). *Identity formation, agency, and culture: A social psychological synthesis*. Mahwah, NJ: Erlbaum.

Cunningham, M., & Swanson, D. P. (2010). Educational resilience in African American adolescents. *The Journal of Negro Education, 79*(4), 473–487.

Darling, C. (2015, April 29). Movie review: "Avengers: Age of Ultron." *Star-Telegram*. Retrieved from http://www.star-telegram.com/entertainment/arts-culture/article19881744.html

Dell'Antonia, K. J. (2016, March 22). "Impossible" homework assignment? Let your child do it. *The New York Times*. Retrieved from http://well.blogs.nytimes.com/2016/03/22/fourth-grade-book-report-let-your-fourth-grader-do-it/

Douglass, F. (1845). *Narrative of the life of Frederick Douglass, an American slave, written by himself.* Boston, MA: Anti-Slavery Office.

Dubner, S. J., & Levitt, S. D. (2006). A star is made: The birth-month soccer anomaly. *The New York Times Magazine*. Retrieved from http://www.nytimes.com/2006/05/07/magazine/07wwln_freak.html

Duke, N. K., & Roberts, K. L. (2010). The genre-specific nature of reading. In D. Wyse, R. Andrews, & J. Hoffman (Eds.), *The Routledge international handbook of English, language, and literacy teaching* (pp. 74–86). Abingdon, UK: Routledge.

Dweck. C. (2006). *Mindset: The new psychology of success*. New York, NY: Ballantine Books.

Eisner, W. (2006). *New York: The big city*. New York, NY: Norton.

Engelbert, P. (Ed.). (1997). *Astronomy & space: From the big bang to the big crunch.* Farmington Hills, MI: Gale.

Enzensberger, H. M. (1997). *The number devil: A mathematical adventure.* New York, NY: Holt.

Ericsson, A., & Pool, R. (2016a). Malcolm Gladwell got us wrong. *Salon*, April 10. Retrieved from http://www.salon.com/2016/04/10/malcolm_gladwell_got_us_wrong_our_research_was_key_to_the_10000_hour_rule_but_heres_what_got_oversimplified/

Ericsson, A., & Pool, R. (2016b). *Peak: Secrets from the new science of expertise*. New York, NY: Houghton Mifflin Harcourt.

Erikson, E. H. (1968). *Identity: Youth and crisis*. New York: W.W. Norton.

Feil, E. (2007). The world is in their hands. In D. W. Moore, D. J. Short, M. W. Smith, & A. W. Tatum (Eds.), *Hampton-Brown EDGE Level B*. Carmel, CA: National Geographic School Publishing/Hampton Brown.

Freire, P. (1970). *Pedagogy of the oppressed.* New York, NY: Bloomsbury.

Gee, J. P. (1990). *Social linguistics and literacies: Ideology in discourses.* London, UK: Taylor and Francis.

Giroux, H. A. (2002). Rethinking cultural politics and radical pedagogy in the work of Antonio Gramsci. In C. Borg, J. Buttigieg, & P. Mayo (Eds.), *Gramsci and education* (pp. 41–65). Lanham, MD: Rowman & Littlefield.

Gladwell, M. (2008). *Outliers*. New York, NY: Little, Brown.

Gonchar, M. (2015, August 25). What is a hero? *The New York Times.* Retrieved from http://learning.blogs.nytimes.com/2015/08/25/what-is-a-hero/

Guthrie, J. T., Klauda, S. L., & Morrison, D. A. (2012). Motivation, achievement, and classroom contexts for information book reading. In J. T Guthrie, A. Wigfield, & S. L. Klauda (Eds.), *Adolescents' engagement in academic literacy* (Report No. 7, pp. 1–51). Retrieved from http://www.cori.umd.edu/research-publications/2012_adolescents_engagement_ebook.pdf

Haskell, R. (2000). *Transfer of learning: Cognition, instruction, and reasoning.* San Diego, CA: Academic Press.

Hillocks, G. (1995). *Teaching writing as reflective practice.* New York, NY: Teachers College Press.

Hillocks, G. (1983). *Research on written composition.* Urbana, IL: National Council of Teachers of English.

Hillocks, G. (1980). Toward a hierarchy of skills in the comprehension of literature. *English Journal,* 69(3), 54–59.

Hirsch, E. D., Jr. (1988). *Cultural literacy: What every American needs to know*. New York, NY: Vintage Books.

Imbrenda, J. (2016a). *For argument's sake: Creating a pathway to college for urban adolescents* (Unpublished doctoral dissertation). Philadelphia, PA: Temple University.

Imbrenda, J. (2016b). The blackbird whistling or just after? Vygotsky's tool and sign as an analytic for writing. *Written Communication,* 33(1), 68–91.

Johnston, P. (2012). *Opening minds: Using language to change lives.* Portland, ME: Stenhouse.

Johnston, P., & Afflerbach, P. (1985). The process of constructing main ideas from texts. *Cognition and Instruction*, 2(3–4), 207–232.

Kennedy, J. F. (1961, January 20). *Inaugural address.* Retrieved from http://avalon.law.yale.edu/20th_century/kennedy.asp

Kincheloe, J. (2008). *Critical pedagogy primer* (4th ed.). New York, NY: Peter Lang.

Kintsch, W. (2005). An overview of top-down and bottom-up effects in comprehension: The CI perspective. *Discourse Processes*, 39, 125–128.

Langer, J. A. (2001). Beating the odds: Teaching middle and high school students to read and write well. *American Educational Research Journal*, 38, 837–880.

Lave, J., & Wenger, E. (1991). *Situated learning: Legitimate peripheral participation.* New York, NY: Cambridge University Press.

Lincoln, A. (1865, March 4). *Second inaugural address.* Retrieved from http://avalon.law.yale.edu/19th_century/lincoln2.asp

Lincoln, A. (1863, November 19). The Gettysburg address. Retrieved from http://avalon.law.yale.edu/19th_century/gettyb.asp

Louv, R. (2008). *Last child in the woods: Saving our children from nature-deficit disorder.* Chapel Hill, NC: Algonquin Books.

Marra, A. (2013). *A constellation of vital phenomena.* New York, NY: Hogarth.

Meyer, J. H. F., & Land, R. (2003). *Threshold concepts and troublesome knowledge: Linkages to ways of thinking and practising within the disciplines* [Occasional Report 4]. Universities of Edinburgh, Coventry, and Durham: ETL Project.

Mukherjee, S. (2010). *The emperor of all maladies: A biography of cancer.* New York, NY: Scribner.

Murphy, J. (1995). *The great fire.* New York, NY: Scholastic.

Perkins, D., & Salomon, G. (1988). *Educational Leadership*, 46(1), 22–32.

Petroski, H. (2003). The evolution of the grocery bag. *American Scholar*, 72(4), 99.

Petry, A. (1983). *Harriet Tubman: Conductor on the Underground Railroad.* New York, NY: HarperCollins. (Original work published 1955)

Pitney, J. J. (2013, August 25). References and allusions in the "I Have a Dream" speech. *Bessette Pitney Text.* Retrieved from http://www.bessettepitney.net/2013/08/references-and-allusions-in-i-have.html

Rabinowitz, P. (1987). *Before reading.* Ithaca, NY: Cornell University Press.

Rabinowitz, P., & Smith, M. W. (1998). *Authorizing readers: Resistance and respect in the teaching of literature.* New York, NY: Teachers College Press.

Raphael, T. (1982). Question answering strategies for children. *Reading Teacher*, 36(2), 186–190.

Reynolds, R. E. (1992) Selective attention and prose learning: Theoretical and empirical research. *Educational Psychology Review*, 4, 345–391.

Richtel, M. (2014). *A deadly wandering.* New York, NY: HarperCollins.

Rideout, V. J., Foehr, U. G., & Roberts, D. F. (2009). *Generation M^2: Media in the lives of 8- to 18-year-olds.* Menlo Park, CA: Kaiser Family Foundation.

Rosenblatt, L. (1978). *The reader, the text, the poem.* Carbondale: Southern Illinois University Press.

Schachter, E., & Galili-Schachter, I. (2012). Identity literacy: Reading and teaching texts as resources for identity formation. *Teachers College Record, 114*(5). Retrieved from http://eric.ed.gov/?id=EJ1000018

Schwartz, S. J. (2001). The evolution of Eriksonian and neo-Eriksonian identity theory and research: A review and integration. *Identity: An International Journal of Theory and Research*, 1, 7–58.

Science Buddies. (2016). *Sample abstract.* Retrieved from http://www.sciencebuddies.org/science-fair-projects/project_sample_abstract.shtml

Sheinkin, S. (2012). *Bomb: The race to build—and steal—the world's most dangerous weapon.* New York, NY: Flash Point.

Smith, W. W., Appleman, D., & Wilhelm, J. (2014). *Uncommon core: Where the authors of the standards go wrong about instruction—and how you can get it right.* Thousand Oaks, CA: Corwin.

Smith, M. W., & Wilhelm, J. (2010). *Fresh takes on teaching literary elements: How to teach what really matters about character, setting, point of view, and theme*. New York, NY: Scholastic.

Smith, M. W., & Wilhelm, J. D. (2007). *Getting it right: Fresh approaches to teaching language use and grammar.* New York, NY: Scholastic.

Smith, M. W., & Wilhelm, J. (2006). *Going with the flow: How to engage boys (and girls) in their literacy learning*. Portsmouth, NH: Heinemann.

Smith, M. W., & Wilhelm. J. (2002). *"Reading don't fix no Chevys": Literacy in the lives of young men.* Portsmouth, NH: Heinemann.

Smith, M. W., Wilhelm, J., & Fredricksen, J. (2012). *Oh yeah? putting argument to work both in school and out.* Portsmouth, NH: Heinemann.

Sternberg, R. J. (1990). *Metaphors of mind: Conceptions of the nature of intelligence*. New York, NY: Cambridge University Press.

Street, B. V. (1995). *Social literacies: Critical approaches to literacy in development, ethnography and education*. New York, NY: Routledge.

Tharp, R., & Gallimore, R. (1990). *Rousing minds to life: Teaching, learning and schooling in social context.* Cambridge, UK: Cambridge University Press.

Thomson, J. (1987). *Understanding teenagers' reading: Reading processes and the teaching of literature.* Melbourne, Australia: Methuen.

Valsiner, J. (2007, December 1). *Locating the self . . . looking for the impossible? Or maybe the impossible is the only possibility.* Paper presented at the *Culturalization of the Self* conference, Chemnitz, Germany.

Van Patter, B. (2005). *Looking at paintings:* Children's games. Retrieved from http://www.brucevanpatter.com/brueghel_painting.html

Why did Taylor Swift go pop? (2014, October 5). *Music Times.* Retrieved from http://www.musictimes.com/articles/11421/20141005/why-taylor-swift-go-pop-1989-star-explains-new-interview.htm

Wiggins, G., & McTighe, J. (2005). *Understanding by design*. Alexandria, VA: ASCD.

Wilhelm, J. (2016). *You gotta be the book: Teaching engaged and reflective reading with adolescents* (3rd ed.). New York, NY: Teachers College Press.

Wilhelm, J. (2012a). *Action strategies for deepening comprehension.* New York, NY: Scholastic.

Wilhelm, J. (2012b). *Enriching comprehension with visualization* (2nd ed.). New York, NY: Scholastic.

Wilhelm, J. (2012c). *Improving comprehension with think alouds* (2nd ed.). New York, NY: Scholastic.

Wilhelm, J. (2007). *Engaging readers and writers with inquiry*. New York, NY: Scholastic.

Wilhelm, J., Baker, T., & Dube, J. (2001). *Strategic reading*. Portsmouth, NH: Heinemann.

Wilhelm, J., Douglas, W., & Fry, S. (2014). *The activist learner: Inquiry, literacy, and service to make learning matter.* New York, NY: Teachers College Press.

Wilhelm, J., & Novak, B. (2011). *Teaching literacy for love and wisdom: Being the book and being the change.* New York, NY: Teachers College Press.

Wilhelm, J., & Smith, M. (with S. Fransen). (2014). *Reading unbound: Why kids need to read what they want—and why we should let them*. New York, NY: Scholastic.

Wilhelm, J., Smith, M., & Fredricksen, J. (2013). *Get it done! Writing and analyzing informational texts to make things happen*. Portsmouth, NH: Heinemann.

Wilhelm, J., Wilhelm, P., & Boas, E. (2009). *Inquiring minds learn to read and write: 50 problem-based literacy & learning strategies.* New York, NY: Scholastic.

Wills, G. (n.d.). The words that remade America: The significance of the Gettysburg Address. *The Atlantic*. Retrieved from http://www.theatlantic.com/magazine/archive/2012/02/the-words-that-remade-america/308801/

Wills, G. (1992). *Lincoln at Gettysburg: The words that remade America.* New York, NY: Simon & Schuster.

Wollstonecraft, M. (1792). *A vindication of the rights of women.* Boston, MA: Peter Edes.

INDEX

Helping educators make the greatest impact

CORWIN HAS ONE MISSION: to enhance education through intentional professional learning.

We build long-term relationships with our authors, educators, clients, and associations who partner with us to develop and continuously improve the best evidence-based practices that establish and support lifelong learning.

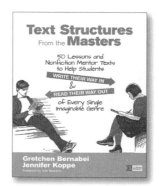

Bring Jeffrey D. Wilhelm to your school or district!

Areas of Expertise

- Teaching nonfiction across content areas with reader's rules of notice
- Reaching and assisting reluctant and struggling readers
- Teaching with inquiry
- Teaching writing: argument, informational and narrative texts
- Motivation
- Teacher research

Jeffrey can help you

- Learn how and why to use frontloading techniques to motivate readers, accessing and building their background knowledge as a resource for reading
- Explore new strategies for teaching reading, including ideas for reluctant readers
- Have a deeper understanding of the reading process
- Explore various visual techniques to assist students to greater comprehension

About the Consultant

Dr. Jeffrey D. Wilhelm is an internationally known teacher, author, and presenter. A classroom teacher for fifteen years, Dr. Wilhelm is currently Distinguished Professor of English Education at Boise State University. He has authored or co-authored more than 40 texts about literacy teaching and learning and has won both the National Council of Teachers of English Promising Research Award and the Russell Award for Distinguished Research. He is particularly interested in supporting the learning of reluctant students.

WHAT YOUR COLLEAGUES SAY

"Dr. Wilhelm's workshop was a hit! We heard a lot of positive feedback. The best was from a secondary English Language Arts teacher close to retirement who said, 'I wish I would have known this before—I could teach another thirty years.'"

—Helene Prefontaine, Superintendent of Education

"This workshop was by far the best professional development session I've ever been to. I would love to model my teaching off of Dr. Wilhelm's further. He is what most teachers go into the profession hoping to be like, but often give up, because they don't know the strategies and lack the super-charged 'growth mindset.' Thanks again, Dr. Wilhelm, for your help, for your example, and most importantly, for your inspiration!"

—Chad (teacher in PA)

"Thank you, Dr. Wilhelm, for all you do for us evolving teachers. You do a fabulous job in imparting your passion and clear designs of teaching."

—Ardis (teacher)

To bring Jeffrey D. Wilhelm to your school, call 800-831-6640

CL CORWIN LITERACY

N169H5